M000221848

U.S. International Trade Policy

Contents

CHAPTER ONE

Introduction

Merchants have no country. The mere spot that they stand on does not constitute so strong an attachment as that from which they draw their gains.
—Thomas Jefferson

The fact that you have picked up this book and are reading the first sentence indicates that you are interested in U.S. international trade policy. That's understandable, as trade policy is important for almost any country. For most people, an awareness of the importance of international trade policy comes from reading, or trying to read, articles in business publications such as the *Wall Street Journal*, *The Economist*, or an Internet news service such as Bloomberg or Reuters. *Trying* to read is the key phrase. Embedded in an article about international trade policy are a number of assumptions about the background information that the intended reader possesses. If the reader doesn't have this background information, then trying to read these articles becomes an uncomfortable experience. For most of us, it is like reading a text on thermodynamics: we can read the words, but we don't necessarily understand what they mean. In this case the situation can be even more frustrating. Many of us have just enough information to partially understand what is being said. However, we frequently can't completely understand an article because gaps in our knowledge are present that prevent us from fully grasping what is being said. Unfortunately, in many cases the problem is not just the reader, but also the person who wrote the article. Most writers on trade policy for business publications are not specialists in the area. A persistent problem then becomes the articles themselves. Reading these pieces can leave one with the uncomfortable feeling that the writer has an uncertain grasp of the material. This leads to a lot of articles on international trade policy that are incomplete or written in an unclear way. As we will see moving through this book, understanding international trade policy involves a rather broad skill set that many business journalists simply do not possess. <u>At the worst, the whole situation can be uncomfort-ably like the blind leading the blind</u>. One of the markets for this book is not only the readers of articles on international trade policy but also those who have to write these articles.

In a roundabout way, this leads us to the fundamental purpose of this book. With a few notable exceptions, one usually doesn't read about international trade policy for fun. Most people are reading about the subject because to a greater or lesser extent it touches their professional lives. If this is the case, then there is the potential problem mentioned earlier. You're reading about it because it matters to you, but you cannot completely understand what you are reading. If you are trying to connect something to your professional life and the connection isn't good, then this could lead to serious mistakes. To emphasize the potential of the problem, consider an important event in international trade policy. In 2001, China signed an agreement to join the World Trade Organization (WTO).[1] In the first case, most people have only a vague idea of what the WTO is and what it does. However, even if you are firm on that information, another bit of misunderstanding is common. <u>Any country that joins the WTO is given a reasonable period of time to get the country's trade policy in compliance with WTO rules</u>. In this case China was given 10 years to fully comply. Further, a timetable is spelled out in excruciating detail in the accession schedule that is associated with any country joining the WTO. A lack of understanding of this process led to some predictable confusion and not a few unfortunate business decisions. Most assumed that China had joined the WTO and was at that point in full compliance with WTO rules. A large part of the problem was that most of what was written on the subject in the business press never mentioned the 10-year accession schedule. This is just one of many examples. International trade policy is full of areas where a lack of understanding of basic rules or processes can, at best, lead to confusion and, at worst, lead to poor decisions.

Beyond these problems of policy and law are the fundamentals of international economics. Many professionals who are quite competent in the details of international trade policy still have only a vague understanding of the economics that is the background for the law. This lack of knowledge is understandable. The typical professional usually has had no more than two principles of economics courses: microeconomics and macroeconomics. International economics is a broad subarea in economics that likewise has two components. The microeconomic aspects of international economics are generically known as international trade. A basic knowledge of international trade is a fundamental building block for understanding international trade policy. The other subarea is known as international finance. To avoid misunderstanding, international finance is not about finance in the way most people use the term to refer to banking and other financial markets. In this case, it is concerned with the balance of payments, exchange rates, and open economy macroeconomics. Once again, the gap in knowledge for most is twofold. First, it is a sad reality that although international economics theoretically is covered in principles of economics, it is usually relegated to the final part of the course. One can guess what's coming next. The material frequently is never covered. This problem is exacerbated by the instructors. Typically, instructors in principles of economics courses have had little or no training in international economics. This is a subarea of the discipline, and many economists were only exposed to the subject in principles of economics (see earlier). Now we have an unfortunate feedback loop where even economists know little about the subject and it is difficult to pass on to students information that instructors themselves don't know.

This leads us to the fundamental organization of the book. Like international economics, the book is loosely divided into two parts. In the next four chapters, the fundamentals of international economics that one needs to know are presented. The goal here is to provide you with the basic tools that will allow you to understand the economic background in which trade policy operates. After laying this foundation, the last half of the book provides the basics of international trade policy that one is likely to encounter in a professional career. To be clear, the book is not comprehensive. There are always trade-offs among length, readability, and breadth of coverage. Very few have the inclination or the time to read a 600-page book. Length has an unfortunate correlation with the sort of dense prose that both academics and lawyers prefer. Unfortunately, that sort of writing has an uncomfortable similarity to medications for insomnia. The trade-off is reducing length also reduces the breadth and depth of coverage. The solution to this dilemma is to provide references to other works for those that need a more thorough coverage of additional topics.

In this introductory chapter, we will present both the organization of the material on international trade policy and thus the subsequent organization of the book. We begin with a look at the world economy. From there we introduce some of the basics of international economics that affect international trade policy. To do this, we will be covering several important topics in in the following way. International trade policy and the public policy discussions of it are full of economic nonsense. As a result, a useful way to proceed is to deal with this nonsense at the beginning. In the process, we'll learn the economic principles behind good international trade policy so that one can understand what one is reading and hearing about the subject.

What Is Globalization?

A commonly heard word in discussions of international trade is *globalization*. Everyone uses the term, but what does it mean? An interesting exercise illustrates the point. The next time you hear the term globalization, ask the person what it means. This is almost guaranteed to create an awkward moment. To turn this around, could you write a sentence or short paragraph that defines globalization? In one sense, everyone knows what this word means but usually only in a vague manner. For the most part, globalization is usually taken to mean that international transactions of one sort or another are becoming increasingly important. Now think of this in terms of international trade policy. If globalization is becoming more important over time, then international trade policy likewise is becoming more important. This illustrates an unfortunate reality. People associated with international trade policy only have a loose grasp of a fundamental concept. In our case, we would like to be more precise about this term. In the first part of this section we clarify the term *globalization*. Following this, we discuss various aspects of globalization and how they relate to what we will cover as we move through the book. In the last part of this section we will cover how to think about the controversy surrounding globalization. This final point is critical as controversies over international trade policy frequently have their roots in the debate over globalization.

First, globalization can be thought of in two ways. One way is to discuss globalization at the national level. Table 1.1 shows exports plus imports of goods as a percentage of gross domestic product (GDP) for a sample of 40 countries. Countries with a high ratio are generally more open to the world economy than countries with a low ratio. Notice that the ratios are not uniform. Some countries are noticeably more open than others. Further, these ratios also change over time. In most cases, the ratio tends to rise at a faster or slower rate for each country. For countries where the ratio is rising rapidly, the structure of the economy is likely to be changing rapidly because industries linked to exports will be expanding. As we will see, countries with rapidly growing exports will likely have rapidly growing imports as well. In this case, some industries will be experiencing more competition from imports. These latter changes can be difficult for a country to manage. Globalization, or the increasing openness of an economy, may bring changes that are not universally positive. The link to international

Table 1.1 Exports Plus Imports as a Percentage of
GDP for Selected Countries

	Country	Exports Plus Imports as a Percentage of GDP
1	Singapore	409.2
2	Hong Kong	398.2
3	Luxembourg	309.3
4	Hungary	186.1
5	Ireland	172.4
6	Belgium	161.0
7	Netherlands	145.7
8	Taiwan	127.6
9	Austria	104.7
10	Denmark	103.6
11	Honduras	102.9
12	Nicaragua	100.7
13	Switzerland	99.4
14	Philippines	96.4
15	Sweden	96.4
16	Korea	92.1
17	Costa Rica	90.9
18	Germany	89.9
19	Finland	85.4
20	Poland	84.3
21	Israel	83.2
22	Chile	82.6
23	Iceland	77.1
24	China	76.8
25	Norway	73.6
26	Portugal	71.8
27	Canada	67.9
28	Ecuador	65.0
29	Mexico	62.3
30	Indonesia	61.6
31	United Kingdom	57.3
32	Spain	57.1

(continued)

Table 1.1   Exports Plus Imports as a Percentage of
GDP for Selected (*continued*)

	Country	Exports Plus Imports as a Percentage of GDP
33	Italy	55.4
34	France	55.0
35	Greece	53.0
36	South Africa	51.2
37	Australia	47.9
38	Turkey	46.8
39	Japan	29.3
40	United States	29.2

Source: Heston et al. (2013).

trade policy is obvious. Import competing firms will be clamoring for protection. Firms that are exporting are going to be interested in increasing their access to foreign markets. The "middle man" in this is the national government.

If the globalization of countries is now common, this implies that the same is true of the world economy. The concept of globalization can be extended to the world economy as well. The sample of countries shown in the table is not unique; the same thing is happening on a global basis. This is illustrated in Figure 1.1. In this figure, world exports of goods are shown as a percentage of world output from 1950 to 2012. During this period, world exports have increased from approximately 12 percent to 26 percent of world output. International trade is becoming an increasingly important component of total economic activity for both individual countries and the world economy. In part, this is a function of the reduction of the barriers to trade or changes in international trade policy. Also, this means that international trade policy is becoming more important.

The concept of globalization is complex and involves more than international trade alone. It has other aspects that are not purely linked to international trade. Not only goods and services move in the world economy; resources do as well. Some common examples would be the movement of people and money for foreign direct investment. In a related vein, there are large movements in the world economy of portfolio capital. Globalization also affects the way the economies of countries function in terms of the growth rate of GDP and changes in a country's overall price level. A well-established correlation in macroeconomics is that openness as defined

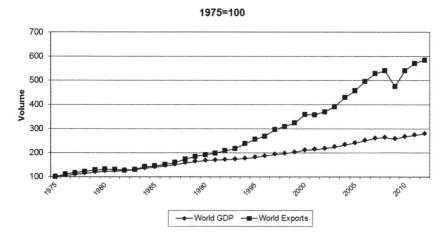

Figure 1.1 The Relationship between World Trade and GDP.
Source: Adapted from World Trade Organization (2014).

earlier and economic growth are positively correlated. If one is inclined to doubt this, think about the state or province that you live in. If the entity were a separate country and could not trade freely with the rest of the country, what would happen to economic output? A similar logic applies to the price level. Without trade, the overall price level in any country would be higher. For certain critical products, such as coffee, the absence of trade would produce consequences that are terrible to think about. Finally, globalization is especially important for developing countries. For countries that are developed, globalization is still an important issue. However, for the developing countries, integration into the world economy is critical for their economic development. Because most of the world's population resides in the developing countries, international trade policy is even more critical than it is for the developed countries.

From this, it is obvious that globalization is a complex issue. In order to examine it in a coherent manner, it is useful to think in the economic terms of benefits and costs. This is a natural way of thinking about most things to an economist. Economic phenomena always have both benefits and costs. The trick is to consider *both* and to analyze concepts like globalization in this way. As we will see, most international transactions improve welfare as long as they are voluntary. By definition, an international transaction is one that involves market participants in more than one country. Market participants such as individuals or businesses do not normally engage in transactions where the costs outweigh the benefits. International transactions occur because both parties expect the transaction to improve their welfare.

If globalization is such a positive thing, then one may well ask why it is so controversial. As we have pointed out, globalization has both benefits and costs. A consistent theme of this book will be to point out both. However, as we will see, in many cases it is much easier to see the costs than to identify the benefits. For example, the closing of a manufacturing plant is highly visible. On the other hand, the hiring of new workers or the expansion of an existing plant to increase exports would go practically unnoticed. One of the purposes of this book is to teach you to see both the benefits and the costs more clearly. With this information, you will be able to more clearly assess and judge the positive and negative sides of globalization. As we will see, on balance globalization is a positive thing. However, to be honest it is necessary to be clear about the costs. We will see that globalization, in all its forms, provides one more example of the economist's saying that there is no such thing as a free lunch. The same can be said of international trade policy. Changes in policy have both benefits and costs. Much of what follows in the next few chapters is learning to see both and apply them to the actions of governments.

Macroeconomics and Trade

To begin this section, one needs to understand that economics is, like medicine, a very broad field. If one meets someone who is a doctor, there is a natural follow-up question: What branch of medicine do you practice? Virtually, the same is true of economists. Economics is fragmented into a number of specializations. A common thread runs through all of them, but most economists study different aspects of the overall economy. Macroeconomics is a large part of the economics profession, and it is different. Unlike most economists, macroeconomists are concerned with the operation of the *entire* economy and not just a part. This part of the profession is large because the interest in the subject is great. It is difficult to get through a day without hearing or seeing a bit of macroeconomic information. It is also hard. It is one thing to explain international trade. Explaining the business cycle is a bit more difficult. Among economists, macroeconomics and international economics have some relationship. We've already mentioned that international trade can affect economic growth and the price level. However, these relationships usually are not large and occur mostly in the long run. For example, an economy that is relatively closed would tend to grow, but at a slightly lower rate than it would if it were more open. The same is true of inflation. Everything else being equal, more open economies would tend to have less inflation. Cheaper goods could be purchased from other countries. A more subtle but significant effect is that domestic producers faced with foreign competition tend to produce better products at lower prices. Consider what kind of car you would be driving and what it would cost if imports of cars from Japan and Korea were banned from the domestic market.

Where macroeconomics, international economics, and trade policy really intersect is with respect to trade balances.[2] As we will see in the next chapter, the intersection is only between the first two. Domestic macroeconomic conditions have a substantial impact on a country's imports. In a similar manner, macroeconomic conditions in other countries affect domestic exports. This is where things tend to go wrong in the reporting of trade balances. In both macroeconomics and international economics, the *overall* trade balance is of importance. The extent to which it is important is related to the data presented in Table 1.1. For example, the trade balance is much more important for Belgium than it is for the United States. Unfortunately in the popular press there tends to be a focus on the trade balance with particular countries. Much of the focus of the next chapter is to show that country-specific trade balances are practically useless information. Overall trade balances can be quite important, but our trade balance with a particular country or a region is of little consequence.

However, sometimes this sort of economic mistake becomes conventional wisdom and has significant adverse effects. This is the case with specific trade balances. A trade deficit with another country that is large all too frequently leads to proposed charges that the other country is engaging in "unfair" trade practices. As we will see later in the book, there is the very real possibility that unfair trade practices are a part of world trade. However, such practices have their effects primarily at the narrowly defined industry level. The possibility that systematic unfair trade practices could lead to a trade deficit with another country is small. Nonetheless, governments are frequently tempted to react to these country-specific trade imbalances using international trade policy. The fact that this almost never happens indicates that policy makers in the area of international trade policy sometimes have a better grasp of economic reality than their rhetoric would indicate.

Why Trade?

International trade policy exists because countries trade with one another. Organized international trade has a history that goes back thousands of years. In a simple sense, it is easy to understand why trade occurs. Any exchange, be it domestic or international, occurs because both parties benefit from it. If this was not the case, trade wouldn't occur. The buyer is improving their welfare, and the seller is making a profit. Now think a bit about some of the things you have heard about international trade. Suppose that country A is buying goods from country B. How often have you heard someone either say outright or at least imply that country A has been made worse off by purchasing goods from country B? Only a bit of reflection would indicate this is nonsense. The buyers in country B are almost always firms in the private sector. Are they likely to systematically buy products that make the firm worse off? This might happen every once in a while because everybody makes mistakes. If it does occur, it is not likely to happen again. If firms and individuals attempt to maximize their welfare by either buying from a foreigner or selling to a foreigner, it is not only in their best interest, but it maximizes the welfare of each country. This is precisely the problem with much of international trade policy. If policy makers, politicians, and the public cannot grasp this fundamental reality, then international trade policy is unlikely to be optimal.

In the simple sense described earlier, it is obvious why international trade occurs. However, economists have spent the last 200 years trying to understand why international trade occurs at an even more fundamental level. In an interesting reversal of the usual sequence, a public policy dispute over international trade policy laid the groundwork for research on what causes international trade. As a result, the theory of international trade and international trade policy are more closely connected than is usually the case. A basic understanding of the principles of international trade becomes an essential prelude to understanding international trade policy. As a bonus, this information is invaluable in understanding much of how the world economy works. In the jargon of economics, there is a significant positive externality in learning basic international trade theory. It is very useful in a variety of contexts—so useful, in fact, that we will take two chapters to walk through the classic and more modern extensions of why nations trade.

What Causes Trade Barriers?

From the earlier material, one can already guess what the optimal trade policy for any country is. To reinforce this point, let's consider a simple thought experiment. The United States is currently composed of 50 individual states. Under federal law there are few barriers to the movement of goods and services among these states. The total output of these states is the GDP of the United States. Now assume that states were allowed to act on the impulse described earlier and started to erect barriers to "imports" from other states. If this went on for a while, what would happen to the GDP of the United States? Intuitively, all of us can see what would happen: GDP would fall. A concrete example is the European Union (EU). For nearly 50 years, the EU has been attempting to replicate the economic system of free trade and common regulations in order to increase economic growth. The bottom line is that free trade increases prosperity. The strong implication of this is that the optimal international trade policy is free trade.

If the optimal international trade policy is free trade, then a world full of barriers to trade is something of a puzzle. Because these barriers lower overall economic welfare, one would think that they wouldn't exist. They exist because of two fundamental factors that governments have to deal with. First, overall is a key word. In economics everything has costs and benefits. The benefit of free trade is that it maximizes economic welfare. However, obtaining these benefits is not free. Some sectors of the economy gain and others lose. Overall, the gains are greater than the losses, but the losses are very real. This sets up the politics of international trade policy. The sectors of the economy that lose due to international trade put pressure on the government to change international trade policy in a way that will mitigate their losses. To the extent that they are successful, you end up with an international trade policy that falls short of the ideal of free trade. If one can learn to understand this trade-off and watch it play out in policy debates, then one can understand what is happening much more easily.

The Evolution of U.S. Trade Policy

U.S. international trade policy in the 21st century did not appear suddenly. Our current trade policy is an ongoing process of change that has been going on for over 200 years. U.S. international trade policy for much of the country's history had two distinct characteristics. First, unlike now, tariff revenue was the primary source of funds for the operation of the federal government. In a sense, trade policy was once much more complicated than it is today. Imagine mixing trade policy together with the personal and corporate income tax code and you can get a sense of the difficulties. Second, trade policy primarily was determined by Congress. If this sounds messy, it was. We will cover the history of U.S. international trade policy in Chapter 6, partially because it is very useful for understanding some of the seemingly complicated politics over trade issues.

As with many government policies, international trade policy underwent a fundamental change during the 1930s. The onset of the Great Depression coincided with a global trade war. Unfortunately, the war was started by the United States. Given the politics of international trade policy at the time, this conflict had its roots in Congress. The result was a sea change in the relationship between the executive and legislative branches of the U.S. government. <u>Our current international trade policy system is much more driven by the executive branch</u> than was true before the Great Depression. However, these relationships are to a certain extent embodied in law but partially a result of how the law is implemented. In the 21st century, the balance of power between the executive and legislative branches on international trade policy is shifting. To understand this shift, it is very useful to understand the history that led both to our current arrangements and the political strain on those arrangements.

Who Determines U.S. Trade Policy?

In the United States the issue of who administers trade policy is complicated. To understand this, consider the situation that would exist in a "typical" country in the rest of the world. First, the typical governmental structure is a parliamentary system. In such a system there is usually either a party of the center left or right or a coalition of parties that has a majority in parliament. After the political dust has settled post-election, there is a prime minister who is not directly elected and who oversees the actions of the various ministries in the government and appoints the other ministers. In virtually every country but the United States, there is either a ministry of international trade or a ministry of trade and industry. In this situation it is very clear who is overseeing international trade policy for the country. The trade minister is responsible for policy in this area subject to the oversight of the prime minister and the governing party/coalition. This is a straightforward arrangement, and the party/individual responsible for international trade policy is clear.

The situation in the United States is much less clear. First, the United States has a republican form of government, which can lead to different parties in charge of the executive and legislative branches of government. Now suppose that one would like to see a certain change in U.S. trade policy. Does one try to influence the executive branch or the legislative branch? With respect to the legislative branch, it is often the case that different political parties are in charge of the Senate and the House of Representatives. On most occasions, a change in international trade policy requires the agreement of both parties simultaneously in order to obtain any movement. In a sense, this is no different than the usual problem of getting movement on any issue out of the U.S. political process. Historically, Congress was in charge of international trade policy. However, for decades after the Great

Depression the president primarily was responsible for initiating changes in policy. More recently, Congress has shown a propensity to reassert its traditional role in determining policy. Combining a republican form of government with the complicated history of U.S. international trade policy yields no clear-cut answer to the question of who determines U.S. trade policy in the 21st century.

Institutions That Administer U.S. Trade Policy

As seen earlier, the United States is unique in its lack of a ministry or department of international trade. In a later chapter, we will see that there is a high-ranking official in the executive branch that functions something like a minister of trade in most countries. However, this official is primarily responsible for the conduct of trade negotiations. A particularly difficult aspect of their job is attempting to coordinate the activities of other government agencies that influence international trade. Anyone with even of modicum of experience in an organization can instantly recognize that this is not likely to be an enviable position. Although the official is in charge of coordinating trade policy, they do not necessarily have the authority to direct their activities.

The day-to-day administration of U.S. international trade policy is thus in the hands of a number of different departments scattered around the U.S. government. Just to name a few, some offices are heavily involved in the administration of international trade policy in the departments of Commerce, Treasury, Agriculture, and others. One of the more important offices involved in the administration of international trade policy, the International Trade Commission (ITC), is a standalone agency. A typical example can illustrate the difficulties this can cause. Suppose that the United States negotiates a free-trade agreement with a foreign country. A broad provision of these agreements is free trade in services. As a result, the Treasury Department is involved because this includes the freedom of foreign financial institutions to work in the U.S. market, and they will be responsible for regulating the activities of foreign firms. The Department of Transportation is involved because the agreement may involve foreign trucks using U.S. roads. The involvement of the Department of Agriculture in the administration of imports of food is an obvious example. To be polite, the administration of U.S. international trade policy has the potential to be a difficult task that may sometimes create problems. Chapter 9 will introduce the major departments and agencies that administer U.S. trade policy. However, even a complete chapter will only provide one with a broad outline of the internal workings of trade policy. A true Department of International Trade has been a policy proposal for decades. However, this probably makes too much sense to become reality.

The Future of U.S. Trade Policy

The general direction of international trade policy in the United States is reasonably clear.

First, as you will see in the following case study, the U.S. economy is becoming ever more open. Both imports and exports as a percentage of GDP have been rising for decades. As you saw in Table 1.1 these ratios are not particularly high when compared with other countries in the Organisation for Economic Co-operation and Development (OECD).[3] Exports will be particularly important for the United States in the future. As a developed country with an aging population, the potential for firms to grow sales and profits in the domestic market is limited. In this environment, exports to the rest of the world will be the easiest way for U.S. firms to rapidly increase sales. This is particularly true of the low- and middle-income countries where economic growth is faster. These countries also have the world's highest trade barriers, so the engagement of the United States in international trade negotiations with these countries is understandable. Second, there has been a consistent trend toward fewer trade restrictions in the world since the late 1940s. At times this movement has been faster or slower but the basic trend never changes. Given this movement toward freer trade, it is not really in the best interest of any country to stop liberalizing. For a country that puts any value on economic growth, attempting to stop liberalizing trade isn't really an option. As we will see, obtaining easier access to foreign markets is a bargain. The other side of the bargain is liberalizing access to your market. Stopping the latter, by definition, means stopping the former as well.

Although the direction of change in international trade policy is clear, the details of these changes are not. In the second half of the 20th century, world trade was made freer by the process of a large number of countries engaging in difficult and protracted trade negotiations. Although this process was difficult, it produced substantial reductions in trade barriers. Unfortunately, in the 21st century that process is no longer producing reductions in trade barriers. What is seemingly the wave of the future is a large number of mostly bilateral trade agreements where two countries essentially eliminate trade barriers. Such negotiations are easier to accomplish. However, they are turning world trade into a "spaghetti bowl" of smaller trade agreements that make policy and decision making much more complicated for both the public and private sectors. In such a world, a lack of understanding of international trade policy can be a large problem. Hopefully, what follows will help to reduce that problem.

Case Study: Globalization and the Position of the United States in the World Economy

The United States has a truly unique position in the world economy for a number of reasons. First, the sheer size of the U.S. economy makes it important. The GDP of the United States is approximately $18 trillion. The second largest economy is China's, with a GDP of approximately $11 trillion. The U.S. economy accounts for nearly a quarter of the world's economic output. Second, the United States is also the world's largest exporter. In 2013, the United States exported and imported approximately $1,593 billion and $2,295 billion in goods and services, respectively. In both an absolute and a relative sense, the United States is the world's largest trading nation. In the concern over U.S. trade deficits, these facts are frequently overlooked. Third, the United States has the world's largest financial market. Consequently, a substantial amount of the capital flows and currency trading directly or indirectly involves these financial markets. Finally, the dollar is the dominant vehicle currency for transactions in the world economy. A vehicle currency is a currency used indirectly in international exchanges because it is stable and easy to trade.[4]

Despite these statistics, the discussion of international trade and the U.S. economy has been a focus of controversy for some time. If the United States is simultaneously the world's largest economy and the world's largest trading nation, why should international trade issues remain so controversial? Figure 1.2 is useful in resolving this seeming paradox. The chart tracks two conflicting trends for the U.S. economy. First, over the last 50 years the percentage of the U.S. economy that produces exports has risen from approximately 2 percent to nearly 14 percent. For industries that emphasize exports, this increasing "openness" of the U.S. economy has created opportunities for increased sales and profits. However, for the part of the economy that produces domestic goods that compete with imports, clothing, steel, and lumber, for example, the adjustment to this new level of competition has been difficult, as sales and profits have fallen. Although trade is beneficial to the economy as a whole, the same cannot be said for all segments of the economy. Perhaps the chronic trade deficits the United States has run over the last 20 years have focused too much attention on import competition and not enough attention on the United States as a successful exporter of goods and services.

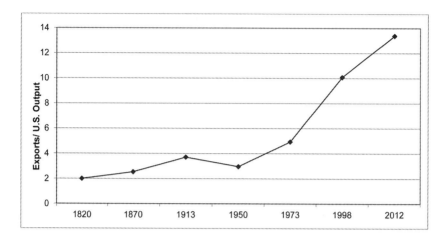

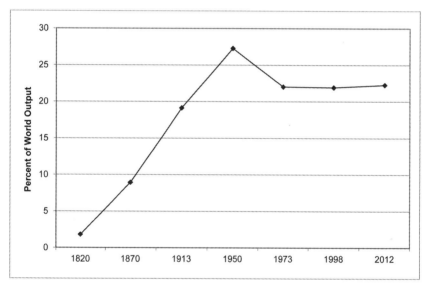

Figure 1.2 Trade and the U.S. Economy. Top: U.S. Exports as a Percentage of U.S. Output. Bottom: U.S. Output as a Percentage of World Output.
Source: Maddison (2001) and World Bank (2014).

The second part of the chart tracks U.S. GDP as a percentage of the economic output of the world economy. In the middle of the 20th century, the U.S. economy was approximately 27 percent of the economy of the world. During that period, the United States was not just a relatively large economy—it was the dominant economy. In the ensuing 50 years, the U.S. economy has become "smaller" relative to the rest of the world economy.

This means that for some time the economy of the rest of the world has grown faster than that of the United States. Whether or not this relative decline is of any importance has served as the subject of some debate.[5] However, being the world's largest economy, being the world's largest trading nation, and having one of the highest standards of living in the world is not a particularly terrible position for a country to be in.

A closer examination of the chart reveals that the time frame covers more than 100 years. This historical perspective is intentional. If one examines the position of the U.S. economy in the late 19th century, the parallels with the late 20th century are interesting. In terms of both trade as a percentage of GDP and U.S. GDP relative to the rest of the world, the U.S. position today is not so different from what it was 100 years ago. At that time, the United States was the world's largest economy. Also, exports were approximately 40 percent as important a component in GDP as they are now. Looking at a longer stretch of history, the position of the U.S. economy as a relatively "closed" economy seems abnormal. The same may be true for the dominant position that the U.S. economy had in the mid-20th century. Despite the U.S. economy's large size, its dominance in the mid-20th century may have been something of an aberration created by the lingering effects of the Great Depression and World War II. Although the position of the United States in the world economy is now somewhat different from what it was 20 or 30 years ago, this position may, in a longer historical view, be more typical.[6]

Notes

1. The website for the WTO at www.wto.org contains a wealth of information about the history and activities of the organization.

2. For now we will use the generic term trade balance. Things are actually a bit more complicated and will be explained in more detail in the next chapter.

3. Throughout the book we will use the acronym OECD as a convenient way of describing the group of high-income countries.

4. For more details, see Devereux and Shi (2008).

5. For example, see Kennedy (1987).

6. For a more extensive treatment of these subjects, see Irwin (1996).

Bibliography

Devereux, Michael B. and Shouyong Shi. 2008. "Vehicle Currency." *Federal Reserve Bank of Dallas Globalization and Monetary Policy Institute Working Paper No. 10.*

Heston, Alan, Robert Summers, and Bettina Aten. 2013. Penn World Table Version 6.2. Philadelphia: University of Pennsylvania.

Irwin, Douglas A. 1996. "The United States in a Global Economy? A Century's Perspective," *American Economic Review* 86 (May): 41–46.

Kennedy, Paul M. 1987. *The Rise and Fall of the Great Powers.* New York: Random House.

Maddison, Angus. 2001. *The World Economy: A Millennial Perspective.* Paris: Organisation for Economic Co-operation and Development.

World Bank. 2014. *World Development Indicators.* Washington, D.C.: World Bank.

World Trade Organization. 2014. *International Trade Statistics, 2014.* Geneva: World Trade Organization.

CHAPTER TWO

Trade Balances and Macroeconomic Imbalances

The produce of a country exchanges for the produce of other countries, at such values as are required in order that the whole of her exports may exactly pay for the whole of her imports.

—John Stuart Mill

Introduction

One of the most important tasks in learning about international trade policy is learning how to place it into the broader context of international economics. For almost everyone, this is a critical point of confusion. The media is filled with terms such as <u>WTO, trade balance, free-trade agreement, exchange rate, current account,</u> etc. This short list is set up deliberately to emphasize a point. Every other term is related to a different part of international economics. The first and third are international trade. The second and last are international finance. This distinction is critically important for trade policy. If you think that the WTO and exchange rates are related in any sense, the potential for confusion is huge. Their frequent confusion about these topics is sadly understandable. This is especially true for those reading about international economic issues. In many cases, they are confused because the journalists writing about international economic issues are confused. It is all too easy to find articles in respectable business publications that contain shockingly basic mistakes in international economics. It is not quite the blind leading the blind, but sometimes it is perilously close. At least journalists usually are trying to get it right. Once one moves into the political sphere, clarity and understanding deteriorate rapidly. For economists, listening to politicians talk about international trade policy is frequently a comedic form of entertainment. Either they observe a massive level of ignorance or political considerations have become paramount, or we observe some combination of the two.

The purpose of this chapter is to get you to the point where you can understand that trade balances aren't really related to international trade policy. It is an unfortunate reality that a lot that is written about trade policy is wrong from the start. At the beginning, there is an assumption that barriers to trade affect overall imports and exports. As we will see in this chapter, that just isn't the case. This basic misconception does not yield favorable outcomes. International trade policy that is driven by this misconception can lead to unfortunate levels of protectionism. On a more daily basis, it just leads to bad writing about what is happening and how the world works. A really common example of this is every month the government reports the trade balance. Because this number virtually always is a deficit, the overall balance is followed by a discussion of the "causes" of the deficit. With all seriousness the journalist goes on to list the deficit with particular countries. The deficit has now been "explained." The overall deficit was large because of large bilateral deficits with some of the major trading partners. As we will see later, this is total nonsense. Our main purpose here is to be able to separate trade balances from trade policy. However, a bonus is involved. If you understand trade balances, then you can much better understand the macroeconomics of the United States and other countries.

To accomplish our goal, the chapter is divided into four parts. The first part involves learning the jargon of the balance of payments. This material can be tedious but it is essential. A lot of reporting on the world economy involves trade balances, and the jargon of the balance of payments frequently is used in the wrong way. If you have the balance of payments jargon straight in your head, it is a lot easier to understand what you are reading or hearing. The balance of payments is something that is created domestically. Surpluses and deficits are mostly made at home, and the results are something like a residual of production and consumption. An important way that the overall economy interacts with the rest of the world is through importing and exporting goods and services. If one can put imports and exports into a broader context, it really helps one to understand how the overall economy works. This knowledge then allows you to put international trade policy into its proper perspective. It is important and can affect imports and exports, but in a more limited way than is usually thought.

The Balance of Payments Accounts

Just as a country's national income accounts keep track of gross domestic product (GDP), savings, investment, taxes, and government spending, the balance of payments accounts keep track of the international transactions. The overall balance of payments includes a number of different important subcomponent accounts. It is composed of the balance on current account, the balance on financial account, and the balance on capital account. The balance on current account is a record of transactions that includes payments for goods, services, and other items described later. The balance on financial account is a record of transactions that includes payments related to financial assets such as bonds. It also includes transactions involving the sale or acquisition of foreign nonfinancial assets like land. The balance on capital account is a record of other activities resulting in transfers of wealth between countries. There is a third component known as the balance on capital account. This includes nonmarket international asset transfers, including debt forgiveness and the transfer of bank accounts by foreign citizens when immigrating to the United States. However, it is normally very small and will be excluded from most of our discussion later.

[handwritten margin note: current financial capital]

At the most basic level, the balance of payments is a record of all economic transactions derived from the exchange of goods, services, income, and assets between residents of one country and the rest of the world. The balance of payments accounts record the total inflows and outflows of money (dollars) to and from foreign countries. The inflows and outflows are relatively large for the United States. Indeed, tracking every dollar would be impossible. One needs to keep in mind that the balance of payments statistics for the United States or any country are a rough approximation of the magnitude of these flows rather than an exact number resulting from a precise accounting system. Although we are using the term *accounting* in association with the balance of payments accounts, in this context the term means something very different from the typical jargon of accounting. As a result, our first objective is to describe the terminology in the balance of payments statement. Our second objective is to ascertain what a country's balance of payments accounts tell us about the country's domestic economy. As we will show, one can learn a lot about a country's economy from analyzing its balance of payments statement. Indirectly, any persistent trend in a country's balance of payments may have an influence on how a country attempts to change its international trade policy.

The Balance on Current Account

Table 2.1 shows a summary of the balance of payments statistics for the United States in the year 2013. The first two rows in the table are merchandise exports and merchandise imports. Notice that the former is a positive number and the latter is a negative number. This is because merchandise

Table 2.1   U.S. International Transactions, 2013 ($ Billions)

Current Account Transactions	
Exports of merchandise	$1,592.8
Imports of merchandise	–2,294.5
Merchandise trade balance	–701.7
Exports of services	687.4
Imports of services	–462.1
Balance on services	225.3
Balance on goods and services	–476.4
Income receipts on U.S. assets abroad	780.1
Income payments of foreign assets in the United States	–580.5
Balance on investment income	199.7
Balance on goods, services, and income	–276.7
Unilateral transfers, net	–123.5
Balance on current account	–400.2
Capital account transactions, net	.4
Financial Account Transactions	
Net U.S. acquisition of financial assets, excluding financial derivatives	644.8
Net U.S. incurrence of liabilities, excluding financial derivatives	1,017.7
Balance on Financial Account	370.7
Statistical discrepancy	30.0

Source: Bureau of Economic Analysis (2014).

exports create an inflow of dollars (money) as other countries pay for U.S. goods. On the other hand, merchandise imports create an outflow of dollars (money) as the United States pays for foreign-produced goods. The principle that inflows are recorded as a positive number and outflows as a negative number holds true for the rest of the items in the balance of payments. When the United States sells goods, services, or assets to foreigners, these sales create an inflow of dollars (money), and a plus sign is attached to the number. The reverse occurs, when the United States buys foreign goods, services, or assets, as the purchases create an outflow of dollars (money), and a negative sign is attached to the number.

The difference between merchandise exports ($1,592.8 billion) and imports (–$2,294.5 billion) yields the merchandise trade balance. As Table 2.1 indicates the United States had a merchandise trade deficit of

−$701.7 billion. In 2013, the United States was a net importer of merchandise (goods), which means that merchandise imports were larger than exports. As column 2 in Table 2.2 indicates, the United States had a merchandise trade surplus for the three years indicated in the 1960s. In the early 1970s, the United States had a merchandise trade deficit. Over time this deficit has become larger as merchandise imports have grown at a faster rate than merchandise exports. This has had an impact on U.S. international trade policy since the 1980s. Prior to that time the U.S. government was much more aggressive in pursuing free trade. The persistent merchandise trade deficits have slowed the drive to freer trade. As we will see later, this is a misplaced emphasis, but it would be naïve to assume that it does not matter.

Merchandise trade does not represent all of the inflows and outflows of dollars to and from the economy. The next three rows of Table 2.1 summarize the international service flows. U.S. citizens traveling overseas take dollars out of the United States (outflow). When foreign citizens travel to Disney World, they bring their currency into the United States (inflow). We do not think of travel expenses or tourism as imports and exports, but they are because they create outflows and inflows of dollars. In addition, some companies are engaged in the provision of services across national borders. These companies may be compensated for these services in the form of fees. For example, an accounting firm's principal activity may be the sale of professional services. If some of these sales occur in other countries, this would create an inflow of money into the country. In other cases, individuals or companies may be receiving payments in the form of royalties or licensing fees for the sale of intellectual property. These sorts of payments must be accounted for as they create inflows and outflows of money. In 2013, service exports of $687.4 billion included travel and transportation services the United States provided to foreigners and fees and royalties the United States received from foreigners. U.S. imports of these services from other countries amounted to −$462.1 billion. The balance on services (the difference between exports and imports of services) was $225.3 billion. This positive balance indicates that the United States had a surplus in services. As column 3 in Table 2.2 shows, the United States consistently has a surplus service balance, and this surplus has grown over time. These large and growing surpluses in services have affected U.S. trade policy. In a later chapter, we will consider the details of the numerous free-trade agreements that the United States has negotiated with other countries. One of the prominent features of these agreements is the inclusion of free trade in services. The data earlier indicate why this is the case.

Table 2.2 Summary of U.S. International Transactions, 1964–2012 ($ Billions)

Year	Merchandise Trade Balance	Service Balance	Goods and Service Balance	Investment Income Balance	Unilateral Transfers Balance	Current Account Balance
1964	6.8	−.8	6.0	5.0	−4.2	6.8
1966	3.8	−.9	2.9	5.0	−5.0	3.0
1968	.6	−.4	.3	6.0	−5.6	.6
1970	2.6	−.3	2.3	6.2	−6.2	2.3
1972	−6.4	1.0	−5.4	8.2	−8.5	−5.8
1974	−5.5	1.2	−4.3	15.5	−9.2	2.0
1976	−9.5	3.4	−6.1	16.1	−5.7	4.3
1978	−33.9	4.2	−29.8	20.4	−5.8	−15.1
1980	−25.5	6.1	−19.4	30.1	−8.3	2.3
1982	−36.5	12.3	−24.2	35.2	−16.5	−5.5
1984	−112.5	3.4	−109.1	35.1	−20.3	−94.3
1986	−145.1	6.6	−138.5	15.5	−24.1	−147.2
1988	−127.0	12.4	−114.6	18.7	−25.3	−121.2
1990	−111.0	30.1	−80.9	8.6	−26.7	−79.0
1992	−96.9	57.7	−39.2	24.2	−35.1	−50.1
1994	−165.8	667.3	−98.5	17.1	−40.3	−121.6
1996	−191.0	86.9	−104.1	22.3	−43.0	−124.8
1998	−248.2	82.1	−166.1	4.3	−53.2	−215.1
2000	−454.7	74.9	−379.8	21.1	−58.6	−417.4
2002	−485.0	61.2	−423.70	27.7	−63.6	−459.6
2004	−669.6	57.5	−612.1	56.4	−84.4	−640.1
2006	−837.3	75.6	−761.75	43.3	−88.3	−806.7
2008	−832.5	123.8	−708.7	146.1	−124.1	−686.6
2010	−648.7	154.0	−494.7	177.7	−126.9	−443.9
2012	−742.1	204.5	−537.6	203.0	−126.1	−460.7

Source: Bureau of Economic Analysis (2014).

The Undercounting of Exports

For the United States, the balance on goods and services was −$476.4 billion in 2013. It is quite likely that this number is too large—in other words, that the deficit is being reported as higher than it actually is. The same logic would hold for a country reporting a trade surplus. In this case, the reported surplus is probably too low. This would also affect the numbers reported in the current account. The United States provides a convenient example of how this happens.

The export of goods is usually undercounted by a nontrivial amount. The U.S. Department of Commerce has reported that the U.S. exports of goods may be undercounted by as much as 10 percent. For 2013, this would represent uncounted exports of approximately $160 billion. If this is the case, then the merchandise trade deficit is being reported as considerably larger than it actually is. To a large extent, this occurs because U.S. exporters are not obligated to report *individual* exports with a value of less than $2,500. This would mean, for example, that Amazon.com would not have to report any sales of books overseas as exports unless an individual order was in excess of $2,500. As more and more small businesses become exporters, the problem may only get worse.

The undercounting of exports is even more severe with respect to services. In part this is a function of how service exports are counted. If a services exporter sells a service to a foreign buyer that is not related to the domestic company, this is recorded as an export of services. However, if a domestic company "sells" a service to a foreign subsidiary of the same company, this is not an export of services. Essentially, intracompany transactions that cross national borders are not counted as an export of services even though the foreign subsidiary may have to pay for that service. The exact size of the undercounting of exports of services is debatable, but it is not likely to be small. The undercounted exports of goods and services means that the U.S. trade deficit and the current account deficit reported previously are significantly overestimated.

This is not just a problem for the United States. It is an interesting anomaly that the world always runs a current account deficit with itself. This means that the world economy is reporting outflows of money that are greater than the inflows. Unless we are trading with another planet, exports must be undercounted in the world economy relative to imports. Given the growth of world trade, as described in Chapter 1, it is becoming increasingly important for governments to obtain a clearer picture of the amount of trade in goods and services. Exports are a large part of GDP in most countries, and an undercount of exports means an undercount of GDP. An important part of managing an economy consists of keeping GDP at an appropriate level. To this end, accurate balance of payments data would be helpful.

Combining the surplus of the service balance with the merchandise trade deficit yields the balance on goods and services of −$476.4 billion. This deficit indicates that the United States transferred fewer goods and services to other countries than it received from them in 2006. Column 4 in Table 2.2 lists the balance on goods and services for the United States from 1964–2006. The United States had a surplus balance on goods and services for the years indicated in the 1960s, and beginning in the early 1970s, this surplus changed into a deficit for the United States.

The U.S. Department of Commerce reports the balance on goods and services (monthly), and it is widely reported in the business media. However, monthly trade statistics should be viewed cautiously for two reasons. First, as we will see, this balance does not count all of the international inflows and outflows. Second, these monthly statistics are quite volatile. A large change in the balance on goods and services from one month to the next really does not mean much, as one month of data does not constitute a trend.

The next section of Table 2.1 shows the inflows and outflows of money associated with U.S. investment in other countries and foreign investment in the United States. Over the years, U.S. citizens have invested a substantial amount of money abroad in real and financial assets. Investments in real assets are called foreign direct investment (FDI). FDI by a firm or individuals generates a stream of profits that eventually will be repatriated back to the United States. Financial investments by U.S. residents overseas also yield a stream of interest payments, dividend payments, and capital gains—all of which are referred to as "receipts." These receipts are recorded as income receipts on U.S. assets abroad. This is recorded as a positive number because it is an inflow of money to the United States.

The other side of investment income is payments to foreigners on their assets in the United States. These payments are recorded as a negative number, as the payments go to citizens or firms in foreign countries. The net of the receipts and payments can create a positive or negative number for the balance on investment income, the difference between income earned on foreign assets and payments to foreign residents on their assets. In 2013, the United States had a balance on investment income of $199.7 billion. Row 5 in Table 2.2 shows the U.S. investment income balance since 1964. This balance for the United States was in surplus from 1964 through 2012. The reasons for the change in this balance are outlined later. Combining the surplus of the balance on investment income with the deficit of the balance on goods and services yields a balance on goods, services, and income of −$276.7 billion.

The next item in the balance of payments statements is unilateral transfers. Unilateral transfers are the inflows and outflows from the United States where there are no services rendered. Unilateral transfers include U.S. government pensions paid to U.S. residents living abroad and economic as well as military grants to foreign countries. U.S. residents create part of the outflow of this balance when they send money overseas to support family members or as part of nongovernmental charitable activities. Conversely, there are inflows of money into the United States. Because more U.S. residents make more transfers to foreigners than foreigners make to U.S. residents, the United States consistently has a negative unilateral transfers balance. As Table 2.3 shows, the net of unilateral transfers to and from foreigners was −$123.5 billion in 2013. The addition of unilateral transfers to the balance on goods, services, and income yields the balance on current account. The United States had a current account deficit of −$400.2 billion. For the U.S. economy this means that outflows of money related to trade in goods and services, investment income, and unilateral transfers were smaller than the inflows of money. For all countries, this balance is the most comprehensive view of a country's total trade flows. Unfortunately, there is a tendency to confuse the current account balance with either the merchandise trade balance or the balance on goods and services. The case of the United States in 1980 is a prime example of this kind of potential confusion. In that year, the United States had a deficit in its merchandise trade balance. However, it also had a surplus in investment income that compensated for the deficit in merchandise trade. Did the United States have a current account surplus or deficit in that year? It had a current account surplus: the total inflow of money on trade in goods and services plus investment income and unilateral transfers was greater than the total of outflows.

If the current account balance gives a much better picture of a country's international trade than does the balance on goods and services, why doesn't it receive more public attention? For the United States, part of the problem is how the numbers are reported. The Department of Commerce reports the balance on goods and services monthly, and the information receives some notice in the media. However, the current account balance is reported quarterly with the GDP statistics. Quite understandably, the focus of the press release is on what has happened to GDP in the previous quarter, and the information on the current account balance is much less widely reported. Although the monthly balance on goods and services statistics are of some interest to economists, the government, and the business community, the quarterly reporting of the current account balance is a better indicator of the country's trade position.

Remittances

Buried in the dry details of the current account balance are unilateral transfers. As indicated in the text, this category includes both government and personal transfer payments either leaving or entering the country. On the government side, these transfers are primarily the official development assistance (ODA) provided by the United States to developing countries. Currently, global ODA is around $100 billion. Traditionally, we think of ODA as the bulk of unilateral transfers. In reality, ODA is becoming the minority of unilateral transfers by a substantial margin. Over the last 20 years, the private transfers, known as remittances, overtook ODA. Globally, remittances are now over $500 billion and growing much more rapidly than ODA. As one would expect, over $400 billion of this is flowing to the developing countries. The developing countries of Asia receive over half of the total, with the remainder distributed evenly among the rest of the developing countries.

These flows are enormously important to many of the recipient countries. The migrants are moving and sending remittances for a variety of reasons. One reason is simple altruism. Others include compensation for previous services rendered or the repayment of loans. Remittances also are used as insurance by households against adverse shocks. Life in a poor country is uncertain, and remittances can be an important buffer against adversity. A motive for remittances that is important is the use of the money for investment—oftentimes in a small business. An active literature studies the extent to which remittances are used for consumption or investment. If the latter, then it is conceivable that remittances should be positively related to economic growth. However, the evidence on this is mixed. What is undeniable is that remittances are absolutely crucial for a number of developing countries. There are at least 30 countries in the world where remittances are at least 5 percent of GDP. There are at least 20 countries where they are 10 percent of GDP. The vast majority of these countries are small, low-income countries where the remittances make a substantial contribution to the standard of living. For these countries it is not uncommon for remittances to cover 20 percent of imports and also be equivalent to 30 percent of exports. For a developed country, unilateral transfers are a minor part of the current account balance. Now consider a country such as Honduras. Remittances are nearly 20 percent of GDP. Remittances cover 30 percent of imports and are equivalent to 40 percent of exports. For Honduras, unilateral transfers are somewhat more than just another line in the current account balance.

The Balance on Capital and Financial Accounts

Even though the current account balance is the most important part of the balance of payments, it is still only a part. We have not covered all possible transfers of dollars into and out of the United States. For instance, what if a U.S. citizen buys a foreign asset? Suppose that a U.S. company purchases land and builds a manufacturing plant in Mexico. Would this transaction be recorded in the current account balance? The answer is no, because a manufacturing plant is not an import. You cannot move the plant from Mexico to the United States. The reverse is also true. When foreigners purchase U.S. assets, these transactions are not recorded in the current account. Such transactions include both FDI and purchases of financial assets such as bonds. These transactions are recorded in what is known as the financial account. The same is true of many governmental transactions. If the U.S. government purchases property in a foreign country, this is a capital account transaction. Something similar occurs when central banks buy or sell foreign exchange. All of these transactions are recorded in a country's capital or financial accounts.

The capital account in Table 2.1 shows the net of capital account transactions. Capital transactions are inflows and outflows of money associated with certain types of nonfinancial assets. These include debt forgiveness and the assets that immigrants bring into the country and emigrants take out of the country. In 2013, the net of these capital transactions was $0.4 billion. This represents a net outflow of money from the United States and enters the balance of payments with a positive sign. If we add the current account balance to the capital account balance, we find that the United States has an excess of outflows over inflows of −$399.8 billion. Because overall outflows and inflows of money must balance, this outflow must be matched by a $815.4 billion inflow in the bottom section of the balance of payments statement, which is called the financial account.

Table 2.1 shows the transactions included in the financial account. This measures the difference between purchases of assets abroad by the United States and sales of U.S. assets to foreigners. Below the financial account is the change in assets abroad. This item totals all of the purchases of foreign assets that U.S. citizens and the U.S. government made during a year. It shows up as a negative number because these transactions create an outflow of money (dollars) as U.S. citizens receive the assets and foreign citizens receive the money. These purchases have risen dramatically, from less than $100 billion in 1980 to $644.8 billion in 2013. This rise was accounted for by a large increase in U.S. private assets abroad. Changes in government assets are included but have not been important since the 1970s.

The next item in the capital account is the change in foreign assets. This item records all of the purchases of U.S. assets by foreigners and foreign central banks. It is a positive number, indicating that these transactions create an inflow of money (dollars) from abroad as U.S. citizens receive the money and the foreign citizens receive the assets. In 1980, foreigners purchased roughly $50.3 billion in U.S. assets. In 2013, foreigners purchased $1,017.7 billion in U.S. assets. In 2013, the U.S. financial account balance was in surplus by $370.7 billion.

The final item in the balance of payments accounts, statistical discrepancy, captures any net inflows or outflows that the U.S. government failed to record. The U.S. government recognizes it failed to record some transactions when the total inflows and outflows of dollars (money) are not equal. In 2013 unrecorded (or misrecorded) international transactions generated a statistical discrepancy of $30 billion. The current account balance was in deficit by $400.2 billion, the capital account was in deficit by $0.4 billion, and the financial account was in surplus by $370.7 billion. Obviously, the U.S. government missed some of the international flows. However, the government has no way of knowing which flows it missed—goods, services, investment income, unilateral transfers, or capital. To make the balance of payments balance, we use the statistical discrepancy to force these inflows and outflows to be equal.

Balancing the Balance of Payments

The rule that total inflows and outflows need to be equal is governed by an interesting logical concept. If the current account balance is negative, then the capital and financial account balance must be positive. The reverse is also true. A country running a deficit on trade in goods and services must somehow "finance" this deficit by borrowing from foreigners. Remember that a deficit in trade in goods and services means that a country is consuming more than it is producing. In 1980, the United States was "paying" for the trade deficit with investment income. Looking at the capital and financial accounts for the same year, the United States was investing more overseas than foreigners were investing in the United States.

Current account surpluses must be balanced as well. A current account surplus means a capital and financial account deficit. Investors in a country will have to purchase foreign assets in excess of what foreigners are purchasing in that country. This may not necessarily be advantageous because the capital account surplus means that there will be less capital for investors to invest in their own country since capital will be moving to other countries. Because rates of economic growth are sensitive to capital investment, growth may slow at some point in the future. Also, exporting capital may lower the rate of growth of productivity and the growth of real wages. However, exporting capital may lead to rising investment income, which would enable the country to consume more in the future.

From these relationships, we may more thoroughly discuss U.S. international trade policy. Virtually all of the discussion attempting to link trade policy to the balance of payments is focused on a subset of the total inflows and outflows of money. The merchandise trade balance is an important subset of the total flows, but it is far from the entire picture. As time passes, trade in services is becoming increasingly important relative to trade in goods. Investment income is important for a developed country because they are typically net lenders to the rest of the world. In a world where labor is increasingly mobile internationally, remittances that are a large part of unilateral transfers are going to represent an outflow of money to other countries. Although the current account is considered in total, we still have not touched the financial account. Flows of FDI are now an important part of the economic workings of the world economy. With global financial markets, flows of portfolio capital are essential to the functioning of the world economy.

What this means is that international trade policy is just one part of a complicated mosaic of a country's international economic policy. Trade policy can have a limited impact on merchandise trade and perhaps trade in services. After that point in a balance of payments statement, there are still a lot of different inflows and outflows. The reality is that few of these are affected by trade policy. Many, if not most, of them are affected by other government policies. In particular, macroeconomic policy has a large impact on both the current and financial accounts. Our task now is to show how changes in the domestic economy influence various components of both accounts. These effects can occasionally have an influence on the international trade policy of a country.

Exporters and Importers of Capital

It is commonplace to think of countries as exporters and importers of goods and services. What is much less common is to consider countries as exporters and importers of capital. This is perfectly understandable. A lot of information is disseminated about the merchandise trade balance, and to a lesser extent, the current account balance. However, flows of capital are just as important as the flows of goods, services, and income. Now that you understand the relationship between the current account and the financial

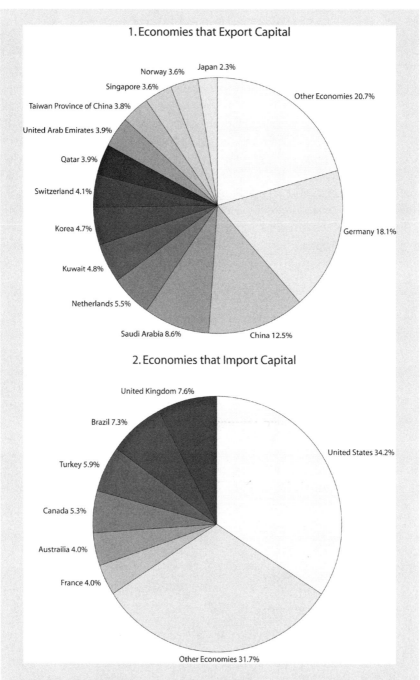

1. Economies that Export Capital

Japan 2.3%
Norway 3.6%
Singapore 3.6%
Taiwan Province of China 3.8%
United Arab Emirates 3.9%
Qatar 3.9%
Switzerland 4.1%
Korea 4.7%
Kuwait 4.8%
Netherlands 5.5%
Saudi Arabia 8.6%
China 12.5%
Germany 18.1%
Other Economies 20.7%

2. Economies that Import Capital

United Kingdom 7.6%
Brazil 7.3%
Turkey 5.9%
Canada 5.3%
Austrailia 4.0%
France 4.0%
Other Economies 31.7%
United States 34.2%

Figure 2.1 Major Net Exporters and Importers of Capital, 2013.
Source: International Monetary Fund (2014).

account, this should make sense. However, the data presented in Table 2.1 pertain to a single country: the United States. Any one country can be a net importer or exporter of capital. Just as trade flows for the world have to balance, the same is true for capital flows. The data on overall capital flows in the world economy are much less commonly reported. Fortunately, the International Monetary Fund tracks global flows of capital over a year. The data on these flows are shown in Figure 2.1.

All countries both import and export capital, so the percentages shown in the two figures represent net capital flows or the balance on financial account. The three largest net exporters of capital are Germany, China, and Saudi Arabia. These three countries account for over a third of the net capital exported in the world. Another half of the capital exported is accounted for by only 10 countries in the Middle East, Europe, and Asia. To summarize the concentration of capital exports, only 13 countries account for nearly 80 percent of the world total of capital exports. The data on capital imports are even more concentrated. The United States accounts for over a third of capital imports. Another third is concentrated in just six countries: the United Kingdom, Brazil, Turkey, Canada, Australia, and France. This concentration of both imports and exports of world capital flows is an interesting, yet often overlooked, aspect of the world economy.

The Relationship between Domestic Production and Consumption

International trade policy has an effect on imports and exports. However, as we saw from the balance of payments statement earlier, both imports and exports are very large numbers. The barriers to trade that are embodied in international trade policy can affect those numbers in a small way. What we need to focus on now is the major factors that determine the extent to which a country engages in international trade. In essence, we are attempting to answer the question of why a country's total imports and exports are what they are. If one reads what is in the media, one can get the impression that imports into the United States are a function of very low U.S. tariffs or the nefarious international trade policies of other countries. A less frequently seen view is that U.S. exports are largely a function of trade barriers in other countries. There is a bit of truth in both statements, but imports and exports primarily are determined by other, more fundamental, factors. It is these factors that we now need to address. The total volume of imports and exports is important, but what is critically important is their relationship to GDP. Simply put, what is important is the percentage of GDP that is involved in foreign trade. More technically, the important numbers are the ratio of exports to GDP and the ratio of imports to GDP. To understand these ratios, let's spend some time thinking about the denominator in them.

National income accounting refers to the calculation of GDP for a country and the subdivision of GDP into various components. Included in the various components of GDP are exports and imports. However, exports and imports cannot be treated in isolation because they are also related to the other components of GDP. Understanding these relationships will make it easier for you to interpret how economic events affect not only international trade but also the overall economy. In the first part of this section, we will briefly review some of the issues to consider when calculating GDP. Next, we define the major components of GDP, and then we examine the interactions among them in a way that highlights the role of international trade in a country's economy.

The Components of GDP

Another way of examining the GDP of a country is to consider its various components. GDP can be calculated by summing the different types of expenditures that occur within a country. Thus, it can be represented using the following identity:

$$Y = C + I + G + (X - M)$$

In this relationship, Y represents GDP (total production). C represents the public's consumption of goods and services. This type of expenditure is composed of spending by individuals and families on a daily basis. I represents two types of investment spending. The first type is investment by business firms in equipment, software, structures, and changes in business inventories. The second type of investment spending is expenditures on housing, which is referred to as residential investment. G represents the purchase of goods and services by local, state, and federal governments. X and M represent exports and imports of goods and services, respectively, and net exports is defined as [exports (X) minus imports (M)]. Figure 2.2 shows the four different components of U.S. GDP for 2013. As the figure indicates, public consumption was approximately 71 percent of GDP. Investment and government spending accounted for approximately 17 percent and 18 percent, respectively. Finally, exports minus imports accounted for a negative 6 percent of GDP, indicating that the United States imported more goods and services than it exported. Although we

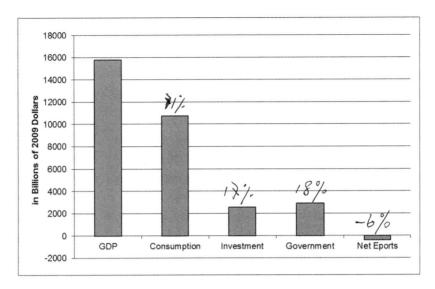

Figure 2.2   The Components of U.S. GDP.
Source: Bureau of Economic Analysis (2014).

illustrate the shares of the four components of U.S. GDP for 2013 in Figure 2.2, it is important to note that the shares of the components are constantly changing.

Until 1970, the sum of U.S. exports and imports rarely amounted to more than one-tenth of GDP. As Figure 2.3 indicates, since 1970, the real volume of trade has grown at more than twice the rate of output. In other words, the ratios of both X and M to GDP have been rising because exports and imports have been growing faster than GDP. This growth of trade has caused an increase in the share of GDP devoted to exports and imports. By 2010, exports accounted for 10 percent of GDP and imports were equivalent to 16 percent of GDP. In 1959, exports and imports together were less than 5 percent of GDP. When we speak of the "globalization" of the U.S. economy, we are referring to these growth trends in total imports and exports. Given these trends, it is clear why trade policy has become a more important subject. In the next section, we examine how the components of GDP interact with one another.

GDP and the Trade Balance

Now that we have examined the components of GDP, we can consider how they interact with one another. In order to do this, we will begin our

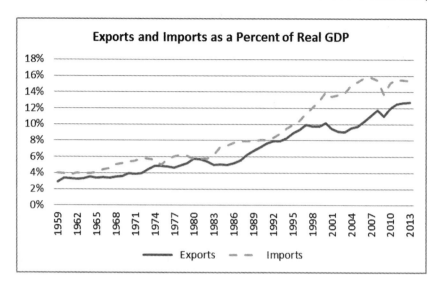

Figure 2.3   Exports and Imports as a Percentage of GDP.
Source: Bureau of Economic Analysis (2014).

discussion by analyzing how these components add up to GDP. Because the sum of all the components of GDP must equal GDP, the relationship can be expressed as an identity. This will help us to more clearly see the role of international trade in an open economy. Exports and imports are just a part of a country's total economic activity (GDP), but putting them together with the other components of GDP allows us to understand their role as a part of the total.

GDP in a Closed Economy

In a closed economy, firms must use any final good or service that individuals do not consume or the government does not purchase to produce new plants and equipment. The easiest way to express this for a closed economy (an economy that does not trade) is:

$$Y = C + I + G$$

where Y, or GDP, equals the sum of consumption, investment, and government spending. This equation holds in a closed economy because we have assumed that the public or government consumed and/or the business sector invested all output.

a trade surplus must be reducing its indebtedness or accumulating more claims on foreign countries. Again, the main point is that a country's trade surplus is not really reflecting anything more profound than a mismatch between domestic production and domestic consumption.

We can see an example of this by viewing statistics for country Beta in Table 2.3. Domestic production (Y) for this country is larger than the sum of domestic spending (C, I, and G), so country Beta will have a trade surplus. Given the two countries in Table 2.3, which country is better off? There is a tendency to believe that surpluses are inherently good and deficits are inherently bad, so it is logical to assume that the country with a trade surplus is clearly better off. However, the answer to the question is not quite that simple.

Intertemporal Trade

When a country has a trade deficit, it is consuming more than it is producing. Whether a deficit (or surplus for that matter) is good for a country depends on several factors. Generally, one of the purposes of economic activity is to provide a higher standard of living for the country's residents. In part, a higher standard of living is measured by the amount of goods and services residents consume. When a country has a trade deficit in a given year, it has consumed more than it produced during that year. Production and consumption should balance over the long run, but they do not need to balance every year. If a country has a trade deficit, it is *importing present consumption*. At some point in time, it will have to pay for the deficit by producing more than it consumes, which will produce a trade surplus. When this occurs, the country will be exporting future consumption. Thus, a trade deficit is the process of importing present consumption coupled with exporting future consumption. This trading of consumption and production over longer periods is known as intertemporal trade. In our example, Alpha has chosen to consume more now and less sometime in the future.

A country with a trade surplus is currently producing more output than it is consuming. As such, this country is *exporting present consumption* to other countries. At some point the residents of the country will be able to run a trade deficit and import consumption. The result is that a country with a trade surplus is exporting current consumption and importing future consumption. Viewed in this manner, trade imbalances simply denote a country's preferences for present versus future consumption. These preferences are expressed as the result of the choices that consumers, the government, and businesses make on a daily basis.

Saving, Investment, the Government Budget, and the Trade Balance

So far we have examined total domestic spending and its relationship to total output. However, we can rearrange the relationship of GDP and its components for an open economy in a way that lets us further explore the relationship between net exports and the rest of the economy. Up to this point, we have been using GDP to measure a country's total final output. GDP also measures a country's total income. The income is attributed to the factors of production in the form of rent, wages, interest, and profits. The public in turn spends this income on goods and services. As such, money moves in a circular flow from businesses to the public and back again.

Although a country's total income equals GDP, not all of society's total income is immediately spent on goods and services. Some income is temporarily withdrawn from this circular flow. This income that is not spent on goods and services is referred to as leakages from the circular flow. There are three sources of leakages from the circular flow. First, residents of the country may choose to save a portion of their current income. This saving (S) represents a withdrawal of spending on goods and services. Second, like saving, taxes (T) involve using part of the economy's income for purposes other than consumption by the public. Finally, imports (M) represent reduced spending on domestically produced goods and services.

However, these outflows from the circular flow do not disappear from the economy. Businesses, government, and foreigners engage in activities that inject the spending back into the circular flow. These activities can be thought of as injections into the circular flow. Investment (I) represents investment goods to businesses along with investment in housing. Investment is one way in which savings are put back into the circular flow. For example, banks perform the function of accepting savings from the public that may be loaned to businesses and/or the housing sector. Another injection of spending in an economy is the amount of government spending (G) on final goods and services. Government spending does not include spending in the form of transfer payments. This is because the recipients of the transfer payments in turn spend the money and the spending would be double-counted. Again, government spending is the way taxes are reinjected into the economy. The last injection of spending into the economy is foreign purchases of domestically produced goods and services—exports (X). The injection of exports replaces the leakage of imports.

For any economy, the sum of the leakages from the circular flow must equal the sum of the injections into the circular flow; therefore,

$$S + T + M = G + I + X$$

In this equation the sum of saving, taxes, and imports will equal the sum of government spending, investment, and exports. However, saving (S) will not necessarily equal investment (I), government taxes (T) will not necessarily equal government spending (G), and exports (X) will not necessarily equal imports (M). This allows us to rearrange the terms to highlight the trade balance:

$$X - M = S - I + T - G$$

In this case, the trade balance becomes the mismatch between private saving (S), government saving (T − G), and investment (I). When the leakages from spending (S + T) are greater than the injections of spending (G + I), then the trade balance (X − M) will be positive. When the sum of saving and taxes is less than the sum of government spending and investment, the trade balance (X − M) will be negative. This equation illustrates that the trade balance is just the difference between the sum of leakages from spending (S + T) and injections to spending (G + I) within the economy.

Examining trade imbalances (X − M) in this manner gives us another way of looking at what causes them. For example, consider a country with a trade deficit. A trade deficit indicates that the country's economy has an excess of domestic spending compared to domestic production. To reduce the trade imbalance, the country could produce more goods and services than it consumes. In the short run, increasing total production past some point is not very easy to do. This maximum level of production of goods and services in any economy is difficult to alter in the short run. Reducing the trade deficit in the short run requires that the country reduce domestic spending.

Adjustments to Trade Imbalances

What the leakage and injection approach indicates is that a country with a trade deficit or surplus has four potential adjustments in the leakages and injections that can be made to reduce the imbalance. Let us examine each of these adjustments listed in Table 2.4. In the table, adjustments to deficits or surpluses are given in the first and second columns, respectively. Keep in mind that these adjustments are not mutually exclusive. Most of the time, the adjustment to a trade imbalance involves movements in more than one of the leakages and/or injections at the same time.

Table 2.4   Potential Adjustments to Reduce Trade Imbalances

Deficit	Surplus
Increase private savings	Decrease private savings
or	or
Increase government taxes	Decrease government taxes
or	or
Decrease business investment	Increase business investment
or	or
Decrease government spending	Increase government spending

First, everything else being equal, increasing the level of saving would tend to reduce the trade deficit. As the level of savings increases on the right side of the equation, there would have to be a change in X – M on the left side of the equation. For example, in the United States, personal saving as a share of income averaged approximately 9 percent during the 1970s. The average saving rate fell to approximately 6 percent during the 1980s, fell to approximately 5 percent during the 1990s, and has remained lower than this in the 21st century. This decline in the national saving rate has contributed to the U.S. trade deficit. For this and other reasons, the U.S. government would like to see an increase in the private saving rate. This is a difficult change in policy for the government to implement because it is not completely clear how to use government policy to increase the amount of saving. The other side of saving is consumption. Increasing saving and decreasing consumption are opposite sides of the same coin. An increase in saving (a decrease in consumption) would tend to reduce the size of a trade deficit.

A second adjustment to reduce a trade deficit would be to change the level of investment. If investment spending falls with no change in savings or the government budget, the trade balance would tend to become smaller. However, there is a potential cost involved in terms of long-run economic growth. An increase in investment tends to increase real GDP. As a result, reducing the level of investment to reduce a trade deficit is not something that economic policy makers generally advocate. The short-run solution of decreasing investment spending may cause long-run economic growth to decline, so the cure to the trade deficit may be worse than the deficit itself. Increasing the level of investment spending relative to savings may worsen the trade deficit, but it may also improve a country's economic growth.

A third adjustment to reduce the trade deficit would be to increase taxes. Increasing taxes without increasing government spending would either reduce the government budget deficit or produce a government surplus. As a result, increasing taxes would either reduce the amount government has to borrow or reduce any previously accumulated government debt. The result of increasing taxes without increasing government spending is similar to an increase in the level of saving. In this case, the means of increasing the level of saving are clear. This would tend to reduce a trade deficit in the same manner as increasing the level of savings.

Changing government spending is a fourth potential adjustment. Reducing the level of government spending would tend to reduce the trade deficit, and reducing government spending in conjunction with raising taxes has the potential to reduce the trade deficit to a greater extent than either policy used in isolation. Further, this combination of strategies avoids the uncertainties of increasing the private saving rate and the undesirability of reducing investment.

The second column of Table 2.4 outlines the possible adjustments for a country with a persistent trade surplus. These are the opposite of the adjustments involved in reducing a deficit. Decreasing the level of savings would tend to reduce a trade surplus. This makes sense because the alternative to saving is consumption. If the public saves less, it will tend to spend more on both domestic and foreign goods and services. An increase in investment would also tend to reduce a trade surplus. Such an increase both reduces a trade imbalance and increases the economy's long-run growth potential. The public sector can also take actions to reduce a trade surplus. Increasing the level of government spending and/or reducing taxes would tend to either reduce a government budget surplus or increase the size of the deficit. Government budget decisions will not automatically reduce a trade surplus, but they can influence it.

The Current Account Balance and International Trade Policy

From the previous material, you should now have a good understanding of the balance of payments. On a very fundamental level, the trade balance is a function of an imbalance between what a country produces and what it consumes. Consumption and investment are determined in private markets by the actions of a vast number of consumers and businesses. The government budget deficit or surplus is determined by the political system. In a democracy, one would assume that the decisions made by the government reflect the preferences of the majority of voters. As a result, a country with a trade deficit is a country where the population has collectively made this choice. For a host of reasons, the country decides to consume more than they produce. This could occur either because of the actions of the private or the public sector. A combination of consumption, investment, government spending, and taxes will produce this result. The flip side of this choice is a financial account surplus. By choosing a trade deficit, the country has also chosen to borrow the difference from the rest of the world. This is not necessarily a bad choice. The public has chosen to consume more now and less later. The same choice may have been made in the public sector if the government is running a budget deficit. An analogous situation exists with respect to countries with trade surpluses. The collective actions of consumers and producers yields a situation where the country is producing more than it is consuming. Likewise, the government budget is influencing the trade balance. Again, some combination of consumption, investment, government spending, and taxes is occurring to produce this result. For these countries, the other side of this decision is a financial account deficit. A financial account deficit means that a country is exporting capital to the rest of the world. In one sense, being a net creditor nation carries the implication of sound economic management. In another sense, it is not as positive. Money is being invested in other countries and not in the domestic market.

Trade deficits or surpluses are a function of macroeconomic imbalances. Imbalance is usually a word with negative connotations, but in this case an imbalance is normal. It would be an odd situation if a country had a perfect balance. In the realm of macroeconomics, the question is not a trade deficit or surplus, but more a question of size and persistence. Trade imbalances that are less than 3 percent of GDP are not large enough even to be of much concern to policy makers either domestically or internationally. The problem is more of an issue when the imbalance is large and lasts for years. The next question becomes one of government policy with respect to consumption versus savings. A government intent upon a trade surplus could pursue policies designed to reduce consumption and increase savings. A combination of high taxes on consumption coupled with tax preferences for savings would tend to increase the size of a trade surplus. In addition, these policies could be supplemented by the government running persistent budget surpluses. Such policies carry the risk that the attendant financial account deficits could reduce domestic investment and future growth. A more common problem is trade deficits that are both large and persistent. A key issue here is how they are "financed." Large inflows of FDI are less of a risk because this investment is unlikely to leave in the short run. A much bigger risk is a large trade deficit financed by inflows of portfolio capital. Portfolio capital is money that is invested in financial assets such as stocks and bonds. Such short-term inflows can all too easily turn into outflows. As a result, trade deficits in the 4 to 6 percent of GDP range are considered risky, especially if they are persistent. As you can see from the material earlier, there can be an uncomfortable relationship between the trade deficit and a government budget deficit. In the absence of a large pool of savings, large government budget deficits can start affecting not only the domestic economy but also the country's economic interactions with the rest of the world.

The reality of trade imbalances should be clear at this point. Persistent trade imbalances are not the result of the usual list of suspects such as unfair foreign competition and high trade barriers in foreign markets. These factors tend to have an influence on trade in particular industries but little, if any, effect on a country's overall trade balance. However, in the United States and elsewhere trade imbalances often are attributed to factors that have little to do with the reality of the situation. Since the 1970s, the United States has had virtually perpetual trade deficits. Usually they are sufficiently small that they are of little concern. However, in the years when they became large, as defined earlier, the focus of the government was on the policies of governments outside the country. In the 1970s, the problem was defined as Organization of the Petroleum Exporting Countries (OPEC) raising the price of oil. In the 1980s and 1990s, the problem was defined as Japanese trade policy that focused on exports. More recently, the problem is alleged to be "currency manipulation" by the Chinese. Most of this falls under the category of convenient excuses. A country with a low national saving rate and perpetual government budget deficits has an uncomfortably high probability of running a trade deficit. Not accidentally, the years where the trade deficit has been the largest have coincided with years where the government budget deficit has also been large.

What this all means is that international trade policy normally has little effect on the overall balance of trade. This understanding is essential to be able to ignore the litany of news attempting to link the two. If international trade policy doesn't affect overall trade flows much, then what does it affect? The answer is that international trade policy can have very significant effects at the level of the industry or the firm. For most industries in most countries, a change in domestic trade barriers for a specific industry will have a noticeable impact on production and profits in that industry. This can be even truer for individual firms within the industry. This is because in most industries, firms are not homogeneous. The same thing is true for changes in the international trade policy of foreign countries. Domestic industries may be able to export more or less as international trade policy in other countries changes. Now that we have covered what international trade policy does not have much of an effect on, we turn our attention to the underlying economics behind international trade.

This is important because it forms the basis for international trade policy, both good and bad.

Case Study: Macroeconomic Imbalances and Trade

In the material earlier, we related overall trade imbalances to a set of macroeconomic imbalances in an economy. Let's now take that information and apply it to the world's four largest economies in the 21st century: China, Germany, Japan, and the United States. These four countries are especially relevant as they also are the major countries involved in world trade. They are also frequently mentioned in international trade policy for all the wrong reasons. China runs large trade surpluses and often is accused of unfair trade practices and/or currency manipulation. Within Europe, Germany's trade surpluses are a source of some controversy. Many feel that the euro especially favors German trade relations. Japan's reputation as both a relatively closed economy and a country that uses industrial policy to gain unfair trade advantages has endured since the 1980s. Of course, the United States runs perpetual trade deficits. The government has a tendency to blame deficits on unfair trade practices and currency manipulation by foreign governments.

As one might expect, Table 2.5 tells a different and much simpler story. China has an astonishing gross saving rate. With this much saving, it is really hard to believe the trade surplus is so small. The reason is simple. Domestic investment is at levels rarely seen in any country at any time. The story is similar for Germany. For a developed country, savings in Germany is high. Also, the government budget deficit is quite small. The result is a trade surplus of 7 percent of GDP. This is both a very high number and it is persistent. Given the size of the surplus and its persistence, it is odd that the complaints from Germany's trading partners are so muted. Japan has savings that are nearly as large as Germany's. The difference is in the final column. The government budget deficit in Japan is horrendous. This is not

Table 2.5   Trade Balances for Four Large Economies

	S	X − M	G − T
China	51	2.3	N/A
Germany	24.2	7.0	−0.4
Japan	21.5	1.0	−8.3
United States	16.5	−2.7	−7.6

Source: World Bank (2015).

an anomaly. Since the early 1990s, Japanese government budget deficits have been extremely large. The result is that even with high savings, the trade surplus is unremarkable. The U.S. statistics live up to our expectations. Saving is relatively small. The government budget deficit for this year (2012) is large, but, unlike Japan, a deficit of this size is not normal and is shrinking. The result for the trade balance is business as usual for the United States. It all fits with the information earlier. A final thought exercise is this. If all of these countries eliminated all of their barriers to trade, what would happen to $X - M$? The answer is not much. However, there would be wrenching changes for industries and firms.

Bibliography

Bureau of Economic Analysis. 2014. *National Income and Product Accounts*. Washington, D.C.: U.S. Government Printing Office. www.bea.gov.

International Monetary Fund. 2014. *Global Financial Stability Report*. Washington, D.C.: International Monetary Fund.

World Bank. 2015. *World Development Indicators*. Washington, D.C.: World Bank.

CHAPTER THREE

Comparative Advantage

It is the maxim of every prudent master of a family, never to attempt to make at home what it will cost him more to make than to buy. The taylor does not attempt to make his own shoes, but buys them from the shoemaker. The shoemaker does not attempt to make his own clothes, but employs a taylor. The farmer attempts to make neither the one or the other, but employs those different artificers. . . . What is prudence in the conduct of every private family, can scarce be folly in that of a great kingdom. If a foreign country can supply us with a commodity cheaper than we can make it, better buy it of them with some part of the produce of our own industry, employed in a way we have some advantage.

—Adam Smith

Introduction

We learned in the previous chapter that the trade balance of a country is not much affected by international trade policy. If a country is running a trade deficit or a trade surplus, this is primarily a function of some type of macroeconomic imbalance in an economy. This does not mean that international trade policy is unimportant. What it implies is that it operates at another level. In a world free of trade barriers, firms and industries would tend to be located where the good or service could be produced in the optimal location. This optimal location is related to where goods and services can be produced most efficiently for all economies that are trading. The solution to this problem is more complex than it may seem at first glance. However, as a general rule, it is in everyone's best interest for production to occur where it would naturally flow in a free market. To demonstrate this point, consider this scenario. The United States essentially is a free-trade area composed of 50 states, the District of Columbia, and some associated territories. For the most part, the production of goods and services within this area is determined by market forces. Once goods and services are produced, they can then be freely traded within this area. Now consider the alternative situation. Suppose all of these entities were sovereign countries. In the usual way, each of these countries would have their own system of trade barriers. First, on an intuitive level, what would be the total output of the United States under these two scenarios? Intuitively output would be higher under free trade than under a regime where each state was allowed to erect barriers to trade.

Unfortunately, governments may not like production to be allocated or determined by the market. We are using production instead of trade in this scenario for a reason. Market forces first determine the best locations for production. Keep in mind that what we call trade theory is in reality a theory of the location of production. Once production occurs, then trade becomes something like a residual. If you know where production is occurring or not occurring, you automatically know where exports are originating and their destination. Over time, the optimal location of production can change as the factors that determine it change. Production and trade are not static but dynamic. The cost of the factors of production such as labor and capital can change over time. New technology can lead to the rise of whole new industries and the decline of others. Transportation costs can change, allowing both goods and services to be traded or to be traded in greater volumes. In short, international trade is a natural extension of capitalism on a global basis. It also creates what the economist Joseph Schumpeter called "creative destruction." Creative destruction means that for new industries to grow, it is necessary for old industries to decline. This process of creative destruction is constantly at work in a domestic market. International trade just adds another factor to the process.

The unfortunate reality is that most of what international trade policy is about is interfering with the process of creative destruction. Changes in the domestic economy as firms and industries compete with one another create changes in the location of production. In most cases, the losses incurred by some firms and industries in this process occur without much attention from the government. However, the process is different if market forces outside of the country impose losses on domestic firms and industries. In these cases, governments are quick to use various barriers to trade to prevent or at least mitigate those losses. If trade policy is about acting on the changes in the economy brought about by international trade, it is useful to take a step back and understand how the process starts. In this chapter, we consider the fundamental causes of international trade. Before we begin that, let's consider the first widespread application of trade policy in modern history that is still with us in the 21st century.

The Scourge of Mercantilism

> *The ideas of economists and political philosophers, both when they are right and when they are wrong, are more powerful than is commonly understood. Indeed the world is ruled by little else. Practical men, who believe themselves to be quite exempt from any intellectual influence, are usually the slaves of some defunct economist.*
>
> —John Maynard Keynes

Why do individuals in many countries consider interregional trade to be more acceptable than international trade? To answer this question, we need to look back to the 16th and 17th centuries when the doctrine of mercantilism dominated political and economic thought throughout the world. The doctrine of mercantilism is based on the premise that a country can promote its self-interest by discouraging imports and encouraging exports in order to increase its wealth. Underlying the mercantilists' view of international trade was the belief that a person's wealth or a country's wealth was based on their holdings of precious metals, which were gold and silver. Because gold and silver circulated as money, a country could increase its wealth by exporting more goods than it imported. This would occur as:

- Exports created inflows of gold and silver—foreigners' payments for domestic goods
- Imports created outflows of gold and silver—domestic residents' payments to foreigners for their goods

When a country's exports exceeded its imports, its stock of gold and silver rose, and the country's wealth increased. This situation implied that international trade was a zero-sum game, in the sense that exports were "good" and imports were "not good at all." To encourage a net inflow of gold and silver, the mercantilists advocated regulating international trade in a way that would promote large exports and small imports, yielding a favorable trade balance. To accomplish this, trade barriers would be used to restrict imports and cheap raw materials, and low wages would be used to encourage low-cost exports. Today, there are still traces of the old mercantilist doctrine in evidence around the world. For example, public officials who argue that exports are "good" because they create jobs in a country and imports are "not good" as they take jobs from the same country still view international trade as a zero-sum game. Adam Smith challenged this view of international trade in the late 18th century when he formulated the concept of mutually beneficial trade between countries based on absolute advantage. His original purpose was to refute the mercantilist view of international trade and to demonstrate that trade between countries was beneficial to both. In the 21st century the echoes of mercantilism are all too easy to find. Listen to virtually any politician in any country talk about international trade, and the mercantilist mind-set is in the background. As a result, international trade policy is basically about an old debate outlined next.

International Trade Versus Interregional Trade

Why do countries trade with one another? For that matter, why does one region of a country trade with another region of the same country? Among the various regions of the United States, there is a tremendous flow of goods and services. The Southeast sells cotton to regions where cotton cannot grow. Northern California sells wine to the rest of the United States where conditions are less favorable for producing wine. New York City sells financial services to other regions where the cost of these services is higher.

Interregional trade and international trade are similar. For example, Massachusetts buys cotton from Mississippi for the same reason the United States buys coffee from Brazil. It makes little economic sense for a country to produce a good that can be purchased from another country at a lower price. The difference lies in the perception that trade between two regions of the same country, such as the United States, is *us buying from and selling to ourselves*, whereas trade between one country and another country is *us buying from and selling to them—another country*. For example, many Americans have trouble endorsing purchases of foreign steel, clothing, cars, meat, sugar, and other foreign goods because they may lead to a loss of U.S. jobs in those industries. Also, there are varying degrees of opposition to U.S. sales of Alaskan oil to Japan, U.S. weapons to foreign governments, and technological expertise to Russia. This difference in perception is illustrated in this anecdote by Ingram (1983):

> A domestic entrepreneur announces that he has discovered a method of transforming agricultural products into electronic products. The agricultural products are fed into one side of a big black box and transformed electronic products of all kinds come out of the other side of the box. (You need to suspend disbelief to appreciate the idea that we are developing.) This method of transforming goods is a great innovation for society. Although this means a loss of jobs for the domestic electronics industry, the public nevertheless accepts it as a reasonable price for economic progress. However, eventually it is discovered that

the agricultural goods are not transformed within the black box. What actually occurs is that the entrepreneur takes the agricultural products going into the black box, and without anyone noticing, he sells them abroad. The entrepreneur then uses the income from those sales to buy foreign electronic goods at a much lower cost and those electronic goods come out of the black box. When the public finds out what the entrepreneur is doing, he is denounced as a fraud and a destroyer of domestic jobs.

For more than 200 years, economists have tried to convince the public and policy makers that countries trade for the same reason that individuals do. Countries, like individuals, are not equally capable of producing every good or service that they want or need. All countries, like individuals, can benefit if each country specializes in producing those goods that it can produce best and satisfy their other wants and needs by trading for them. Specialization and trade make total world output of goods and services larger than it would be without trade. One goal of this chapter is to show how international trade is not like a poker game where one person's gain is another person's loss. Rather, in international trade all countries gain and are better off than they would be if they pursued the alternative: buying and selling goods restricted to their own domestic markets.

Adam Smith and Absolute Advantage

In the late 18th century, Adam Smith formulated the concept of mutually beneficial trade between countries. His original purpose was to refute the mercantilist view of international trade and to provide a case for free trade between countries. According to Adam Smith, in order for two individuals, two regions, or two countries to trade with one another, both must gain from the exchange. Smith wanted to show that international trade was not a zero-sum game like poker, but an *n*-sum game where all countries can benefit. To do this he created the concept of absolute advantage, which is the ability of a country to use fewer resources to produce a good than other countries. In this section, we will demonstrate exactly how this is possible.

Absolute Advantage

To illustrate Adam Smith's idea of the mutual gains from trade, we will assume that there are only two countries, the United States and India, and that both countries produce just two goods, machines (M) and cloth (C).

Table 3.1   Absolute Advantage

Country	One Person Per Day of Labor Produces	
	Machines	Cloth
United States	5 machines	10 yards of cloth
India	2 machines	15 yards of cloth

Suppose, further, that labor within a country is homogeneous and is the only factor of production used to produce both machines and cloth. In addition, suppose that the United States and India have a fixed amount of labor to produce the goods and that within the United States and India labor is fully employed. Also, the level of technology used to produce the goods is constant. With free trade, goods can move freely between the United States and India, but labor is mobile only within a country and remains immobile between countries. Transportation costs between countries are zero, and the two countries engage in barter trade, where goods are exchanged for other goods without the use of money.

Given these assumptions, Table 3.1 demonstrates the mutually benefi-cial gains from trade. The first row shows that one worker in the United States can produce either 5 machines or 10 yards of cloth in one day. The second row shows that one worker in India can produce either 2 machines or 15 yards of cloth in one day. Comparing the two countries, U.S. workers are more productive in machine production and Indian workers are more productive in cloth. In this situation, the United States has an absolute advantage in machine production because it can produce more machines than India can with a given amount of labor. As a result, the United States can produce lower-cost machines. Likewise, India has an absolute advan-tage in cloth production and it can produce lower-cost cloth because India can produce more cloth than the United States with a given amount of labor.

The Gains from Specialization and Trade with Absolute Advantage

Assuming that trade opens up between the two countries, the United States could benefit from importing cloth from India and exporting machines to India. India could benefit from importing machines from the United States and exporting cloth to the United States. Each country would, in its own self-interest, import the cheaper product in an attempt to profit from trade. This is an important point in our analysis. In our example, for each worker that the United States transfers from cloth production to machine production, U.S. output of machines increases by 5 units and U.S. output of cloth falls by 10 yards. For each worker that India transfers from machine production to cloth production, Indian cloth production increases by 15 yards and Indian machine production falls by 2 units. These results are shown in Table 3.2. As the table indicates, world output increases by 3 machines and 5 yards of cloth. This increase in output occurs as each country transfers one worker into the production of the good in which it has an absolute advantage. The gains from trade are the increase in world output that results from each country specializing its production according to its absolute advantage. This increase in output would be allocated between the two countries through the process of international trade. The United States would export machines and import cloth, and India would export cloth and import machines.

In our example, what causes the difference in labor productivity and the difference in costs between each country is not crucial. Adam Smith's concept of cost, and the one that we use in our example, is based on the labor theory of value. The labor theory of value assumes that labor is the only relevant factor of production. This implies that the cost of a product depends solely on the amount of labor needed to produce it. Workers who produce more output per day produce less costly goods. Specialization and trade by countries based on absolute advantage result in the world using its resources more efficiently and cause an increase in world output that is distributed to the two countries through international trade. However, absolute advantage can explain only a small part of international trade. For example, absolute advantage can explain international trade based on a country's climate or natural resources, such as Brazil's capacity to export coffee or South Africa's capacity to export diamonds. In the next section we will present a more generalized case of the gains from international trade.

To return to the beginning of this section, recall what Smith was trying to accomplish. The concept of mercantilism had existed for hundreds of

Table 3.2 Change in World Output Resulting from Specialization

Country	Change in the Production of	
	Machines	**Cloth**
United States	+5 machines	−10 yards of cloth
India	−2 machines	+15 yards of cloth
Change in World Output	+3 machines	+5 yards of cloth

years, and it was the received wisdom to the late 18th century. At the time it seemed obvious that a country would maximize its welfare by exporting more and importing less. The genius of Smith was twofold. First, he had the insight to see that trade with any country was mutually beneficial. Second, he had the courage to put that in print. It is difficult to express how important his work is even in the 21st century. For over 200 years, economists have been trying to persuade anyone who would listen that free trade will maximize a country's welfare. Also notice that it will maximize the welfare of the world. Even today, this argument must be forcefully and consistently made. In the end, much of international trade policy is still about the debate over free trade illustrated in this segment.

Football Games, Rats, and Economic Theory

For many, the term "economic theory" is often associated with unrealistic assumptions. However, economic theory is not nearly as "unrealistic" or removed from reality as it is frequently perceived to be. The purpose of any theory, economic or otherwise, is to explain and to predict events. All of us use "theory" every day—we just don't usually realize it.

The first step in the process of developing a theory is abstraction. Most economic events, such as international trade, are influenced by a myriad of factors. In most cases there are too many factors to consider simultaneously. International trade is a good example. Virtually millions of factors influence the international trade of a country. That's why it is important to first limit the number of factors to be considered to a manageable number. Once this is accomplished, the second task is to formulate a theory of how these factors interact to explain past economic events such as exports and imports of a country. Finally, it is desirable to test the theory against real-world data to see if it does explain past exports and imports of a country. With a little luck the theory then *might* be useful in predicting future exports and imports of a country.

The "unrealism" of economic theory is usually perceived to be a result of the first part of the process (abstraction). However, abstraction is necessary. Many events are influenced by too many factors to be considered simultaneously. Football games are a good example. How many factors can influence the outcome of a football game? Literally thousands of greater or lesser factors could influence the outcome. The next time you hear people discussing who will win a football game, or any other type of athletic contest, you will probably be hearing theory at work. A person with an opinion on the outcome cannot consider all possible factors. Listen carefully and you'll hear abstraction. He or she has picked out a few important factors from all possible factors and used this limited number to arrive at a prediction. Arguments over the outcomes of athletic contests are usually over differences in the factors that the abstraction process produced. Notice also that people focus on important factors and "unrealistically" ignore many things that can influence the game's outcome.

The principle is general. When you buy a car, do you consider *all* possible features of every car on the market? Most likely not, as this would be "unrealistic." Similarly, we cannot consider every factor that would influence international trade. We have to limit ourselves to a few main factors in much the same way that we do when analyzing the outcomes of football games. The only real difference is that economists are simply more precise about exactly what the assumptions are.

Trade Based on Comparative Advantage

Comparative advantage is one of the few things in economics that is true, but not obvious.

—*Paul Samuelson*

Smith's explanation of mutually beneficial trade is an effective case for free trade. However, Smith's analysis leaves an unanswered question. Why would trade occur between two countries if one country had an absolute advantage in the production of both goods? In the late 18th and early 19th centuries, the United Kingdom was the most advanced country in the world with an absolute advantage in the production of most goods. This was the heart of the mercantilist counterattack on trade based on absolute advantage. For a large country like the United States there are echoes of that counterattack even today. Given this situation, why would the United Kingdom trade with a less productive area such as the American colonies? This rebuttal to Smith had two advantages. First, it took decades for an effective rebuttal to be developed. It came in the form of the concept of comparative advantage. It was left to David Ricardo (1817), a British economist, to develop the answer. Expanding upon Adam Smith's work based on absolute advantage, Ricardo formulated the theory of comparative advantage. It is not a particularly difficult concept.

However, the quote at the beginning of the section is more than usually pertinent. The concept of comparative advantage is very true but not obvious. As we will see, it is hiding in plain sight. It is not just about international trade but also forms the basis of *all* exchange. Understanding this concept isn't just helpful in understanding international trade policy; it is an invaluable life skill.

Comparative Advantage

To see how comparative advantage works, refer to Table 3.3 where the data show that one U.S. worker can produce either 5 machines or 15 yards of cloth per day (first row) and that one Indian worker can produce 1 machine or 5 yards of cloth per day (second row). When comparing the two countries in Table 3.3, notice that the United States has an absolute advantage in the production of both machines and cloth. If you were using the concept of absolute advantage alone as the basis for trade, no trade would occur between the United States and India. However, Ricardo's theory of comparative advantage shows that mutually beneficial trade can still occur between these countries.

As the table indicates, U.S. labor has a 5 to 1 absolute advantage in the production of machines. In other words, U.S. workers can produce 5 machines for every 1 machine produced by Indian workers. U.S. labor also has a 15 to 5 or 3 to 1 absolute advantage in the production of cloth. This means that U.S. workers can produce 3 yards of cloth for every 1 yard of cloth produced by Indian workers. India has an absolute disadvantage in the production of machines and cloth. That is, U.S. workers can produce more machines and more yards of cloth than workers in India.

In this example, the United States has a greater absolute advantage in producing machines than it does in producing cloth. However, India's absolute disadvantage is smaller in producing cloth than in producing machines. Notice we are comparing the degree of absolute advantage or disadvantage in the production of both goods between these countries. Using Ricardo's logic, the United States has a comparative advantage in machines because its degree of absolute advantage is higher and a comparative disadvantage in cloth because its degree of absolute advantage is lower. Similarly, India has a comparative advantage in cloth because its degree of absolute disadvantage is lower, and it has a comparative disadvantage in

Table 3.3   Comparative Advantage

Country	One Person Per Day of Labor Produces		
	Machines	Cloth	Relative Cost
United States	5 machines	15 yards of cloth	1M = 3C 1/3M = 1C
India	1 machine	5 yards of cloth	1M = 5C 1/5M = 1C

machines because its degree of absolute disadvantage is higher. Comparative advantage, as opposed to absolute advantage, is a relative relationship.

Ricardo illustrated the principle of comparative advantage with the following example:

> Two men can make shoes and hats, and one is superior to the other in both employments; but in making hats he can only exceed his competitor by one-fifth, or 20 percent, and in making shoes he can excel him by one-third or 33⅓ percent. Will it not be for the interest of both that the superior man should employ himself exclusively in making shoes, and the inferior man in making hats?

If Babe Ruth had played baseball 100 years earlier, Ricardo might have used him to illustrate comparative advantage. Babe Ruth began his baseball career as a pitcher for the Boston Red Sox. As a pitcher he won 89 games in six seasons, but he was also an outstanding hitter. The New York Yankees traded for the Babe and turned him into an outfielder so he could specialize in his greater advantage, hitting. As a result he once hit 60 home runs in one season and 714 home runs in his career. In the same way, the United States has a comparative advantage in the production of machines and should specialize in producing machines. India has a comparative advantage in the production of cloth and should specialize in producing cloth.

The Gains from Specialization and Trade with Comparative Advantage

Now, assuming that trade opens up between the United States and India, the United States could benefit from importing cloth from and exporting machines to India. India could benefit from importing machines from and exporting cloth to the United States. For each worker that the United States transfers from cloth production to machine production, U.S. output of machines increases by 5 units and U.S. cloth production falls by 15 yards. As India transfers 3 workers from machine production to cloth production, Indian cloth production increases by 15 yards of cloth and Indian machine production falls by 3 units. In this case, there is a net increase in world output, since cloth production remains constant and machine production increases by 2 units. These results are shown in Table 3.4. Again, the gain from specialization and trade is the increase in world output that results from each country specializing production according to its comparative advantage. This increase in output would be allocated between the two countries through the process of international trade.

Table 3.4   Change in World Output Resulting from
Specialization According to Comparative Advantage

| | Change in the Production of | |
Country	Machines	Cloth
United States	+5 machines	−15 yards of cloth
India	−3 machines	+15 yards of cloth
Change in World Output	+2 machines	0 yards of cloth

The Distribution of the Gains from Trade

Using this information, we can now turn our attention to one problem that makes international trade policy so difficult. We have shown earlier that free trade between the United States and India produces gains for both countries and the world. The analysis so far has left unanswered questions. How are the gains from trade distributed among the two countries? Second, how are the gains from trade distributed within the two countries? In a purely economic sense, the two questions are of less significance. Economists usually are interested in maximizing the total economic welfare of a country and the world. The distribution of these gains among countries or within a particular country is of less interest. This is not just cold-hearted rationality. Any trade, domestic or international, invariably improves welfare if it is voluntary. If I exchange money for goods or services, both myself and the merchant are better off. Neither of us would engage in a trade that would make us worse off. If this is the case, then increasing welfare becomes a question of maximizing the number of exchanges. Wealthy societies are wealthy because their citizens engage in a large number of exchanges. In contrast, a pervasive feature of poor countries is that the volume of exchange is low. In this case, international trade is just a special case of a general principle. Because these exchanges are international trade, there are some special aspects of distributing the gains from trade that need to be considered.

First, there is the question of the distribution of gains among countries. In our example earlier, the United States and India will trade at any price between 1M = 3C and 1M = 5C. Neither country would trade outside these limits as they could obtain either cloth or machines more cheaply in the domestic market. This ensures that if trade occurs, both countries are better off because they can obtain more goods by trading than is possible with no international trade. The question we left unanswered was what the price would be if the two countries began trading. This has always been a theoretical, although not practical, problem with the model. The theory can tell us what the limits to trade are, but it cannot, *a priori*, tell us what the price will be. The final price at which trade occurs is dependent on the relative intensity of demand. Suppose that the U.S. demand for cloth is more intense than India's demand for machines. In this case, the U.S. buyers would bid up the price of cloth closer to 1/3M = 1C. They would be willing to give up more machines to get cloth. The gains from trade are not evenly distributed. As the ratio gets closer and closer to the internal price in the United States, India is obtaining more of the gains from trade. The reverse would be true. If India had a relatively intense demand for machines, Indian buyers would be willing to trade more cloth for machines. This would move the price closer to 1M = 5C. In this case, the United States would be obtaining more of the gains from trade. The general principle is that the closer the price is to a country's own internal price ratio, the less of the gains from trade the country is receiving.

This creates an uncomfortable possibility. It is entirely possible that two countries could trade and both countries become better off. However, one of the two countries may benefit considerably more from trade than the other. The United States and India example may provide a useful example. The United States has the largest gross domestic product (GDP) in the world and a comparably high income. It is standard microeconomics that one of the primary determinants of demand is income. India is the reverse. The GDP of India is smaller than the state of California. The result is likely to be that the U.S. demand for cloth is higher than India's demand for machines. In this case, U.S. buyers would bid up the price of cloth relative to machines. If this occurs, then India would reap most of the gains from trade. A domestic example might help reinforce the idea. Suppose that both California and New Mexico became countries and started limiting trade with the rest of the world. Which of the two states would be most harmed by this change? Both would be worse off, but anyone could guess that the damage to New Mexico would be far higher. This line of thought creates two problems for international trade policy. First, it is a sad reality that the developing countries have been slow to liberalize trade. From the example earlier, it is clear that the world's poorer countries can gain more from trade than the richer countries. The second issue is more general. A large part of international trade policy is about countries negotiating trade agreements. In some cases, the disparity described earlier may be a stumbling block to negotiations. All of us engage in trades where we sense that we are obtaining a relatively small amount of the total benefits. We still trade because the alternative is worse. The problem for a country is that if the gains from a trade agreement are small, then the incentive for the country to negotiate is likewise small. If the other country is going to obtain the majority of the gains, then a country may not pursue further liberalization for the same reason that a consumer may avoid these types of exchanges. However, such a situation still leaves potential gains from trade lying on the table. Avoiding these sorts of exchanges falls into the category of seeing $1 on the sidewalk and not picking it up because it is not $20.

Expanding Comparative Advantage: The Factor-Proportions Theory

So far, we have shown that two countries can benefit from trade if each country specializes in the production of a good that it can produce at a lower comparative cost than the other country. They also may benefit if they import a good or goods that necessitate a higher comparative cost to produce. In a world with free trade, the activities of businesses and individuals will produce these benefits for the country as a by-product of their desire to make a profit. International trade will increase until the point where all profitable opportunities for trade are exhausted. The model developed in the previous chapter was able to produce these results.

However, the model left us with some important but unanswered questions. What determines a country's comparative advantage? How does international trade affect the size of an economy's various industries? How does international trade affect the payments or returns to the factors of production such as labor and capital? How does international trade affect the distribution of income within a country? The answers to these questions form the basis of any discussion of international trade policy. The model presented in this section allows us to look much more closely at how international trade affects the domestic economy of a country that trades.

The Factor-Proportions Theory

For nearly 100 years economists could explain trade based on comparative advantage, but they could not explain what *caused* comparative advantage. In the early part of the twentieth century two Swedish economists, Eli Heckscher (1919) and Bertil Ohlin (1933), explained the causes of comparative advantage. Paul Samuelson (1948) later refined their basic idea, which is referred to as the factor-proportions theory. The factor-proportions theory states that a country's comparative advantage is determined by its initial resource endowments.

We begin our analysis with the simplest version of the factor-proportions theory. We can relate the research on the basic theory and yield the same valid results. As is usual in economics, the basic theory is built on a set of assumptions. These assumptions are important for two reasons. First, it is necessary to look at the theory in its most basic form in order for it to be easily understood. Second, much of what we do in the next several chapters involves changing one or more of these assumptions. As we will see, the theory is much more "realistic" than the basic version outlined later. The reality of these assumptions is less of an issue than the results. The basic results of the model are a good starting point for explaining what causes comparative advantage and its application to international trade policy

To illustrate the factor-proportions theory of trade, we will assume that:

- As before, the United States and India each produce two goods, machines (M) and cloth (C), respectively.
- The production and consumption of the goods occur under perfect competition both in the product and factor markets. This means that:
  - Firms are price takers and their individual actions cannot influence conditions in their respective markets
  - The prices of the two goods and the prices paid to the factors of production are determined by supply and demand in each market
  - In the long run, the prices of the goods are equal to their respective costs of production.
- There are no transportation costs, taxes on trade, or other obstructions to the free flow of goods between the two countries.
- The introduction of international trade does not cause complete specialization in the production of one of the goods in either country. Both countries will continue to produce both goods.
- Consumers in the two countries have equal tastes and preferences. This means that when the price of machines in terms of cloth is the same in the two countries, both countries will consume the same proportion of the two goods.
- Both countries are endowed with two homogeneous factors of production, capital (K) and labor (L), and both resources are employed in the production of the two goods
- The technology available to produce the two goods is the same in both countries, and each good is produced under constant returns to scale. Constant returns to scale is a production condition in which proportionate changes in the factors of production lead to proportionate changes in output. In this case, if the amount of labor and capital used to produce cloth doubles, then the output of cloth doubles.
- Labor and capital are mobile domestically. This means that within each country, labor and capital can flow freely from one industry to the other. As a result, both industries within a country will pay the same wage rate and the same return to capital.
- Labor and capital cannot move between the two countries. This allows for differences in wage rates and the return to capital between the two countries. It

also rules out the possibility of eliminating wage differences between countries through migration.

- The production techniques available to produce machines and cloth in both countries are such that the production of machines is everywhere capital intensive and the production of cloth is everywhere labor intensive. This means that the production of machines tends to use a lot of capital relative to labor—in other words, it has a high capital-to-labor ratio (K/L). The production of cloth, on the other hand, requires a substantial amount of labor relative to capital—in other words, the K/L ratio for cloth is low relative to that for the production of machines.

- The United States is a relatively capital-abundant country, and India is a relatively labor-abundant country. This means that the capital-to-labor ratio in the United States is greater than the capital-to-labor ratio in India. The important point here is not whether the United States has more units of capital than India, but whether the United States has a larger capital-to-labor ratio than India. To illustrate, the capital-to-labor ratio in the United States is approximately $292,659 and the capital-to-labor ratio in India is approximately $20,374. In this case, the United States is capital abundant relative to India and India is labor abundant relative to the United States.

  Referring to Table 3.5, you can see that the production of machines and cloth occurs using a fixed ratio of the factors of production. Notice that the production of machines in both countries requires more units of capital than units of labor. Further, the capital-to-labor, or K/L, ratio for the machine industry is 2.5 (= 10/4). In both countries, the production of cloth requires more inputs of labor than capital, and the cloth industry's K/L ratio is 0.5 (= 4/8). Comparing the K/L ratios, one observes that the cloth industry's K/L ratio (= 0.5) is low relative to the K/L ratio of the machine industry (= 2.5). This indicates that the production of machines in both the United States and India is relatively capital intensive.

In the factor-proportions theory of international trade, the K/L ratio of a country plays an important role in determining the relative abundance of capital and labor in that country. One of the reasons that the theory we describe later can explain international trade is that the various countries of the world have widely differing capital-to-labor ratios. These ratios are

Table 3.5   Production Conditions in the United States and India

Country	Input Requirements to Produce	
	1 Machine	10 Yards of Cloth
United States	10 units of capital	4 units of capital
+ 4 days of labor	+ 8 days of labor	
India	10 units of capital	4 units of capital
+ 4 days of labor	+ 8 days of labor	

Table 3.6 Capital Stock per Worker in 2011 (in 2005 PPP Dollars)

High-income Country	Capital-to-labor Ratio	Middle- & Low-income Country	Capital-to-labor Ratio
Spain	$380,328	Turkey	$115,815
Italy	341,831	Poland	104,372
France	327,443	Chile	91,959
Japan	297,565	Mexico	85,597
United States	292,659	Thailand	58,165
Netherlands	290,043	Philippines	34,872
Switzerland	258,467	India	20,374
Australia	250,949	Nigeria	8,517
United Kingdom	222,406	Kenya	7,588
Canada	198,930		

Source: Heston et al. (2013).

presented in Table 3.6. The countries shown on the left side of the table are all high-income countries, whereas those on the right are middle- and low-income countries. The lowest K/L ratio for the group of high-income countries is almost $200,000 for the Canada. On the other hand, the highest K/L ratio for a middle- to low-income country is nearly $116,000. The K/L ratios for Kenya and Nigeria are less than $10,000. Our point is that some countries are relatively capital abundant or relatively labor abundant. These substantial differences among countries serve to make the theory of comparative advantage described later much more realistic.

The Factor-Proportions Theorem

Given our assumptions, we can explain what determines a country's comparative advantage. We assumed that consumers in the United States and India have equal demand conditions for machines and cloth. Because of this assumption, the supply of resources, as reflected by each country's resource endowments, will be the sole determinant of factor prices. This means that before the United States and India trade with one another, capital would be relatively less expensive in the capital-abundant country and labor would be relatively less expensive in the labor-abundant country. In the United States, capital would be relatively cheap and labor would be expensive. The reverse would be true for India: capital would be relatively expensive and labor would be cheap. This is reflected in the ratio of the payment made to labor—wages—and the payment made to capital—which economists call rent. In this case, the ratio is higher in the United States than in India. This can be seen in the following relationship:

$$\left[\frac{\text{Wages in U.S.}}{\text{Rent in U.S.}} \right] \rangle \left[\frac{\text{Wages in India}}{\text{Rent in India}} \right]$$

Because the wage–rent ratios are different, a country will have a lower opportunity cost of production in goods where the production technique requires greater quantities of the abundant factor and smaller quantities of the scarce factor. In our example, the United States will have a lower opportunity cost in goods produced using more capital and less labor. India's opportunity cost will be lower in goods produced using more labor and less capital. This leads to the following two important conclusions concerning the United States and India:

- The United States has a comparative advantage in the production of machines because the production of machines is capital intensive and the United States has an abundance of capital.
- India has a comparative advantage in the production of cloth because the production of cloth is labor intensive and India has an abundance of labor.

The abundance of a particular factor of production in a country tends to make that factor less expensive relative to the cost of that same factor in other countries. Given this, a country will tend to produce and export goods that intensively use their less expensive factor of production. The factor-proportions theorem can be expressed in the following way:

A country will have a comparative advantage in goods whose production intensively uses its relatively abundant factor of production. A country will have a comparative disadvantage in goods whose production intensively uses its relatively scarce factor of production.

This is one of the most powerful statements in international economics. If you examine the U.S. pattern of trade, much of what the United States imports are goods from countries where labor is abundant relative to capital. The reverse also is true. Much of what the United States exports are capital-intensive goods. We have reached this conclusion using a simplified model with only two countries, two goods, and two factors of production, but the results can be generalized to many factors and many goods.

This theory provides an explanation of what determines a country's comparative advantage—but keep in mind the other side of the coin, comparative disadvantage. A country will have a comparative disadvantage in the production of goods that intensively uses its scarce factor of production. We usually focus on a country's comparative advantage. However, comparative disadvantage is just as important in generating the gains from trade. Comparative disadvantage is a critical factor in international trade policy. As we will see in a later chapter, governments have a strong incentive to protect comparative-disadvantage industries. In most discussions of international trade there is a strong bias in terms of focusing on comparative advantage. Because we are concerned with international trade policy, we will need to take that traditional bias and turn it on its head so to speak.

Factor-Price Equalization and the Distribution of Income

The premise of the factor-proportions theory is that comparative advantage and international trade occur because countries are endowed with different factor proportions. Employing the results of the theory, we also can illustrate several other phenomena associated with international trade. For example, what happens to the relative size of industries as an economy moves from autarky to free trade? What happens to the payments or returns to factors of production such as labor and capital within an economy? What is the relationship between international trade and the distribution of income within a country?

Factor-Price Equalization

In the discussion of comparative advantage given in the previous section, there was an obvious result that is now significant. International trade changed the price of machines and cloth in both India and the United States. Essentially, the price of the comparative-advantage good rose in each country and the price of the comparative-disadvantage good fell. This equalization of the prices of the final product sets off something like a chain reaction within the economies of countries that trade. As it turns out, understanding these changes is critical in understanding international trade policy. Within the factor-proportions theory this adjustment to free trade produces a very interesting result known as the factor-price equalization theorem. This theorem states that when international trade occurs between two countries based on different factor proportions, not only will free trade equalize the price of the traded goods, but also the relative factor prices in the two countries will tend to converge. The changes in the relative factor prices will occur over a period of years or decades. Such changes have long-run implications for businesses that want to exploit short-run differences in the costs of production between countries.

To illustrate the factor-price equalization theorem, let's return to our previous example. The United States has a comparative advantage in capital-intensive machine production because it is a capital-abundant country, and India has a comparative advantage in labor-intensive cloth production because it is a labor-abundant country. As trade opens up between the United States and India, the price of cloth and machines in the United States and India equalize as both countries trade at the same terms. Because each country will specialize its production in its comparative-advantage good, the size of the machine and cloth industries in each country will change.

For the United States, machine production expands and cloth production contracts as international trade allows the United States to specialize in the production of machines. For India, machine production contracts and cloth production expands as international trade allows India to specialize in the production of cloth. This change in machine and cloth production within each country changes each country's industrial structure. Industrial structure refers to the percentage of output accounted for by each industry within a country. Without any trade, both the United States and India would have a certain percentage of their total industrial capacity devoted to producing machines and cloth. By allowing international trade, each country specializes its production and changes the percentage that is allocated to machines and cloth.

With international trade, the U.S. machine industry experiences an increase in demand for its output, as the industry will have to supply not only the U.S. market but also—in the form of exports—India's. As a result, the price of machines rises relative to the price of cloth. The U.S. machine industry expands its production to meet this increase in demand. To expand production, the machine industry requires more resources, meaning more capital and more labor. This expansion requires a greater increase in capital relative to the increase in labor because machine production is capital intensive. Assuming the economy is at full employment, the additional resources that the machine industry needs will come from the cloth industry.

As trade opens up, the U.S. cloth industry experiences a decrease in demand for its output, and the price of cloth declines relative to the price of machines. The cloth industry produces less cloth as imports from India replace domestic production. As the cloth industry contracts, it uses less capital and less labor. This contraction releases more labor relative to the release of capital because cloth production is labor intensive. However, this shift of capital and labor from one industry to another is not a perfect fit. The expanding machine industry is capital intensive. To expand, this industry needs a lot of capital and only a little more labor. On the other hand, the contracting cloth industry is releasing a lot of labor and only a little more capital.

Refer to the production conditions shown in Table 3.5. As the cloth industry contracts, it releases 4 units of capital and 8 days of labor. The expanding machine industry requires 10 units of capital and 4 days of labor. In this case, the 4 units of capital supplied is less than the 10 units of capital demanded. The result is a shortage of capital, and the price paid to capital (rent) rises. The opposite occurs in the labor market, where the 8 days of labor supplied is greater than the 4 days of labor demanded. The result is a surplus of labor, and the price paid to labor (wages) falls. Given these conditions, the relative price of the factors of production (the ratio of wages to rent) decreases. The introduction of international trade sets in motion market forces that cause a change in the relative price of machines in terms of cloth. The changes in the prices of the two goods cause changes in the industrial structure of the United States. In turn, this change in the industrial structure causes changes in the prices paid to the factors of production.

A similar situation occurs in India, where the introduction of trade leads to an increase in the price of cloth relative to machines. The change in the price of cloth relative to machines causes changes in India's industrial structure. In India, the production of cloth expands and the production of machines contracts. This change in India's industrial structure causes the price paid to the abundant factor in India (labor) to increase and the price paid to the scarce factor (capital) to decrease. As a result, the relative price of the factors of production (wages/rent) in India increases.

In the United States, labor becomes less costly, and in India it becomes more expensive. The difference in the price of labor between the two countries narrows. The same thing is happening with respect to capital. In the United States, the price paid to capital increases, and in India it decreases. The difference in the price of capital in the two countries also narrows with trade. Would the price of each factor of production in the United States ever reach perfect equality with the price of the corresponding factor in India? Under the very strict assumptions of the factor-proportions theorem, the answer is yes. However, under practical conditions, the answer is no. Absolute factor-price equalization may not occur for a variety of reasons. Among these are less-than-perfect competitive conditions in the product and/or factor markets, differences in technology, and the existence of trans-portation costs and/or trade barriers. Nevertheless, we can view the factor-price equalization theorem as a consistent tendency. This is true because international trade puts market forces in motion that tend to move relative factor prices in the two countries closer together in the long run. They may never reach perfect equality, but the direction of change in relative factor prices is clear. Factor-price equalization is most likely to be observed between countries that are geographically close and have had a large trading relationship for a long time. For example, what is the difference in factor prices between Germany and Austria? The answer is not much. The same holds true for factor prices between the United States and Canada.

The factor-price equalization theorem also has important implications for international trade policy. Due to international trade, comparative-disadvantage industries will tend to shrink. This usually is a slow process where the first step is declining prices and profits. As production and profits fall, firms reduce investment in the industry, the labor force ceases to grow, and real wage growth slows. Over time the lack of investment leads to declines in production capacity and decreases in employment. The process ends with the establishment of a new equilibrium with lower prices, less output, and little or no growth in real wages. In this case, both the firms and the labor force are experiencing declining outcomes. If possible, the industry and its workers will both put pressure on the government to take steps to stop or slow down this process.

Technology, Trade, and Growth

The old saying in economics that "there is no such thing as a free lunch" applies to certain aspects of economic growth. In order for an economy to grow at its potential rate, the market must be allowed to allocate resources in the most efficient way. This is not to say that resources are allocated perfectly at all points in time. They just need to be moving in the right direction. International trade is a very efficient means of enhancing these reallocations. When a country trades, imports push resources out of comparative-disadvantage industries. Exports pull resources into comparative-advantage industries. This produces a positive effect on economic growth. Comparative-advantage industries are more productive than comparative-disadvantage industries. As resources move from the former to the latter, the overall level of production in the economy rises. As this occurs, an economy is able to produce more goods and services with the same level of resources. Another way of putting this is that the overall productivity of the economy rises. Unfortunately, a lot of international trade policy is about reducing the rate at which comparative-disadvantage industries shrink. This mitigates the adverse effects on firms and workers in comparative-disadvantage industries. This is not free. There is a significant cost in terms of lost output as too many resources are still in less productive industries.

In a market economy, the concern for adversely affected firms and workers is understandable. However, it also is somewhat odd. Consider the cell phone that you use. This industry has made the economy much more efficient. These benefits were not free. Prior to the introduction of cell phones there was a large pay phone industry. A large number of firms and workers were involved in the production, distribution, and servicing of pay phones. As a result of the introduction of cell phones, another substantial industry in the country was totally destroyed. Independent firms and divisions of larger firms disappeared. Thousands of workers permanently lost their jobs. This is just a common example of the effects of technological change. All of us intuitively understand that this is the unfortunate price of better technology, and society accepts these losses as the price of progress. For an economist, the losses associated with trade and the losses from technological change are the same. The reasons for these differences in policy responses to these losses pose an interesting question.

Trade and the Distribution of Income

We have just explained how international trade changes the prices paid to the factors of production in the two trading countries. The price paid to the abundant factor of production would rise and the price paid to the scarce factor of production would fall within a country. These factor-price results have significant implications regarding the effects of international trade on a country's distribution of income.

In our example, as trade opens up, the price paid to capital (the abundant factor) in the United States would rise, and the price paid to labor (the scarce factor) in the United States would fall. In India, the price paid to labor (the abundant factor) would rise, and the price paid to capital (the scarce factor) would fall. Carrying this analysis one step further produces an interesting result. Because we assume that labor and capital remain fully employed both before and after trade, the real income of both labor and capital will move in the same direction as the factor-price movements.

In our example, the percentage of national income that capital receives would increase in the United States and the percentage of national income that labor receives would decrease. For India, the percentage of national income that capital receives would fall and the percentage of income that labor receives would increase. The result is that international trade has discernible effects on the distribution of income within a trading country. Specifically, the abundant factor tends to receive a larger share of the income pie and the scarce factor tends to receive a smaller share. This effect is called the Stopler-Samuelson theorem (1941).

International trade enhances a country's total welfare, but the gains from trade are not necessarily equally distributed among the factors of production. In many cases, the changes in the distribution of income may be very subtle, in the sense that the incomes of the abundant factor may be growing faster over time than are the incomes of the scarce factor. The main point is that international trade has the potential to change the distribution of income among the various factors of production in a predictable way. The same type of change would occur in India. As trade opens up, the abundant factor's income would tend to rise and the scarce factor's income would tend to fall. Labor in India would receive a larger percentage of national income, and capital would receive a smaller percentage.

These effects of international trade on factor prices have important implications for international trade policy. In developed countries, the relatively abundant factor of production is capital and the scarce factor is unskilled labor. As a result, those with the potential to gain from free trade are the owners of capital with above-average incomes, and the losers are unskilled labor with the lowest incomes. Understandably, the strongest proponents of protectionism in developed countries are labor unions. Their fierce opposition to the reduction of trade barriers simply is an expression of economic self-interest. Their opposition is reinforced by the owners of capital in comparative-disadvantage industries. If the capital is immobile, or specific to the production of comparative-advantage goods, then business and labor are fighting the same battle for trade restrictions. For the developing countries, international trade tends to increase the incomes of the relatively abundant factor, labor. However, this presents something of a puzzle. In this case, trade has the prospect of reducing the poverty prevalent in many of these countries by increasing wages. The reality is that many of the governments of developing countries are less than enthusiastic about trade negotiations that would allow their comparative-advantage industries greater access to the markets of developed countries. We will return to these issues in later chapters. For now, keep in mind that although international trade improves the welfare of the trading countries, the benefits are not necessarily distributed evenly and may lead to absolute or relative losses for some segments of society.

Trade Adjustment Assistance

If the United States has a comparative disadvantage in the production of goods that intensively use (unskilled or semiskilled) labor, then imports of labor-intensive products will cause labor in the United States to suffer losses of income even though the economy as a whole gains from trade. The abundant factor gains and the scarce factor loses. Paul Samuelson (1962) developed one possible solution to this income redistribution effect. He concluded that the U.S. gains from trade were large enough that society could "bribe" the losers into accepting their losses and still have money left over.

In the United States such a system, known as Trade Adjustment Assistance (TAA), is actually in place. TAA was created under the Trade Act of 1962. Under this legislation, workers who lost jobs caused by trade liberalization were entitled to compensation. The Trade Act of 1974 greatly liberalized the program. Under this act's new rules, displaced workers could qualify for compensation if import competition caused the job loss. Under the liberalized rules, it was easier to be certified as a worker who was displaced by import competition. Certified displaced workers were then entitled to receive extended unemployment compensation and special training benefits. During 2010, the U.S. government provided nearly $1.0 billion in funding for this program which provided benefits for over 227,000 workers. Given the benefits of imports and the modest cost, the program seemed a bargain.

However, research by Clark, et al. (1998), Kletzer (2004), and Ebenstein, et al. (2009) on TAA casts some doubt on the program's economic necessity. TAA is by nature discriminatory—workers who lose their jobs due to import competition become eligible for benefits in excess of what is available to other workers who lose their jobs due to other economic conditions. For example, if your firm closes due to competition from a more efficient domestic competitor, you are out of luck! Similarly, if the industry you work in is in long-run decline, then TAA becomes available only if increased imports also are associated with this decline. Indeed, Robert Lawrence (1984) has found that this is often the case. It is not surprising that Clark, et al. found that there are no significant differences in employment outcomes between workers in manufacturing industries who lost their jobs due to import competition and workers who lost their jobs for other reasons. TAA may be a political necessity, but it does not appear to be an economic necessity.

Trade and Income Inequality

A common economic policy concern is the effect of international trade on the distribution of income. The Stopler-Samuelson theorem indicates that trade should have an impact on the distribution of income. Using the simple model we presented, in a developing country trade has the potential to reallocate income to the abundant factor, labor, in a way that reallocates income to the poor. However, the ability of trade to reallocate income in a high-income country is more troubling. If the abundant factors are capital and human capital, then trade may reallocate income to already high-income groups. As a result, movements to freer trade in high-income countries have become more controversial. Such policy changes have the potential to make the distribution of income more unequal. This is particularly true for many of the countries of the Organisation for Economic Co-operation and Development (OECD) in the late 20th and early 21st centuries. Income inequality has been rising for decades at the same time these economies are becoming more open. Logically, it is easy to make the jump from correlation to causation. However, the effects seem to be small. To understand why this is so, we'll revisit the concept of human capital and use a version of the specific-factors model.

Because income inequality has been rising for decades, it is not surprising that the phenomenon has been extensively studied. The standard explanation of rising inequality is focused on the interaction of human capital and technological change. New technologies developed in the latter part of the 20th century created an increase in demand for highly skilled workers relative to less skilled workers. The response in the labor markets was predictable. The wages of highly skilled workers began to rise relative to less skilled workers. For example, the ratio of the wages of high school–educated workers relative to the wages of college graduates rose dramatically. As wage inequality increased, the distribution of income became more unequal. As shown by Pinketty and Saez (2003), this pattern became especially pronounced beginning in the late 1960s. However, this pattern isn't obvious. What was more obvious was that imports were becoming an ever larger percentage of GDP and a substantial portion of these imports were originating in low-wage countries. Under the circumstances, it was all too easy to blame international trade for downward pressure on wages in U.S. manufacturing and then link that to rising income inequality. The empirical research on trade and income inequality fails to identify that the former is a significant contributor to the latter. The highest estimate in the literature indicates that trade contributed to 20 percent of the rise in income inequality but only in the 1980s. Estimates of these effects using more recent data are finding that they are moving in the predicted direction, but that they are quite small.

There are several reasons this may be the case. First, U.S. imports of unskilled-labor–intensive goods from developing countries are quite small. Given this, it is not surprising the effects of this type of trade on wages and the distribution of income are likewise small. Second, more recent research has focused on the effects of trade on wages at the industry level. Not surprisingly, it has been found that trade puts downward pressure on wages in import-competing industries. This is clearly a hardship for workers in these industries, but, again, this is different from effects on the overall distribution of income. Also, trade may at times depress wages in a local area where an import-competing industry is located. This may cause some loss of economic output in these areas, but the effects on the distribution of income are not large. Recall that on several occasions we have pointed out that trade benefits society overall but that the gains are not uniform. What the research is finding is yet another small loss to society from international trade. In a high-income country, trade is making the distribution of income slightly more unequal. On the other hand, most high-income countries have some form of trade adjustment assistance designed to help workers adversely affected by trade. Many other factors have a larger impact on the distribution of income than international trade. If the distribution of income yielded by market forces, including international trade, is unacceptable, then changing that is best left to more general social policies such as the tax and transfer payments system. Limiting imports to improve the distribution of income would seem to be a policy that would be unlikely to pass any sort of cost/benefit analysis.

Consumption and the Gains from Trade

In this chapter, we have considered how trade influences the distribution of income. We have shown that trade will tend to increase the returns to the abundant factor of production and increase its share in the distribution of income. The reverse would be true for the scarce factor of production. This implies that in a developed country, capital and human capital will gain from trade. In a developing country, labor would tend to gain from trade, whereas capital would tend to receive a lower return and a lower percentage income. However, such gains and losses apply only to income. What is possibly quite important is what is happening on the consumption side. In theory, consumers should gain from trade as imported goods become cheaper. There are potential losses on the consumption side as the price of goods that are exported rise in price.

Although this is theoretically clear, until recently there was virtually no research going on concerning the welfare changes due to international trade that were happening with respect to consumption. Partially, this is a problem with data because it is much easier to study changes in income than changes in consumption. In the case of the former, one simply has to track the amount of income going to various groups and attempt to link changes in income to trade. Consumption is much more difficult to study, as one needs information on the market baskets of goods that various groups within the income distribution consume. Recently, researchers have begun to calculate the gains from trade on the consumption side. Using a sample of 40 large developed and developing countries, Fajgelbaum and Khandelwal (2014) developed a theoretical model and empirical estimates that are both plausible and surprisingly large. The basic idea of their research is that poor consumers consume a market basket that is relatively high in tradable goods and relatively low in services. This makes sense because poor consumers spend a higher proportion of their income on food, clothing, etc. On the other hand, wealthy consumers spend a higher proportion of their income on services, which are not tradable. To summarize, the researchers found that in every country studied, the consumption effects of trade had a pro poor bias. There were substantial differences in the *size* of the effect but not in its direction. One of the most interesting aspects of their study was the effects on different parts of the income distribution. On average, for consumers in the bottom 10th percentile a movement from trade to autarky would cause a 57 percent real income loss. For consumers in the 90th percentile such a change would only cause a 25 percent loss in real income. What is emerging from this research is that the gains and losses to various groups within a country due to international trade are a complex mix of changes in income and changes in the cost of living. Further research on both changes in income and consumption will give us a much clearer picture of how international trade affects both income and consumption.

Beyond Capital and Labor: Human Capital and R&D

The factor-proportions theory provides a logical and obvious explanation of international trade. Unfortunately, economists have learned from experience that a "logical and obvious" explanation of an economic phenomenon can be misleading or wrong. It is not enough for a theory to make sense. It also needs to pass enough empirical tests to give us a sense of confidence about it. We need to be assured that what we think is true is actually true. The empirical testing of the factor-proportions theory of international trade provides an excellent example. Empirical testing of theory is designed to check the validity of a theory. In some cases, the empirical testing leads to a better understanding and/or extensions of the basic theory. As we will show, this has been the case with the factor-proportions theory.

When the factor-proportions theory of international trade was developed in the early 20th century, lack of economic data made empirical testing of economic theory nearly impossible. Economic data that are routinely reported from media outlets such as radio, TV, newspapers, magazines, and the Internet did not become available until after 1945. Similarly the statistical tools used to test economic theory and the means to process the data (computers) were not available until the 1950s and 1960s. Because the factor-proportions theory seemed so logical, most economists accepted it as true before it had been empirically tested.

The Leontief Paradox

Wassily Leontief (1954) conducted the first and most famous empirical test of the factor-proportions theory. What Leontief found was surprising. He reasoned that compared to its trading partners, the United States was a capital-abundant country. Given the factor-proportions theory, the United States should export goods that are capital intensive and import goods that are labor intensive. To test this hypothesis, Leontief calculated how much capital and labor—the K/L ratio—various U.S. industries used in their production. He then compared the K/L ratios of the industries that had a net trade surplus—the net exporters—with the K/L ratios of the industries that had a net trade deficit—the net importers. He expected that U.S. industries with a trade surplus would have a high K/L ratio (capital intensive) relative to U.S. industries with a trade deficit (labor intensive).

Leontief's empirical estimation of the capital-to-labor ratio in U.S. industries with a trade surplus was higher than for industries with a trade deficit. This meant that his empirical result was the reverse of what he had expected. Net export industries in the United States were more labor intensive than were U.S. net import industries. This result has been called the Leontief paradox. This paradox is not some peculiarity of 1947, the year that Leontief did his research. Subsequent empirical studies on the factor-proportions theory—some very recent—have obtained this same perverse result. Leontief's findings caused considerable dismay among economists, who concluded that something was wrong with either the empirical test or the basic theory. The problem turned out to involve both, as we will show in the next section. In identifying the nature of the problem, economists were able to gain a better understanding of how factor abundance influences international trade.

Explanations of the Leontief Paradox

There are a number of possible explanations for Leontief's results. One is that some imports are not based on an abundance of labor or capital, but depend, instead, on the foreign country's possession of natural resources such as oil, diamonds, bauxite, or copper. Many of these natural-resource industries use highly capital-intensive production techniques to extract the product. Because Leontief used only a two-factor model (labor and capital), his results may have been biased. Because the U.S. imports many natural resources, this would help to explain why U.S. imports are capital inten- sive. Another explanation of the paradox is that U.S. trade policy may have created a bias in the results. Many of the most heavily protected industries in the United States are labor intensive (e.g., textiles and apparel). In our earlier discussion of trade and the distribution of income, we showed that the scarce factor of production (labor, for the United States) generally favors trade restrictions. The imposition of trade restrictions on certain labor-intensive goods would be to diminish U.S. imports of labor-intensive products and reduce the overall labor intensity of U.S. imports.

The most important explanations of the Leontief paradox, however, have to do with the skill level of the U.S. workforce and the presence of high technology. Leontief's test found that U.S. exports were labor inten- sive. This conclusion was based on the simple two-factor version of the factor-proportions model. This simple model assumes that labor is homo- geneous, or that one unit of labor is like any other unit of labor. In many cases, assumptions like this do not alter the predictions of economic models. However, in this case it did affect the model's results. Much of the U.S. labor force is highly skilled, or, to state it differently, represents valuable human capital (knowledge and skills). A simple way of examining the human capital that is embodied in labor is to consider a worker's wage in relation to the minimum wage. Most U.S. workers earn wages above the minimum wage. To the extent that any employer pays more than the abso- lute minimum wage, workers must possess something, such as skills, educa- tion, or training, that reflects their value in the labor market. Any payment to labor above the minimum wage can be viewed as a return to some form of human capital. In attempting to explain U.S. exports, it is necessary to take account of the human capital embodied in exports. When human capital is taken into account, U.S. exports appear to be not labor intensive but rather human-capital intensive. Most recently, Romalis (2004) has shown this, but the general result has been known for decades. In addition, U.S. exports appear to be intensive in technology, which represents another factor, different from capital, labor, or human capital. That is, U.S. exports have been shown to be intensive in research and development (R&D), and the level of R&D in an industry is a somewhat coarse but frequently used measurement of that industry's level of technology.

The importance of technology in trade can be considered in a different way. In an important paper, Trefler (1995) indicated that the volume of trade in the world was much smaller than would be predicted by the factor-proportions theory. Essentially, the labor-abundant countries are not exporting as much to the labor-scarce countries as the factor-proportions theory would predict. The differences are not trivial. Relatively speaking, the United States does not import nearly as much labor-intensive goods as the theory would predict. This phenomenon is usually referred to as "missing trade." The resolution of this puzzle ties in with both the technology factor and human capital discussed earlier. What is happening is that workers in the United States are much more efficient than workers in labor-abundant countries. This is partially due to access to better technology coupled with higher levels of human capital. Seen in this light, the supply of labor in the United States is not as small as it seems. The effective labor supply is actually much larger than the number of workers would suggest. This means that the United States is not nearly as labor scarce as the raw data would suggest and correspondingly imports fewer labor-intensive products than a simple version of the factor-proportions theory would predict.

As a result of this research, we can use the factor-proportions theory with some confidence. Most empirical evidence indicates that the basic reasoning embodied in the theory is correct. Countries tend to have a comparative advantage in and export goods whose production intensively uses its abundant factor of production. What needs to be considered is what constitutes a factor of production. Physical capital can be used as a factor essentially as it was described in the simple version of the theory. The same cannot be said for labor. The knowledge and skills that a labor force (human capital) possesses need to be treated as separate factors of production. The same is true for technology. The basic logic embodied in the factor-proportions theory is correct. We just need to broaden the concept of factors of production to include factors other than capital and labor.

Aside from presenting the basic theory of international trade and the related empirical evidence, we can make a final argument for the relevance of the theory. Economists like to use the term "revealed preference." What this means is that one of the best proofs of economic theory is checking to see what economic agents actually do as opposed to what they are predicted to do. Watching the evolution of international trade policy gives a powerful indication that the basic theory is correct. In a developed country, the strongest opposition to freer trade comes from firms and workers in labor-intensive industries. Is it even conceivable that labor-intensive industries in the United States would lobby for free trade? On the other side, the strongest proponents of free trade are industries that are human capital or technology intensive. Likewise, could one imagine Microsoft or Google arguing for protection? The theory presented earlier makes the preferences of industries, firms, and workers with respect to international trade policy more understandable. The theory tells one who gains and who loses from international trade, and the resulting actions of the winners and losers is quite predictable.

Case Study: United States–China Trade

If we compare the resource endowments of the United States to China, we find that the United States possesses abundant skilled labor (human capital) and scarce unskilled labor. China possesses abundant unskilled labor and scarce skilled labor. Thus, the factor-proportions theory would predict that the United States has a comparative advantage and should export goods that intensively use skilled labor in its production and that China has a comparative advantage and should export goods that intensively use unskilled labor in its production.

Table 3.7   The Factor-Proportions Theory and United States–China Trade

Skill Group Industry Examples	Chinese Exports to the United States	U.S. Exports to China
Most skilled		
1. Periodical, office and computing machines	4.8	7.7
2. Aircraft and parts, industrial inorganic chemicals	2.6	48.8
3. Engines and turbines, fats and oils	3.9	21.3
4. Concrete, nonelectric plumbing, and heating	11.5	4.3
5. Watches, clocks, toys, sporting goods	18.9	6.3
6. Wood buildings, blast furnaces, basic steel	8.2	1.3
7. Ship building and repair, furniture and fixtures	4.1	2.8
8. Cigarettes, motor vehicles, iron and steel foundries	5.2	1.8
9. Weaving, wool, leather tanning and finishing	17.2	0.4
10. Children's outerwear, nonrubber footwear	23.5	5.2
Least skilled		

Source: Sachs and Shatz (1994).

Table 3.7 shows the results of a study that tested this prediction based on United States–China trade. In this study, the authors divided a sample of 131 industries into 10 groups based on their skill intensity. Group 1 industries embodied the most skill intensive, and Group 10 industries the least skill intensive. This table provides sample industries for each group and shows each group's share of both U.S. exports to China and China's exports to the United States.

Notice that the pattern of United States–China trade shown in the table fits the prediction of the factor-proportions theory well. U.S. exports to China are concentrated in the high-skilled industries, as industry groups 1 through 3 account for 78 percent of U.S. exports to China. Also, China's exports to the United States are concentrated in the least skilled industries. Industry groups 9 and 10 account for more than 40 percent of China's exports to the United States. The pressure to restrict imports from China is easy to understand from the data.

Bibliography

Clark, Don P., Henry W. Herzog, Jr., and Alan M. Schlottmann. 1998. "Import Competition, Employment Risk, and the Job-Search Outcomes of Trade-Displaced Manufacturing Workers," *Industrial Relations* 37: 182–205.

Ebenstein, Avraham, Ann Harrison, Margaret McMillan, and Shannon Phillips. 2009. "Estimating the Impact of Trade and Offshoring on American Workers Using the Current Population Surveys," NBER Working Paper No. 15107.

Fajgelbaum, Pablo D. and Amit K. Khandelwal. 2014. "Measuring the Unequal Gains from Trade," NBER Working Paper No. 15107.

Heckscher, Eli. 1919. "The Effect of Foreign Trade on the Distribution of Income," *Ekonomisk Tidskrift* 21: 497–512.

Heston, Alan, Robert Summers, and Bettina Aten. 2013. Penn World Table Version 6.2, Center for International Comparisons of Production, Income, and Prices at the University of Pennsylvania.

Ingram, James C. 1983. *International Economics*. New York: Wiley.

Kletzer, Lori G. 2004. "Trade Related Job Loss and Wage Insurance: A Synthetic Review," *Review of International Economics* 12(November): 724–48.

Lawrence, Robert Z. 1984. *Can America Compete?* Washington, D.C.: The Brookings Institution.

Leontief, Wassily. 1954. "Domestic Production and Foreign Trade: The American Capital Position Reexamined," *Economia Internazionale* 7(4): 3–32.

Ohlin, Bertil. 1933. *International and Interregional Trade*. Cambridge, MA: Harvard University Press.

Pinketty, Thomas and Emmanuel Saez. 2003. "Income Inequality in the United States: 1913–1998," *Quarterly Journal of Economics* 118(1): 1–39.

Ricardo, David. 1966. *The Principles of Political Economy and Taxation*, London: Cambridge University Press. This work was first published in 1817.

Romalis, John. 2004. "Factor Proportions and the Structure of Commodity Trade," *American Economic Review* 94: 67–97.

Sachs, Jeffery and Howard Shatz. 1994. "Trade and Jobs in U.S. Manufacturing," *Brookings Papers on Economic Activity* 1(230): 18–53.

Samuelson, Paul A. 1948. "International Trade and the Equalization of Factor Prices," *Economic Journal* 58(288): 163–84.

Samuelson, Paul. 1962. "The Gains from International Trade Once Again," *Economic Journal* 72(288): 820–29.

Stopler, Wolfgang and Paul A. Samuelson. 1941. "Protection and Real Wages," *Review of Economic Studies* 9(5): 58–73.

Trefler, Daniel. 1995. "The Case of the Missing Trade and Other Mysteries," *American Economic Review* 85(5): 1029–46.

CHAPTER FOUR

New Models of International Trade

Most students of international trade have long had at least a sneaking suspicion
that conventional models of comparative advantage do not give an adequate account
of world trade . . . [I]t is hard to reconcile what we see in the manufactures trade
with the assumptions of standard trade theory.

—*Paul Krugman*

Introduction

In our analysis of international trade you have learned why countries have
a comparative advantage in producing different types of goods. The United
States has a comparative advantage in machines and India in cloth because
the two countries are endowed with different factor proportions. Comparative advantage based on the factor-proportions theory is the foundation
of our understanding of the gains from specialization and trade. With this
foundation we can determine the impact that trade has on factor prices and
a country's distribution of income.

However, a large share of international trade is not based on comparative advantage that results from different factor endowments. Countries also
trade essentially the same goods with one another. This is known as intra-industry trade (IIT). For example, Canada and the United States have a large
trading relationship based on exporting and importing automobiles and
automobile parts to one another. In this chapter, we will explain what intra-industry trade is and how it differs from the interindustry trade that we
have considered in the previous three chapters. As we will see, intra-industry
trade is determined by factors that differ from those involved in interindustry trade. As a result, a large part of this chapter is dedicated to explaining why intra-industry trade occurs. Fortunately, the welfare effects of
intra-industry trade are as beneficial as interindustry trade. The good news
for international trade policy is that the adjustments to higher levels of intra-industry trade may not be as high as for interindustry trade. In the latter

part of the chapter we consider two of the latest areas of research in inter-national economics. These relate to transportation costs and the study of international trade at the firm level. Transportation costs and other imped-iments to trade now are filtering into discussions of international trade policy. Reducing transportation costs and other impediments to trade has the potential to increase the gains from trade for both individual coun-tries and the world. The study of firms in international trade is expanding our knowledge of how economies adjust to changes in trade flows. Ulti-mately, it is firms that are the engine of world trade. The more clearly we understand how firms operate in global markets, the higher the probability that government policies with respect to international trade will be more effective.

Intra-industry Trade Versus Interindustry Trade

In the previous chapter, you learned that comparative advantage is based on different factor endowments among countries. The empirical tests of the factor-proportions theory raised some questions regarding the empirical validity of the theory but also stimulated the development of new trade the-ories. More specifically, the factor-proportions theory leaves unexplained a large portion of today's international trade. Up to this point, we have assumed that all international trade is interindustry trade, meaning coun-tries trading different goods with one another. However, a large portion of international trade consists of countries exporting and importing the same goods—this is intra-industry trade. For example, the U.S. imports and exports automobiles, beer, and steel. Intra-industry trade is not an isolated event but rather a pervasive part of international trade for many countries.

Unfortunately, intra-industry trade between countries coupled with the factor-proportions theory as the basis of trade poses a logical problem. The premise of the factor-proportions theory is that each country exports goods in which it has a comparative advantage. This comparative advantage reflects a country's ability to produce the good at a lower opportunity cost. Countries have different opportunity costs because they have different resource endowments. As a result, the factor-proportions theory provides a basis for interindustry trade but not for intra-industry trade.

With intra-industry trade, a country simultaneously imports and exports the same good. This implies that a country simultaneously has a compara-tive advantage *and* a comparative disadvantage in the same good. Using the factor-proportions theory as the sole basis for examining trade, this does not make any sense. Something else must be determining the basis for intra-industry trade. However, explaining intra-industry trade is more complicated than was the case for interindustry trade. We will discuss several theories, each less general than the factor-proportions theory, and each designed to explain intra-industry trade for narrower groups of goods. In order to meaningfully discuss intra-industry trade, we must first define it more carefully.

Defining Intra-industry Trade

Assessments of the importance of intra-industry trade vary because measuring this form of trade is not nearly as straightforward as measuring interindustry trade. For the latter, we can easily determine what goods are imported and exported. We measure such trade by calculating the value of trade in various goods. For example, the United States imports $100,000 of cloth from India and exports $100,000 of machines to India.

On the other hand, the problem in measuring intra-industry trade is that it is two-way trade in the same good. For example, suppose that the United States imports $50,000 in food from India and exports $50,000 in food to India. In this case, a numerical measure of the amount of intra-industry trade in the food industry is necessary. The easiest way to measure intra-industry trade is by means of the intra-industry trade index created by Balassa (1966).

$$\text{Intra-industry trade index} = 1 - |X - M| / X + M$$

For a particular industry, X represents the value of exports and M represents the value of imports. The vertical bars in the numerator of the index denote the absolute value of the difference between the amount exported and the amount imported.

In the previous chapter, a country either imported or exported a particular product. As a starting point, suppose that the United States only imports $100,000 of cloth from India, without exporting anything. In this case the second term in the expression reduces to 1 by dividing ($100,000/ $100,000), and the whole expressions equals 0. This indicates no intra-industry trade in the cloth industry. If the United States only exports $100,000 of machines to India, without importing anything, the second term in the expression reduces to 1 by dividing ($100,000/$100,000), and the whole expression equals 0. This indicates no intra-industry trade in machines. In both cases, all trade is interindustry trade.

However, if the United States exports $50,000 in food to India *and* imports $50,000 in food from India, the result is different. The second term in the expression reduces to 0 by dividing (0/$100,000). The whole expression now equals 1. This indicates that 100 percent of the trade in the food industry is intra-industry trade. Using these two extreme cases, the intra-industry trade index ranges from 0 (no intra-industry trade) to 1 (100 percent of the trade is intra-industry trade). The closer the index is to 1, the more intra-industry trade there is relative to interindustry trade. The closer it is to 0, the less intra-industry trade there is relative to inter-industry trade in the same good or service.

The major shortcoming of using this index to measure the amount of intra-industry trade is that we can get very different values for intra-industry trade depending on how we define the industry or product group. The more broadly we define the industry, the more likely we are to find that a country engages in intra-industry trade. For example, suppose that the United States imports $100,000 worth of men's pants and exports $100,000 worth of women's pants. What is the amount of intra-industry trade? If we define the industry to be the pants industry, the second term in the expression reduces to 0 by dividing (0/$200,000), and the whole expression equals 1. This indicates that 100 percent of the trade in this industry is intra-industry trade. But if we define the men's pants industry and the women's pants industry separately, the intra-industry trade indexes for each industry would equal 0, indicating no intra-industry trade. As a result, measurements of the importance of intra-industry trade can vary depending on how you define the industry or product group. The general principle is that the more broadly one defines the industry, the higher the intra-industry trade index will be. Conversely, the more narrowly the industry is defined, the lower the index will be.

Beyond this definitional issue, there is little doubt that intra-industry trade is an important part of international trade overall. The data in Table 4.1 present estimates of IIT for both the world and the United States. As one would expect, IIT is low for many types of food, beverages, and crude materials that the country does not possess or produce. As the level of processing indicates, IIT tends to be higher for manufactured goods. The data run against the grain of many portrayals of the United States as a country that increasingly only imports manufactured goods. Because the United States has lowered trade barriers since World War II, U.S. imports of manufactured goods have increased substantially, leading to the perception that manufacturing in the United States is dying. The reality is that U.S. exports of manufactured goods are increasing. This shows up in our data as high levels of IIT. The United States is *both* a major importer and exporter of manufactured goods. Compared to the world, the United States is a rather average country with respect to IIT. The overall IIT index for the world and the United States are virtually identical. As one would expect, there are some differences by industry. The overall picture reveals that half of U.S.

Table 4.1   Intra-industry Trade by Industries for the World

Industry	United States	World
Food and live animals	0.45	0.38
Beverages and tobacco	0.31	0.34
Crude materials, inedible, except fuels	0.38	0.27
Mineral fuels, lubricants, and related products	0.14	0.22
Animal and vegetable oils, fats, and waxes	0.27	0.26
Chemicals and related products	0.64	0.59
Manufactured goods, classified by material	0.53	0.52
Machinery and transport equipment	0.59	0.58
Miscellaneous manufactured articles	0.41	0.49
Commodities and transactions not included elsewhere	0.67	0.68
Total	0.51	0.51

Source: Sawyer and Sprinkle (2012).

trade is now IIT with the rest being intra-industry trade. As shown in Sawyer and Sprinkle (2012), most developed countries have even higher IIT indexes, with the average being 0.62. France has the highest index of 76.7. This is merely to show that IIT can reach very high levels of total trade. Further, IIT is a growing phenomenon in world trade. IIT indexes were routinely below 0.20 for most countries in the 1960s. They are still lower for the developing countries, but like the developed countries, their IIT indexes are rising.

Explaining Intra-industry Trade

The famous trade economist H. Peter Gray (1985) once described intra-industry trade as an "untidy phenomenon." What he meant by that remark is that IIT is hard to demonstrate using the sort of convenient mathematical models economists are so fond of. For our purposes, it means that we cannot use a single, unified model of IIT. Unfortunately, there are different kinds of IIT that require somewhat different explanations. In the end, it all makes sense, but it is not quite as clean as explaining interindustry trade. That's the bad news; but for every cost there is a benefit. The benefit here is that a lot of what occurs in international trade will become much more understandable. Interindustry and intra-industry trade are a bit like two sides of the same coin. It's all trade, but it is hard to think of total trade without both. The previous chapter assumed that countries were trading homogeneous goods. As we will see later, there also is IIT in homogeneous goods. The real distinction lies in the existence of differentiated goods. The existence of differentiated goods is the driver of the majority of IIT. In the next section, we'll consider IIT in homogeneous goods and then move on to several explanations of trade in differentiated products.

Intra-industry Trade in Homogeneous Products

So far we have assumed that the goods being traded were homogeneous goods (identical goods). For example, cloth and machines produced in India are identical to cloth and machines produced in the United States. The factor-proportions theory explained why there is interindustry trade in homogeneous goods. We now want to explain why there also is intra-industry trade in these goods. Intra-industry trade in homogeneous goods between countries can occur as a result of one (or more) of four possible circumstances.

First, consider a bulky material such as cement, for which the cost of transportation is high relative to its value. For example, several cement plants are located on each side of the U.S. and Canadian border. Cement users in both Canada and the United States might find it cheaper to buy from a supplier on the other side of the border—that is, a foreign supplier—if that supplier is closer than the nearest domestic supplier. In such cases, exports and imports would show up as intra-industry trade for both Canada and the United States.

Second, homogeneous services can be the basis of intra-industry trade due to the joint production of the service or peculiar technical conditions. For example, a country both exports and imports banking services, shipping services, and insurance services because these services are produced jointly with another traded product. Exports of automobiles from Germany to the United States must be transported and insured. Frequently a bank is involved in financing goods as they move from the German exporter to the U.S. importer. Similarly, a shipment of computers from the United States to Germany must be transported, insured, and financed. The export and import of these goods represent interindustry trade, but the export and import of transportation, insurance, and financing services to move these goods would show up as intra-industry trade in services for both Germany and the United States.

Third, some countries engage in substantial *entrepot* and *re-export* trade. With entrepot trade, goods are imported into a country and later the same good is exported to another country. The country engaging in entrepot trade is providing storage and distribution facilities for an international firm. For example, IBM may ship computers from the United States to a warehouse facility in Singapore. With computers stored in a warehouse in Singapore, IBM can supply other countries in the Far East. Imports and exports of computers by Singapore are classified as entrepot trade. With re-export trade, goods are imported into a country and then subjected to some small transformation that leaves them essentially unchanged prior to exportation to another country. For example, Singapore, Hong Kong, and the Netherlands collect imports and then sort, repack, and label these goods for use in the countries to which they will ultimately be shipped. The receiving countries may, in turn, re-export the goods to countries within the region. In the case of entrepot and re-export trade, the trading country does not actually produce the good, but rather transships it using its own facilities. However, this type of trade is included in a country's imports and exports and increases the reported level of intra-industry trade. This sort of trade is facilitated by the existence of foreign-trade zones (FTZs). FTZs are a part of a country, but they are outside of the usual trade policy restrictions of the country. Goods can be shipped in and out freely. However, goods entering an FTZ cannot be brought into the country and can only be reshipped to another country. Fourth, seasonal or other periodic fluctuations in output or demand can lead to intra-industry trade in homogeneous goods. Examples would include international trade in seasonal fruits and vegetables, electricity, and tourist services.

Intra-industry Trade in Differentiated Products

Foreign trade then is highly beneficial to a country, as it increases the amount and variety of the objects on which revenue may be expended.
—David Ricardo

Most intra-industry trade is trade in differentiated goods between countries. Differentiated goods have features that make them appear different from competing goods in the same industry. Goods can be differentiated in one of two ways. Horizontally differentiated goods are goods that differ among themselves in some slight way, although their prices are similar. For example, candy bars may have the same price but contain very different flavors or ingredients. Vertically differentiated goods are those that have very different physical characteristics and different prices. For example, the prices and physical characteristics of new automobiles vary enormously. In either case, trade is heavily influenced by demand. This is in stark contrast to our earlier models of trade that were most heavily influenced by differences in the cost of production among countries. The common phrase here is that consumers inherently have a "love of variety," which in turn is causing international trade.

In addition, most international trade in differentiated goods occurs under conditions of imperfect competition. A critical distinction between perfect and imperfect competition has to do with the number of firms in the marketplace. Under perfect competition, a firm cannot affect the market price because it is only one of many firms that produce virtually identical goods. Under imperfect competition, a firm is able to influence the price of the product by changing the quantity of goods offered for sale. When a firm in an imperfectly competitive market can influence the price of the product, this means that the firm has some degree of market power. Imperfect competition can occur under three different market structures—monopoly, oligopoly, or monopolistic.

In a monopoly, a firm's market power is derived from being the only firm in the industry that produces a unique product with no close substitutes. Electrical power service, water service, sewer service, natural gas service, cable TV service, and drugs under patent are all examples of monopolies or virtual monopolies. In global markets, a monopoly really isn't a realistic possibility. In an oligopoly there are few firms, and each firm has some market power that is derived from the small number of firms in the industry and high barriers to entry. Automobiles, tires, detergents, and TVs are all differentiated products sold in oligopoly markets in which one firm's actions may cause a reaction on the part of the other firms. Such situations do exist in global markets, but the results are not that different from monopolistic competition except for higher barriers to entry. In an industry characterized by monopolistic competition, there are many firms and each one has some market power derived from product differentiation. For example, there may be 30 women's clothing stores in a city. Each store may be able to differentiate itself by offering different locations, atmosphere, style, quality of the material, or quality of the service. However, each firm must compete with other firms offering close substitutes. The examples in global markets are almost endless. In most cases, consumer goods are characterized by monopolistic competition. Firms face a high degree of competition when they produce differentiated products that can be distinguished from one another by the consuming public. If competition is great enough in the marketplace, the free entry of firms into the market will drive profits for all firms to zero. In this case, the demand for the product produced by any one firm is characterized by a downward-sloping demand curve. As such, the firm is a price searcher in that if the firm raises or lowers its price while the prices of competing products are constant, its sales would dramatically decrease or increase, respectively.

Figure 4.1 illustrates the equilibrium level output for a single firm in this monopolistically competitive market. The demand curve, D, facing the firm is downward sloping, implying that the marginal revenue curve, MR—meaning the change in total revenue as the firm sells one more unit—lies below the demand curve. With the firm producing in the range of decreasing costs, the average cost curve, AC, is declining. With average costs declining, the marginal cost curve—that is, the change in total costs as the firm produces one more unit—lies below the average cost curve.

The firm in this market seeks to produce an output level at which profits are maximized. This means that the firm will select the output level for which marginal revenue equals marginal cost, Q_M. If new firms are free to enter this market, the resulting maximum profits for any one firm are zero. This is shown in Figure 4.1 by the tangency of the average cost and the demand curves at point M. Output Q_M and price P_M represent the best that the firm can achieve, as any other output level results in losses for the firm.

What follows are three theories that serve to explain intra-industry trade. Economies of scale, the product cycle, and overlapping demands all are used to explain intra-industry trade in differentiated products. These theories, however, are not mutually exclusive. Indeed, Paul Krugman won a Nobel Prize in Economics combining two of the three. This means that you

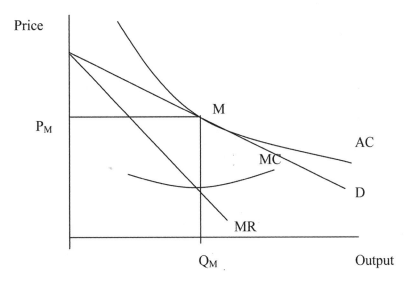

Figure 4.1   Equilibrium with Monopolistic Competition.

may be able to apply more than one of these explanations of intra-industry trade to a particular product or industry.

Trade and Product Variety

In the last chapter, we demonstrated that international trade improves the welfare of countries that trade. In our examples, the United States and India improved their welfare by gaining the ability to obtain goods at a lower price than they could have if the goods had been produced domestically. However, there are other gains from trade that are more difficult to capture in standard economic models. Everyone recognizes the importance of these sorts of gains from trade. The problem is that in many cases they are difficult to quantify. Economists being economists, this is an annoying situation. However, in some cases progress is being made in putting numerical values on these gains.

An example of this is international trade and the variety of goods available to domestic consumers. As we will see in later chapters, international trade is riddled with various barriers to trade. However, over the last 50 years there has been a substantial amount of progress in the world economy in reducing these trade barriers. As trade barriers have fallen, there has been a substantial expansion in the number of countries that individual countries trade with. A recent paper by Broda and Weinstein (2004) illustrates this trend. Table 4.2 reproduces the main result of their study. The 20 countries in the table are the world's largest importers of goods. The data show that for each country, the average number of countries that it imports from since 1972 has increased substantially. The average increase in the number of supplying countries is 49 percent. In this study, the number of countries from which an individual country imports is taken to be a measure of the variety of imports in a particular product category.

These results imply two things: one more obvious and the other less so. Having choices in one's consumption has value to most consumers. This is almost entirely the reason why many markets are characterized by monopolistic competition. For most of us, our welfare would be diminished considerably if the wide variety of goods from which we can choose were curtailed. For many of us, considering life without imported goods is not a pleasant thought. However, there is another benefit of variety that is less obvious and may be quantified to some extent. A larger variety of imported goods tends to put downward pressure on the price of other imports. In other words, the more varieties there are of a product that are imported, the lower will be the price—all else being equal. This makes sense because the presence of a larger number of suppliers will usually cause lower prices in any market. These

Table 4.2 The Impact of Variety

Country	Average Number of Suppliers Per Imported Good		
	1972	1997	Percent Change
United States	31.4	42.7	36.1
Germany	29.1	38.2	31.2
Japan	20.6	28.8	39.9
United Kingdom	30.4	38.4	26.5
France	26.3	35.2	34.2
Italy	23.9	33.5	40.0
Canada	17.8	25.2	41.3
Netherlands	23.6	31.5	33.1
China	4.9	20.7	326.1
Belgium	20.8	27.6	32.8
Hong Kong	15.0	23.7	57.9
Spain	16.6	21.8	31.6
Mexico	9.1	17.3	89.3
Singapore	14.7	23.2	57.6
Former Soviet Union	8.7	27.3	213.7
South Korea	5.9	16.8	185.3
Switzerland	18.7	24.2	28.9
Taiwan	7.7	17.4	126.9
Sweden	18.8	22.8	21.5
Brazil	11.5	19.7	70.7

Source: Adapted from Broda and Weinstein (2004).

effects are subtle but noticeable. Broda and Weinstein (2006) calculate that the increase in the variety of imports has lowered the price of imports by about 1.2 percent per year faster than would otherwise be the case. Given that imports in the United States are a rising percentage of gross domestic product (GDP), these lower prices are having a noticeable effect on overall welfare. Further, Broda and Weinstein estimate that the rising number of varieties available has increased consumer welfare in the United States by about 3 percent. In terms of nominal GDP, this is about $510 billion. More recent research by Blonigen and Soderbery (2010) indicates that the previous estimates may seriously underestimate the gains from intra-industry trade.

Virtually all of the research on this topic relies on government trade data. The problem with this data is that they cannot capture the actual degree of product differentiation in all cases. It would be preferable to use actual market-based data, which would more closely mirror the actual choices consumers make. In this study the authors were able to use very detailed data for the automobile market that are even more detailed than that presented in Table 4.2. The results indicated that the gains to consumers due to increased variety in the automobile market are twice as large as previously reported estimates. In other words, a 3 percent gain in welfare may be a very conservative estimate.

Economies of Scale

A common explanation of international trade in differentiated products is that this form of trade is a result of economies of scale—EOS—in the product's production. Economies of scale means that as the production of a good increases, the cost per unit falls. This phenomenon also is known as increasing returns to scale.

Figure 4.2 shows the effects of economies of scale on international trade. Assume that a U.S. automobile firm and a German automobile firm have identical cost conditions. This means that the firms have the same long-run average cost curve (AC) for this type of car. As the figure indicates, the economies of scale that both firms face result in decreasing unit costs over the first 250,000 cars produced in a year. Past this point, the unit cost of a car remains constant. That point is known as the minimum efficient scale of plant size. This means that 250,000 units of output are required to minimize per-unit cost.

Now, suppose that the U.S. automobile firm produces and sells 75,000 cars in the United States and the German automobile firm produces and sells 75,000 cars in Germany, as indicated by point A. Because cost and price structures are the same, the average cost for both firms is equal at AC_0. At this point, there is no basis for international trade. Now suppose that rising incomes in the United States result in a demand for 150,000 cars while German demand remains constant. The larger demand allows the U.S. firm to produce more output and take advantage of the economies of scale. As output increases from 75,000 cars to 150,000 cars, unit costs for the firm change from AC_0 at point A to AC_1 at point B. Because the U.S. firm is subject to economies of scale, its unit costs have declined. Compared to the German firm, the U.S. firm now can produce cars at a lower cost. With free trade, the United States would now export cars to Germany. As a result,

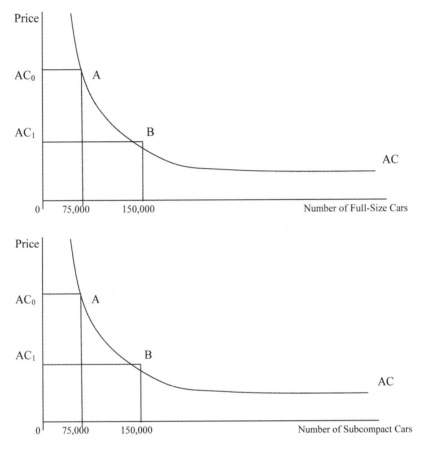

Figure 4.2   Economies of Scale as the Basis for Intra-industry Trade.

we can use economies of scale to explain interindustry trade when initial comparative costs between countries are equal. However, this example of economies of scale and international trade does not explain the existence of intra-industry trade in automobiles between Germany and the United States.

To explain intra-industry trade using economies of scale, consider a situation where both a U.S. automobile firm and a German automobile firm each produce full-size cars and subcompact cars. In addition, assume that both firms have identical cost conditions in the production of both types of cars so that they have the same long-run average cost curves (AC). As Figure 4.2 indicates, the economies of scale that both firms face result in decreasing unit costs for both full-size and subcompact cars. Assume that the U.S. automobile firm produces and sells 75,000 full-size cars in the

United States and the German automobile firm produces and sells 75,000 full-size cars in Germany, as indicated by point A. In addition, assume that the U.S. automobile firm produces and sells 75,000 subcompact cars in the United States and the German automobile firm produces and sells 75,000 subcompact cars in Germany, as indicated by point A. Because cost and price structures are the same, there is no basis for trade.

Now, assume that both Germany and the United States allow free trade in the automobile market. The total demand for full-size and subcompact cars in the combined German and U.S. markets is 150,000 full-size and 150,000 subcompact cars (75,000 cars in Germany and 75,000 cars in the United States). This combined larger demand for full-size cars would allow the U.S. firm to produce more full-size cars and thus take advantage of economies of scale. As the U.S. firm increases output from 75,000 to 150,000 full-size cars, unit costs for the firm change from point A to point B. Because the U.S. firm is subject to economies of scale, its unit costs decline from AC_0 to AC_1. Compared to the German firm, the U.S. firm now can produce full-size cars at a lower cost. In addition, the combined larger demand for subcompact cars would allow the German firm to produce more subcompact cars and likewise take advantage of economies of scale. As the German firm increases output from 75,000 to 150,000 subcompact cars, unit costs for the firm fall from AC_0 to AC_1 (point A to point B). Because the German firm is subject to economies of scale, its unit costs decline. Compared to the U.S. firm, the German firm now can produce subcompact cars at a lower cost. With free trade, the United States would now export full-size cars to Germany, and Germany would export subcompact cars to the United States. As a result, economies of scale can be used to explain intra-industry trade when initial comparative costs between countries are equal.

While our example shows that intra-industry trade can occur between countries because of economies of scale, the actual specialization pattern is indeterminate. In the example, the United States produces full-size cars and Germany produces subcompact cars. As a practical matter, it does not make any difference which firm or which country produces the full-size or subcompact car. In either case, unit costs decline and intra-industry trade will occur between the two countries. Very often, the determination of which country produces which type of good is a result of historical accident or is based on initial consumer tastes and preferences within the domestic economy. In our example, we assumed that the initial comparative costs and demand conditions between the two countries were identical. With differentiated products, identical costs and demand conditions are not necessary for mutually beneficial trade to occur from economies of scale.

There are two sources of economies of scale. One source is *internal* economies of scale for the firm. Scale economies are internal when the firm's increase in output causes a decline in its average cost. A firm that has high fixed costs as a percentage of its total costs will have falling average unit costs as output increases. This cost structure generally occurs when firms use a lot of capital to produce a good relative to labor or other variable factors. For example, most firms in the automobile industry are subject to internal economies of scale. Firms such as General Motors or Toyota produce a large number of automobiles at relatively low prices. Smaller firms such as Porsche or Ferrari have much higher production costs per unit. Similar economies of scale occur in industries that produce intermediate products such as steel and chemicals.

Another source of internal economies of scale occurs in high-technology products where there are high fixed costs associated with research and development (R&D). For example, nearly all of the total costs of computer software are development costs. The variable unit cost of producing and distributing the software may be small relative to the total production costs. In the pharmaceutical industry, the development costs of a new drug are quite high and the variable costs of producing and distributing it are low. In many cases, the first producer to successfully develop the product gains almost all of the market as unit costs decline. The result is that internal economies of scale contribute to the existence of intra-industry trade.

On the other hand, when there are *external* economies of scale, a firm's average unit cost falls as the output of the entire industry rises. As the industry expands output, several factors may influence costs for all firms. Because the industry may depend upon the existence of suppliers or a large pool of labor with the skills necessary in that industry, external economies of scale may explain why firms within an industry tend to cluster geographically as famously described by Porter (1990). Examples include the watch industry in Switzerland, the movie industry in southern California, and the financial services industry in New York City or London. Economies of scale provide a basis for intra-industry trade. In markets characterized by internal or external economies of scale, international trade makes it possible for consumers to enjoy a greater variety of goods while paying a lower price to producers, whose costs are lower because of large-scale production.

The Product Cycle

Another explanation for the occurrence of intra-industry trade between countries is that of the product cycle. In this case, changes in technology or a new product design can change the pattern of imports and exports.

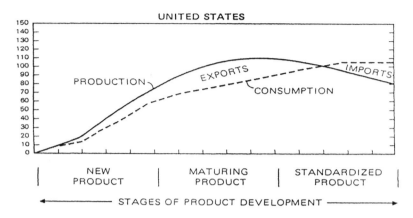

Figure 4.3 The Product Cycle.

The basic idea originally given by Vernon (1966) behind the product cycle is that developed countries tend to specialize in producing new goods based on technological innovations, while the developing countries tend to specialize in the production of already well-established goods. The theory of the product cycle is that as each good moves through its product cycle, there will be changes in the geographical location of where and how the good is produced. The product cycle for a typical good is shown in Figure 4.3.

In the first stage of the product cycle, manufacturers of a "new" product need to be near a high-income market in order to receive consumer feedback. Generally, a firm targets its initial small-scale production at a consumer base with substantial income in the firm's domestic market, such as the United States. At this point, both the product's design and the production process are still evolving. The product may need to be improved and/or the production process may need to be adjusted to determine the most efficient method of production. These design and production enhancements usually require specialized scientific and engineering inputs that are available only in developed countries. During this stage of the product cycle, both consumption and production of a "new" product are likely to occur in a relatively high-income and high-cost-of-production country. Over time, the firm will perfect the product and the production process. At this point the product's consumption and production increase. In addition to serving the domestic market, the firm will begin to export the new product to other countries where there is similar demand from high-income consumers.

In the second stage of the product cycle, the product matures as it becomes more standardized in terms of size, features, and the production process. If foreign demand is sufficiently large, the firm may find it more profitable to produce the product in those foreign markets instead of exporting it. In some circumstances, the country where the product was originally developed may begin importing the product from other high-income countries where production costs are less.

In the third stage of the product cycle, the product and the production process have become so standardized that profit maximization leads firms to produce in the lowest-cost production site. At this point, the standardized production processes can be moved to developing countries where using semiskilled labor in assembly-type operations keeps production costs low. The innovating country now becomes an importer of the product. In the innovating country, attention moves on to a new product at the early stage of its product cycle. Examples of products that have experienced a typical product cycle include radios, TVs, VCRs, and semiconductor chips. The product may have started as a "new" and somewhat unique product in the first phase. In the last stage, the product has become a standardized one so that factor abundance and low-production costs determine its pattern of production and trade.

The concept of the product cycle can be used to explain some of the intra-industry trade both among developed countries and between developing and developed countries. For example, a country may be exporting a new product and at the same time importing a similar product from another country. The United States may be exporting a new sports car to Japan and simultaneously importing another variety of sports car from Japan. With the constant flood of "new" product development in developed countries, intra-industry trade occurs among high-income countries as they exchange these new products with one another. The model also implies that high-income countries will be exporting "newer" versions of the product to developing countries and importing "older" versions of the product from these countries.

Overlapping Demands

A nation that would enrich itself by foreign trade is certainly most likely to do so when its neighbors are all rich, industrious, and commercial nations.
—Adam Smith

The final explanation of intra-industry trade focuses on the importance of demand characteristics in various countries. Staffan Linder (1961) used the concept of overlapping demands to suggest that similarities between countries could be the basis of trade, even though factor prices were the same in both countries.

According to the overlapping demands hypothesis, trade in manufactured goods is likely to be greatest among countries with similar tastes and income levels. Linder argues that firms within a country are primarily oriented toward producing a specific variety of a good for which there is a large home market. As such, a country's tastes and preferences determine the specific variety of product that its firms will produce and that they could then export to foreign consumers. The most promising foreign markets for these exports will be found in countries with tastes and income levels similar to those of the country in which the products are produced. Each country will produce products that primarily serve its home market, but part of the output will be exported to other countries where there is a receptive market.

For example, a U.S. automobile firm will produce an automobile that satisfies the tastes and preferences of most U.S. consumers. However, a small number of U.S. consumers will prefer something other than the domestic version. In Sweden and Germany, automobile producers will produce an automobile that satisfies the tastes and preferences of most Swedish and German consumers, respectively. However, it is likely that in both countries a small number of consumers will prefer something other than the Swedish or German versions. In all three countries, some consumers are not able to purchase the variety of automobile that they prefer. The hypothesis of overlapping demands indicates that in such a case, U.S. producers could produce for their domestic market and export automobiles to Swedish and German consumers who prefer the U.S. automobile. At the same time, Swedish and German producers could export automobiles to U.S. consumers who prefer German and Swedish automobiles. These sorts of overlapping demands can lead to intra-industry trade.

Linder states that within a country, consumers' average income level will determine their general tastes and preferences. Countries with low average incomes will demand lower-quality goods, and countries with high average incomes will demand higher-quality goods. As such, high-income countries are more likely to trade with other high-income countries because there is a greater probability of overlapping demands. For the same reason, low-income countries are more likely to trade with other low-income countries.

Overlapping demands implies that intra-industry trade would be more intense among countries with similar incomes. In general, the theory of overlapping demands can explain the large and growing amount of trade in similar but differentiated goods. These conclusions concerning trade patterns between countries are interesting because they are not based on or predicted by the factor-proportions theory. Everything else being equal, the theory suggests that trade will be more intense between countries that have similar tastes, preferences, and incomes.

The discussion of intra-industry trade and overlapping demands indicates that countries with similar incomes would tend to have a higher percentage of their trade as intra-industry trade. Going back to Table 4.1, it would appear that in general this is the case. However, it was noted in the first part of the chapter that developing countries also engage in a substantial amount of intra-industry trade. Some of these exchanges may be explained as intra-industry trade with other developing countries at a similar level of income. On the other hand, it has been observed that there is a growing amount of intra-industry trade between developed and developing countries. At first glance, this would seem to be a bit odd. The explanation lies in linking vertical product differentiation with overlapping demands. In a developing country, there may be a substantial number of consumers with incomes similar to those that prevail in developed countries. These consumers may be poorly served by the domestic producers, who are producing for the majority taste and preference within the country. Satisfying the needs of these high-income consumers may be most profitably accomplished by importing higher-quality versions of products from developed countries. The reverse is true for the developed countries. In these countries there may be less affluent consumers who desire cheaper varieties of a product. These consumers may not be well served by the domestic producers if the market is too small. The solution may be to import lower-priced versions of the product designed for consumers in low-income countries. The existence of vertical product differentiation and overlapping demands between different groups of consumers in different types of countries helps to explain the growing amount of intra-industry trade between developed and developing countries. Beyond the logic, papers such as Fajgelbaum, Grossman, and Helpman (2011) are using the more formal models preferred by economists to achieve this result.

Empirical Evidence on Intra-industry Trade

The empirical evidence on intra-industry trade confirms the discussion of the theory given earlier. A basic prediction is that countries with higher GDP per capita will engage in more intra-industry trade. In very general terms, one can see this in Table 4.1 at the start of the chapter. The empirical evidence on intra-industry trade strongly confirms this. In essence, the love of variety increases with income. This can be taken one step further.

Intra-industry trade should be positively correlated with the overall size of the markets in the two countries. In other words, the larger the sum of the GDP, the larger the amount of intra-industry trade. This occurs as firms in both countries have more opportunities to exploit a larger overall market. Intra-industry trade should be positively correlated with similarities in income. The more similar GDP per capita is between two countries, the more trade should be intra-industry trade as opposed to interindustry trade. Again, the empirical evidence indicates that this is the case.

More recent research has focused on attempting to separately examine intra-industry trade in horizontally and vertically differentiated goods. Because these two types of goods are different, this may produce different patterns of trade. A theoretical prediction is that trade between two countries with similar GDP per capita should be predominantly in horizontally differentiated goods. This makes sense as consumers in the two countries have similar incomes and should be purchasing goods of similar quality. On the other hand, differences in GDP per capita should result in trade in vertically differentiated goods described in the preceding section. As recently shown by Thorpe and Leitao (2013), dissimilarities in GDP per capita should be associated with vertical product differentiation. The implication of the research is that the characteristics of demand proxied by GDP per capita have a large influence on international trade.

Transportation Costs and Trade

One of the more active areas of research in international trade has been analyzing the effects of transportation costs on trade, prices, and domestic production and consumption. Up to this point, we have assumed that transportation costs between countries are zero. With zero transportation costs and perfect competition, a single world price would be established for a good after free trade opens up between countries. This area of research is now at the point where it is influencing international trade policy. A part of transportation costs involves the cost of moving goods across that line known as a border. In the 21st century there are now ongoing trade negotiations seeking to make border regulations more common. This in turn reduces transportation costs and has the same effects that we will see later.

The effects of transportation costs can be seen by comparing trade in a single good under conditions of zero transportation costs between countries with a condition in which transportation costs are positive. In Figure 4.4, we illustrate the economic effects of transportation costs for both the importing and exporting countries. As we begin our analysis, once again

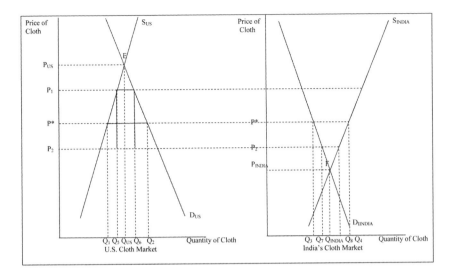

Figure 4.4 Effects of Transportation Costs on International Trade.

consider a world consisting of two countries—India and the United States—and one product—cloth, which is produced and consumed in both countries. Figure 4.4 shows the domestic supply and demand conditions for cloth in the United States and India. The U.S. supply and demand curves for cloth are given in the left-hand panel by S_{US} and D_{US} respectively. The same curves for India are shown in the right-hand panel by S_{INDIA} and D_{INDIA}, respectively. As we have previously illustrated, under free trade with zero transportation costs between the United States and India, the world price of cloth would be equal to P^*. At price P^*, the quantity of cloth supplied in the United States by domestic producers will be Q_1, and the quantity demanded by U.S. consumers will be Q_2. Meanwhile, the quantity of cloth supplied in India will be Q_4 and the quantity demanded will be Q_3. For the international market to clear, the excess demand in the United States, Q_1 to Q_2, must equal the excess supply in India, Q_3 to Q_4. That is, the quantity of cloth available for export from India must be equal to the quantity of cloth imports demanded by the United States.

Now, assume that positive transportation costs are included in the analysis. The effect of these costs will be to place a wedge between the price of cloth in the United States and the price of cloth in India. As such, a single world price of cloth will no longer exist. The difference between the price of cloth in India and the United States exists because in order for Indian exporters to be willing to sell to consumers in the United States, they must receive a price that covers the additional costs of transporting cloth to the

United States. In equilibrium, the difference in cloth prices between the two countries will be equal to the per-unit transportation costs.

Suppose that transportation costs per unit of cloth are equal to T, as illustrated in Figure 4.4. This means that the price of imported cloth by the United States will rise from P* to P_1. As the price of imported cloth rises, the quantity of imported cloth falls from the horizontal difference Q_1 to Q_2 to the smaller amount Q_5 to Q_6. In addition, the net price (the price of imported cloth in the United States minus transportation costs) of exported cloth from India falls. As illustrated in Figure 4.4, the price of cloth in India falls from P* to P_2. India's price of cloth will fall until U.S. imports of cloth (Q_5 to Q_6) equals India's exports of cloth (Q_7 to Q_8.). The difference between the U.S. price, P_1, and India's price, P_2, is equal to the transportation costs, T.

With positive transportation costs, the quantity of cloth traded is lower; imports by the United States and exports by India both have decreased. In addition, the consumption of cloth in the United States has declined and the production of cloth in the United States has increased. For India, the consumption of cloth has increased and the production of cloth has decreased. Thus, the effect of transportation costs is to move the price of cloth and the quantities traded partially back toward the no-trade situation. As such, transportation costs act has a barrier to trade much as tariffs and other nontariff barriers do. Indeed, if transportation costs were equal to or greater than the no-trade price differences between the United States and India, there would be no trade between the two countries. You may be able to think of numerous goods that are not typically traded between countries for just this reason. Often, the analysis of trade between countries distinguishes between tradable and nontradable goods. This distinction is determined by transportation costs between countries. Nontradable goods are those goods whose transportation costs are so large that it makes trade unprofitable—whereas tradable goods are those whose transportation costs are low enough to make it potentially profitable to trade the goods between countries.

The Firm in International Trade

Until recently, economists had very little information on the characteristics of firms engaging in international trade. Fortunately, recent research has produced both an interesting picture of exporting firms and some basic theory on how firm characteristics influence comparative advantage.

Firm Heterogeneity

Collectively, the literature on firms in international trade is referred to as trade with heterogeneous firms, or firm heterogeneity. Behind the models we have been using firms are assumed to be essentially alike, that is, a representative firm. Research beginning in the 1990s paints a different picture of firms and industries in autarky and when international trade exists. Firms in industries are typically *not* homogeneous. In terms of international trade, normally only a minority of firms export. Table 4.3 shows a sample of countries around the world. Detailed studies of the economies of Europe by Mayer and Ottaviano (2008) and others have shown the same sort of pattern. It is now routinely assumed that exporters constitute a minority of manufacturing firms.

As one might expect, there is substantial variation across different industries. Table 4.4 provides data on the percentage of firms within various industries that export for the United States. The lowest percentage shown is 5 percent, whereas the highest is 38 percent. One can notice a similarity in both Tables 4.3 and 4.4. The highest percentage in either table is less than 40 percent. This means that in the vast majority of cases that exporters in almost any industry in any country will be a minority of firms.

A typical description of an industry is where firms differ widely in productivity levels. In other words, more efficient and less efficient firms coexist in the same industry. Using data from Bernard, et al. (2007) allows us to see these differences for a large trading economy, the United States. First, exporting firms are substantially larger than firms that do not export. This is true both in terms of output and employment. However, these firms are primarily engaged in serving the domestic market. The last column of Table 4.4 clearly shows that for the average industry in the United States

Table 4.3 Percentage of Manufacturing Firms That Export

Country	Percentage of Exporting Firms
United States	18.0
Norway	39.2
France	17.4
Japan	20.0
Chile	20.9
Colombia	18.2

Source: World Trade Organization (2008).

Table 4.4   U.S. Manufacturing Exports

	Exporting Firms (Percentage)	Exports/ Shipments
Miscellaneous manufacturing	2	15
Printing and publishing	5	14
Furniture	7	10
Apparel	8	14
Wood products	8	19
Nonmetallic mineral products	9	12
Food manufacturing	12	15
Textile products	12	12
Fabricated metals	14	12
Petroleum and coal	18	12
Beverages and tobacco	23	7
Leather	24	13
Paper	24	9
Textiles	25	13
Transportation equipment	28	13
Plastics and rubber products	28	10
Primary metals	30	10
Chemicals	36	14
Machinery manufacturing	33	16
Computers and related products	38	21
Electrical equipment, appliances	38	13
Average	18	14

Source: Bernard et al. (2007).

the percentage of output that is exported is 14 percent. Further the range around this average is not very large. The lowest percentage is 7 and the highest is 21. Exporters are both a minority of all firms but at the same time their primary business is servicing the domestic market.

Firms that export are substantially different from firms that do not. The reasons for these disparities are easy to find. They are more productive than the majority of firms in their respective industries. The reasons for their higher productivity are not surprising. First, the firms are more capital intensive. As we saw in a previous chapter, this increases value added per worker. In addition, workers in firms that export tend to have higher levels of human capital as they use more highly skilled workers. Not surprisingly, firms that export tend to pay higher wages than firms that do not. They are also better managed. Everything else being equal, these firms produce more output with any given amount of capital and labor. In the jargon of economics, this is referred to as total factor productivity (TFP). With this information about the characteristics of exporting firms, the question is now how to explain the patterns in the data.

The models of firm heterogeneity and trade pioneered by Melitz (2003) show how two concepts introduced earlier interact to produce intra-industry trade. First, we have already considered monopolistic competition as a market structure. Many industries are characterized by a large number of firms producing differentiated products. Each of these firms is insufficiently large to influence either industry price or output. The firms in the industry are each searching for the most profitable price and output levels as shown in the previous chapter. In addition, we showed the effects of economies of scale on a firm. Due to economies of scale, as industry output expands, the average cost declines. As we showed in Figure 4.2, economies of scale in both countries would allow for intra-industry trade even if the cost differences between the two countries were negligible. Behind our discussion was an assumption that firms in the industry in a country are operating under similar cost conditions. However, even with this restrictive assumption, both industries and both countries gain from international trade in differentiated products.

Now let us consider the effects of firm heterogeneity, or the assumption that all firms in an industry are not the same. To do this, first consider a firm that is contemplating entering an industry. Its first problem is that it is uncertain as to what its TFP will be, as well as the TFP of the other firms in the industry. There is an entry cost facing the firm composed of the cost of building a brand and the technology to manufacture it. The firm will enter the industry if its expected profits from entry are high enough to cover this entry cost. Whether or not the firm can successfully do this involves making an estimate of its productivity relative to the existing firms in the industry. However, this is just an expectation. What its actual TFP will be in the industry is uncertain. To solve this problem, the firm will form expectations of profits based on alternative levels of productivity. In the worst-case scenario, the firm expects that it could not survive and does not enter the industry. A second possibility is that the firm would be productive enough to service the domestic market. A final possibility is that the firm would be productive enough to both serve the domestic market and export. As suggested by the empirical evidence, one reasonably might assume that the firm would have to bear additional costs if it wished to export and produce for the domestic market. These costs might be in the form of

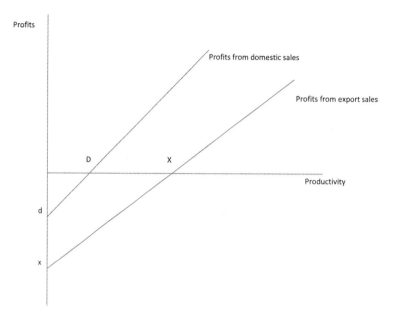

Figure 4.5   Firm Productivity and Profitability.

transportation and insurance costs and other costs associated with selling in a foreign market.

We can demonstrate the situation in Figure 4.5. The figure shows the relationship between the productivity of the firm (TFP) on the horizontal axis relative to the profits of the firm on the vertical axis. Logically, there is a positive relationship between the two, and firms that are more productive also are more profitable. However, a firm with no productivity still has to bear fixed costs of serving the domestic market. With no productivity, this cost is at point d on the vertical axis. The distance between point d and the horizontal axis is the fixed cost. The firm would break even in the domestic market at point D, and profits would continue to rise past that point. The profits from exporting are shown in the curve to the right. Fixed costs associated with exporting are higher than for domestic sales as shown at point x. The difference between d and x is the larger fixed cost of exporting. Losses fall as productivity increases with the breakeven point at X. Again profits would continue to rise past that point. Notice that point X is to the right of point D.

The model provides us with an explanation of industrial structure and of exporters that fits the characteristics of exporting firms described earlier. Any firm to the left of D will either not enter the industry in the first place or exit if is an existing firm. Firms that are to the right of D but to the left of X will service only the domestic market because they cannot make a profit from exporting. Firms to the right of X will both service the domestic market and export. Firms leave the industry, produce for the domestic market, or both serve the domestic market and export depending on their level of productivity. The model explains why exporting firms tend to be larger, as producing for more markets requires that the firm be larger. It also explains why only a minority of firms tend to export. Only the most productive firms can make a profit from exporting after covering the higher costs.

Import Penetration and Firm Behavior

In the model presented earlier, firms that are less productive are less profitable than more productive firms. This would be true even in autarky. In our discussion we focused on differences in profits that could occur if the firm only produced for the domestic market versus both producing for the domestic market and exporting. However, if the industry is characterized by monopolistic competition and intra-industry trade, then there might as well be imports. Presumably this would put even more pressure on the less productive firms. To think about this, let's borrow a common paradigm from the industrial organization literature in economics. This is the structure, conduct, and performance approach to studying the way firms operate in an industry. In this approach, the structure of the industry greatly influences how firms conduct their business. In turn this affects the overall performance of the industry. For example, if the industry is perfectly competitive, then firms must be very efficient just to survive. This leads to good performance of the industry as resources are used very efficiently. On the other end of the spectrum one can imagine that a monopolist doesn't have to be very efficient and perhaps doesn't use resources as carefully. Import competition can alter the structure of an industry. Imports are equivalent to adding more domestic firms, which changes the structure of the industry in a way that makes it more competitive. The result would be that firms in the industry would become more efficient or exit the industry. The final result would be an improvement in the performance of the industry. Since the early 1970s, import penetration in U.S. manufacturing has increased from an average of 6.5 percent to over 35 percent. While all of this is logically true, usually changes in firm behavior are hard to quantify.

Although the research in this area is new, the existing papers are showing predictable responses to imports. Bernard, et al. (2006) found that industrial plant survival and growth in the United States were negatively correlated with imports. Further, they found that firms tended to reallocate production toward more capital-intensive products. Hutzschenreuter and Grone (2009) have found that import penetration may induce firms to limit the scope of their activities and reduce the area that they serve. Liu (2010) shows that import penetration tends to reduce the number of products that firms produce as they reallocate resources within the firm to their most productive use. Finally, Zhou, Booth, and Chang (2013) show that import penetration reduces the propensity of firms to either pay a dividend or, if so, reduce the amount paid. The picture that is emerging from this new literature is that import penetration changes firm behavior in a way that is consistent with economic theory.

Global Value Chains

If one were to look at the label on a manufactured product, two phrases one might see convey something important. The first is "made in" and the second is "assembled in." Throughout our previous discussion of international trade, there was an implicit assumption. That assumption was that all of the products were "made in." In more technical terms, what we were assuming was that all of the value added of the product was occurring in the exporting country. For many manufactured products in international trade, this is not what is happening. What is actually occurring is parts of the product from around the world are being assembled into intermediate or final products and then shipped somewhere else for further assembly or consumption. As a result, when you purchase a product, it may embody components, or value added, from a large number of countries. A famous example is the iPod. Dedrick, Kraemer, and Linden (2010) show that although the iPod is assembled in China, only 2 percent of the value added occurs there. The product is assembled from hundreds of components that are sourced from around the world. This process could occur in two different ways or a combination of the two. First, the process could be likened to a "snake." In this case a crude or intermediate product is shipped from Country A to Country B for further processing. An intermediate good could then be shipped to Country C for further processing or final consumption. This is what many of us think of when considering a global value chain. On the other hand the process can be like a "spider." Here intermediate goods are coming from a number of locations for final assembly. The iPod example demonstrates this process.

The production of manufactured goods in the world is increasingly fragmenting, with the components and final assembly of goods being sliced into smaller parts of the production process. The principles of comparative advantage still apply. The production process is becoming more efficient precisely because of comparative advantage. New communication technology and lower transportation costs now allow countries to export the type of value added in which they have the highest degree of comparative advantage. On the other hand, it allows countries to more easily avoid engaging in activities that they have a comparative disadvantage in. This fragmentation of production may lead to even larger gains from trade than were described earlier in the book. If the United States imports German cars and the producers can obtain cheaper components from another country, then German comparative advantage in cars is even larger and American consumers benefit more.

An empirical example of the effects of the global value chain in an important industry in a large country is shown in Table 4.5. Each of the rows shows the contribution of various types of labor and capital to the final value added in the German car industry. The data are further decomposed to show the contribution to total value added that occurs in Germany and the rest of the world. The data paint an interesting picture. First, notice that only two-thirds of the value added is occurring in Germany. The remaining third of the value added is occurring outside of the country. The cars are clearly "German" but perhaps a bit less so than one might imagine. Over a third of the value added is accounted for by capital. As one would expect, this is a capital-intensive industry. Another third of value added is medium-skilled labor. Highly skilled labor obviously is important, as it accounts for

Table 4.5 The Global Value Chain of German Cars (Percent of Final Output Value)

	1995	2008
German value added	79	66
High-skilled labor	16	17
Medium-skilled labor	34	25
Low-skilled labor	7	4
Capital	21	20
Foreign value added	21	34
High-skilled labor	3	6
Medium-skilled labor	6	9
Low-skilled labor	4	4
Capital	8	15

Source: Timmer et al. (2014).

nearly a quarter of value added. The table also shows the analogous amount of value added for 1995. From the top of the table, the value added in Germany dropped from nearly 80 percent to 66 percent. Foreign value added rose from a bit over 30 percent to over a third. Most of this change was accounted for by the lower contribution of capital and medium-skilled labor in Germany that was transferred to other countries. Germany hardly is alone, as this same process of expanding global value chains is occurring around the world. This process of transferring value added across borders is considered in more detail in the next section.

In this section, we've considered some of the newest research in international economics on the economics of the firm and the role of global value chains in the world economy. These results are remaking the way we think about international trade. The basic theory of international trade presented in the preceding chapter is just as valid, as has always been the case. However, international trade probably always has been somewhat more complex than the basic theory indicates. Countries not only engage in two-way trade of very different products, but also exchange very similar products. In the past, this intra-industry trade was probably quite small. However, in the past several decades, intra-industry trade in the world economy is growing rapidly. A reasonable estimate is that it is now 50 percent of all international trade. This doesn't make the theory of comparative advantage wrong—just somewhat incomplete. Distance and transportation costs have always been an impediment to trade. For most of human history, international trade was confined to products with a high value-to-weight ratio. With relatively high transportation costs, trade is only profitable for these goods. In the 19th century, major improvements in transportation such as railroads and the steamship radically reduced transportation costs for goods with a much lower value-to-weight ratio. In turn, this led to a global boom in international trade. More recently, the advent of containerized cargo and air freight have lowered costs even further. These developments led to the concept of global value chains where the production of a product has been vertically disintegrated. Trade in parts and components is an increasingly important part of international trade. In another vein, the traditional trade theory was focused on how countries traded with one another at the industry level. While not wrong, the traditional theory left a major gap in our understanding of international trade. Partially due to a lack of data, our knowledge of how firms within an industry participate in trade was negligible. The emergence of firm level data is painting a fascinating new picture of international trade. We now know that firms that export are both rare and much more efficient than firms that do not export. Industries in countries that export are not composed of a large number of homogeneous firms. Instead, they are composed of a heterogeneous set of firms of varying degrees of efficiency. Only the most efficient export, and many firms serve only the domestic market. Comparative advantage is something that is not only industry specific but also applies to the spectrum of firms within an industry.

A reasonable question at this point is: How does this new knowledge of international trade affect international trade policy? At this point there is no clear answer to that question. However, some links between the new theory and empirical research may affect international trade policy, either now or in the near future. First, the adjustment of countries to international trade should be easier in the case of intra-industry trade. Firms may be able to survive foreign competition more easily if imports are not necessarily less expensive, just different. On the other hand, firms that produce higher-quality products at reasonable prices may be able to export and expand into foreign markets. In both cases, the adjustments to trade may be more muted in the case of intra-industry trade. Second, the ongoing reduction in international transportation costs will increase all kinds of trade over time. What this means is that the costs of trade are falling even in the absence of explicit decreases in trade barriers. This is one area where international trade policy is being explicitly affected. A part of the costs of trade are the costs of moving goods across borders. These costs can be affected by government policy. World Trade Organization (WTO) negotiations are currently occurring to try to reduce the complexity of moving goods across borders. Finally, the research on the firm in international trade is so new that the effect on trade policy is hard to predict. It is now clear that lower trade barriers would benefit a minority of firms in an industry. On the other hand, these firms tend to be larger, so the positive effects may likewise be large. What is missing from the research at this point is more information on the firm in comparative-disadvantage industries. As we will see in the following chapters, international trade policy is disproportionately affected by what occurs in these industries. The potential of new knowledge about firms in these industries may have a large effect on the conduct of international trade policy.

Case Study: The Steamship and the Box

When we purchase a good that has been imported from another country, there is no need to think about how the good arrived in the store. Part of the progress of civilization is the reduction in the number of things one must think about. Just for a moment, let's consider how those goods arrived in the store. For most of the history of international trade, the transportation of goods between countries was a very laborious process. In the country of origin, groups of workers manually loaded freight from the dock into a boat. This was extremely hard labor that also could be dangerous. Until the 19th century, the ships were wooden sailing vessels that were labor intensive to operate and could only carry a limited amount of cargo. By modern standards, these ships were slow and expensive to operate. The result was that international trade in goods was limited to cargoes with a high value-to-weight ratio. Only relatively light, expensive goods could be profitably traded. At the other end of the voyage, the labor-intensive process of unloading the cargo was followed by reloading the cargo onto some other mode of transportation. The result was very high international transportation costs that reduced trade as indicated in the model earlier.

Two innovations have transformed international transportation costs over the last 200 years and have resulted in huge increases in world trade. Steamships were first used in the early 19th century, but were still expensive to operate. By the middle of the century the introduction of steel hulls and more efficient engines dramatically reduced the cost of operation. In addition, the ships became far larger and were now capable of carrying large quantities of bulk cargo such as grain. The result was an explosion of transatlantic trade both in traditional goods and new goods that were now profitable to trade due to lower transportation costs. O'Rourke and Williamson (1999) found that in the late 19th and early 20th centuries, Atlantic freight rates were dropping by 1.5 percent *per year*. The expansion of railroads in both Europe and North America was further reducing transportation costs by lowering the cost of moving goods from ports to final destinations inland.

As important as the steamship was to world trade, it did not reduce the costs of transferring freight from land transportation to boat and back again. The reduction in this part of transportation costs did not begin until the 1950s. Levinson (2006) has documented the effects of containerized cargo on trade. The ubiquitous metal boxes one sees on trains and trucks were first used only just over 50 years ago. The containers can be loaded at the factory and sealed at that point to reduce the possibility of theft. The container is loaded onto a truck or train and then transported to a port. The containers are then loaded onto the boat using a crane in a highly automated process. Thousands of these containers can be loaded onto a single ship capable of traveling 20 miles per hour with a crew of 20. At the port of destination the process is put in reverse, and the boat is unloaded by crane and the containers moving directly to the train or truck. The net result of these transportation cost improvements is that a cargo container can be shipped almost anywhere in the world using water transportation for between $1,000 and $2,000 dollars.

Bibliography

Balassa, Bela. 1966. "Tariff Reductions and Trade in Manufactures Among the Industrial Countries," *American Economic Review* 56(3): 466–73.

Bernard, Andrew B., J. Bradford Jensen, Stephen J. Redding, and Peter K. Schott. 2007. "Firms in International Trade," *Journal of Economic Perspectives* 21(3): 105–30.

Bernard, Andrew B., J. Bradford Jensen, and Peter K. Schott. 2006. "Survival of the Best Fit: Exposure to Low-Wage Countries and the (uneven) Growth of US Manufacturing Plants," *Journal of International Economics* 68(1): 219–37.

Blonigen, Bruce A. and Anson Soderbery. 2010. "Measuring the Benefits of Foreign Product Variety with an Accurate Variety Set," *Journal of International Economics* 82(2): 168–80.

Broda, Christian and David E. Weinstein. 2004. "Variety Growth and World Welfare," *American Economic Review* 94(2): 139–44.

Broda, Christian and David E. Weinstein. 2006. "Globalization and the Gains from Variety," *Quarterly Journal of Economics* 121(2): 541–88.

Dedrick, Jason, Kenneth L. Kraemer, and Greg Linden. 2010. "Who Profits From Innovation in Global Value Chains? A Study of the iPod and Network PCs," *Industrial and Corporate Change* 19(1): 81–116.

Fajgelbaum, Pablo D., Gene M. Grossman, and Elhanan Helpman. 2011. "Income Distribution, Product Quality, and International Trade," *Journal of Political Economy* 119(4): 721–65.

Gray, H. Peter. 1985. *Free Trade or Protection: A Pragmatic Analysis*. London: Palgrave.

Hutzschenreuter, Thomas and Florian Grone. 2009. "Product and Geographic Scope Changes of Multinational Enterprises in Response to International Competition," *Journal of International Business Studies* 40(7): 1149–70.

Levinson, Marc. 2006. *The Box: How the Shipping Container Made the World Smaller and the World Economy Bigger*. Princeton, NJ: Princeton University Press.

Linder, Staffan B. 1961. *An Essay on Trade and Transformation*. New York: Wiley.

Liu, Runjuan. 2010. "Import Competition and Firm Refocusing," *Canadian Journal of Economics* 43(2): 440–66.

Mayer, Thierry and Gaianmarco Ottaviano. 2008. "The Happy Few: The Internationalization of European Firms," *Intereconomics* 43(3): 135–48.

Melitz, Marc J. 2003. "The Impact of Trade on Intra-Industry Reallocations and Aggregate Industry Productivity," *Econometrica* 71(6): 1695–1725.

O'Rourke, Kevin H. and Jeffrey G. Williamson. 1999. *Globalization and History: The Evolution of a Nineteenth Century Atlantic Economy*. Cambridge, MA: MIT Press.

Porter, Michael. 1990. *The Competitive Advantage of Nations*. New York: Free Press.

Sawyer, W. Charles and Richard L. Sprinkle. 2012. "The Role of Intra-industry Trade in the World Economy," *TCU Department of Economics Working Paper No. 12-03*.

Thorpe, Michael W. and Nuno C. Leitao. 2013. "Determinants of United States' Vertical and Horizontal Intra-Industry Trade," *Global Economy Journal* 13(2): 233–50.

Timmer, Marcel P., Abdul Azeez Erumban, Bart Los, Robert Stehrer, and Gaaitzen J. de Vries. 2014. "Slicing Up Global Value Chains," *Journal of Economic Perspectives* 28(2): 98–118.

Vernon, Raymond. 1966. "International Investment and International Trade in the Product Cycle," *Quarterly Journal of Economics* 50(2): 190–207.

World Trade Organization. 2008. *World Trade Report 2008: Transactional Corporations and the Infrastructure Challenge*. Geneva: World Trade Organization.

Zhou, Jun, Laurence Booth, and Bin Chang. 2013. "Import Competition and Disappearing Dividends," *Journal of International Business Studies* 44(2): 138–54.

CHAPTER FIVE

Barriers to Trade

A protective tariff is immoral and dishonest, because its sole purpose is to increase prices artificially, thereby enabling one citizen to levy unjust tribute from another.
—Cordell Hull

Introduction

So far we have assumed that international trade is similar to trade among regions of a country in that it is not impeded by government action. Also we have shown that free trade leads to the most efficient allocation of world resources and maximizes world output. Unfortunately, governments choose to restrict or influence the international flow of goods and services through the use of trade barriers. The purpose of this chapter is to study of the effects of trade barriers. Our analysis begins by examining the most basic barrier to trade—the tariff. To describe the effects of a tariff, we employ a basic supply-and-demand model of international trade for a single product. This model allows us to focus on the effects that tariffs have with respect to imports, domestic consumption, and domestic production. This allows us to cover some of the common arguments in favor of tariffs and show that there usually is a better public policy option available than imposing tariffs. A similar model can be used to understand the effects of quotas. The final part of the chapter considers the effects of some other government policies that have an impact on international trade.

Tariffs

A tariff is simply a tax on an imported good. Tariffs affect the domestic production and consumption of a good. They also affect the foreign production and consumption of a good. In both countries, the tariff changes the industrial structure. In many respects, the effects of a tariff are no different from those of any other tax imposed by a government. Like many other taxes, tariffs come in different types. In the following section, the various types of tariffs and the methods of valuation used to determine the tariff are briefly explained.

Types of Tariffs

The simplest form of a tariff is a specific tariff. A specific tariff is expressed as a per-unit tax on imported goods, such as 5 cents per liter or $5 per ton. A specific tariff is easy for a government to administer—it is a certain amount of money per unit of whatever is imported. However, if there are large differences in the imported price, the effects of a specific tariff are not uniform across lower- and higher-priced items. For example, a specific tariff of $1,000 imposed on automobiles would yield a high percentage tariff relative to the import price for inexpensive Hyundais and a low percentage tariff relative to the import price of Porsches. In this case, a specific tariff is regressive. Hyundais and Porsches are likely to be purchased by lower-income and higher-income consumers, respectively. In addition, the degree of protection given domestic producers varies with the price of the imported good. In this case, a specific tariff provides domestic producers of low-priced cars more protection than producers of high-priced cars. The result of a specific tariff would be to encourage domestic producers to produce lower-priced goods.

To avoid these problems, governments impose ad valorem tariffs. An ad valorem tariff is expressed as a percentage of the value of the imported good. This constant-percentage tariff avoids the regressive nature of a specific tariff. However, with an ad valorem tariff the valuation of the imported good becomes critical in determining the amount of the tariff. The higher the price of the imported good, the higher the tariff. In this case, importers facing an ad valorem tariff have an incentive to *underinvoice* the price of the imported good. Underinvoicing means reporting a lower value on the imported good than the true market price in order to reduce the amount of the tariff. Underinvoicing also may occur when a multinational corporation ships intermediate products from one country to another. Pricing in intrafirm trade can influence in which country the profits of the multinational corporation are reported and taxed. This means that customs officials must be extremely knowledgeable about the market prices for all imported goods. As a result, ad valorem tariffs are more difficult for a country to administer than are specific tariffs. A tariff that is composed of both a specific tariff and an ad valorem tariff is a compound tariff. An example would be $4 per imported ton plus 3 percent of the value of the imported good.

Such compound tariffs are common on agricultural products, whose prices tend to fluctuate.

Methods of Valuing Imports

One of the issues that a country faces in collecting tariffs is that its customs valuation can be based on one of three different methods of valuing imports. One such method is the free alongside (FAS) price. This valuation method defines the price of the imported good as the foreign country's market price before the good is loaded into the ship, train, truck, or airplane for shipment to the importing country. Another method of valuing imports defines the imported price of the good as the free on board (FOB) price. The FOB price defines the price of the imported good as the foreign country's market price plus the cost of loading the good into the means of conveyance. The third method of valuing imports is the cost, insurance, and freight (CIF) price. This method defines the price of the imported good as the foreign country's market price plus the cost of loading the good into the means of conveyance, plus all inter-country transportation costs up to the importing country's port of entry. Most countries use the CIF price for calculating ad valorem tariffs. However, the United States currently uses the FOB price for calculating ad valorem tariffs.

The Economic Effects of Tariffs

Now, we can use the concepts of consumer and producer surplus to analyze the impact of a tariff. In Figure 5.1, the domestic demand and supply of cloth is illustrated. Before international trade, equilibrium in the domestic cloth market occurs at point E. The equilibrium price and quantity of cloth associated with this point are P and Q, respectively. Now, assume that the country has a comparative disadvantage in the production of cloth and decides to engage in international trade. The country will be able to import at the world price (P_w), which is below its domestic price, P. Point F is the new free-trade equilibrium. This new equilibrium is clearly beneficial for cloth consumers. It is as though a market-wide sale of cloth were occurring as the price of cloth declines from P to P_w. In addition, the quantity of cloth that consumers are willing and able to buy increases from Q to Q_2. However, with free trade, the amount supplied by the domestic cloth industry contracts from Q to Q_1 as the price of cloth declines and imports increase. Let's assume that the domestic government imposes a tariff on cloth of the amount T to restrict imports. The result of this is the price of cloth in

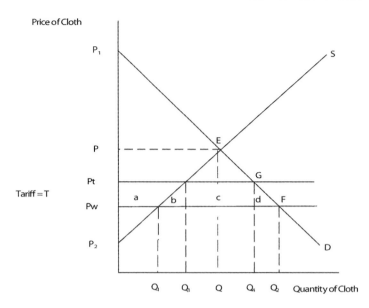

Figure 5.1 Domestic Effects of a Tariff.

the importing country rises from P_w to P_t. The imposition of the tariff results in a new equilibrium at point G.

The higher price of imported cloth has two effects. First, the quantity imported falls from the horizontal difference Q_1 to Q_2 to the smaller amount Q_3 to Q_4. The decline in imports is a result of lower domestic consumption of cloth—Q_2 to Q_4—and greater domestic production—Q_1 to Q_3. Second, consumers of cloth are clearly worse off. The price of cloth has increased and the quantity of cloth consumers buy has declined. As a result, consumer surplus in the country has declined. Specifically, the loss in consumer surplus is represented by the area $(a+b+c+d)$. As a result of the government imposing a tariff, consumers in the country lose. The remaining question is: Who gains? The gainers in the case of a tariff are the domestic government and domestic producers.

The rectangular area c represents the tariff revenue that the domestic government collects. The quantity imported after the tariff is imposed is the horizontal difference between Q_3 and Q_4. The tariff (T) is the difference between the world price, P_w, and the price paid by domestic consumers, P_t. Multiplying the quantity imported by the amount of the tariff gives us the total tariff revenue collected by the government, area c. As a result, the government gains this area and the consumers lose it. If one assumes that the utility derived from government spending is the same as that derived from private consumption, there is no net loss to society as a whole from the consumer losing area c and the government gaining it.

The area a represents a transfer of consumer surplus to producer surplus. This transfer of welfare from consumers to domestic producers represents the domestic producers' gains from a tariff. From the standpoint of the domestic cloth producer, a tariff is not as good as autarky, but it is preferable to free trade. The small triangle (b) represents the cost of resources transferred from their best use to the production of more cloth—Q_1 to Q_3. This represents a loss to society, because in a free market these resources would have been used to produce a product in which the importing country has a comparative advantage. Transferring resources to the tariff-ridden industry necessarily entails a loss of resources to some other, more productive industry. Finally, the area d represents a consumption effect caused by a tariff as consumers purchase less cloth—Q_3 to Q_4.

The areas a and c are redistributed from consumers to producers and government, respectively. The net loss to society and the general loss are composed of the area (b + d). This loss to society is referred to as the dead-weight loss of a tariff. The dead-weight loss of a tariff represents a real loss to the country since it is not transferred to another sector of the economy and represents a waste of resources in economic terms.

Henry George on Free Trade

The U.S. economist Henry George (1839–1897) is best known for his proposed single tax on land. However, he was also an eloquent critic of protectionism in an age when it was rampant. The following are some of his better quotes concerning the folly of protectionism.

"It might be to the interests of [lighting] companies to restrict the number and size of windows, but hardly to the interests of a community. Broken limbs bring fees to surgeons, but would it profit a municipality to prohibit the removal of ice from sidewalks in order to encourage surgery? Economically, what difference is there between restricting the importation of iron to benefit iron-producers and restricting sanitary improvements to benefit undertakers?"

"If to prevent trade were to stimulate industry and promote prosperity, then the localities where he was most isolated would show the first advances of man. The natural protection to home industry afforded by rugged mountain-chains, by burning deserts, or by seas too wide and tempestuous for the frail bark of the early mariner would have given us the first glimmerings of civilization and shown its most rapid growth. But, in fact, it is where trade could best be carried on that we find wealth first accumulating and civilization beginning. It is on accessible harbors, by navigable rivers and much traveled highways that we find cities arising and the arts and sciences developing."

"To have all the ships that left each country sunk before they could reach any other country would, upon protectionist principles, be the quickest means of enriching the whole world, since all countries could then enjoy the maximum of exports with the minimum of imports."

"What protection teaches us, is to do to ourselves in time of peace what enemies seek to do to us in time of war."

"However protection may affect special forms of industry it must necessarily diminish the total return to industry-first by the waste inseparable from encouragement by tariff, and second by the loss due to transfer of capital and labor from occupations which they would choose for themselves to less profitable occupations which they must be bribed to engage in. If we do not see this without reflection, it is because our attention is engaged with but a part of the effects of protection. We see the large smelting-works and the massive mill without realizing that the same taxes which we are told have built them up have made more costly every nail driven and every needle full of thread used throughout the whole country."

Arguments for Tariffs

In Chapter 3, we showed that free trade increases a country's welfare as resources are better utilized by countries that specialize and engage in trade. Our analysis showed that the total output of each individual country would rise. Further, this implies that the economic output of the world would rise. In Chapter 3, we showed the causes of comparative advantage. Comparative advantage occurs because countries are endowed with relatively different amounts of capital, labor, human capital, and/or technology. The result in terms of the economic output of the countries engaging in trade was the same. The total output of the two countries both increased as a result of trade. Under these circumstances, one may well wonder why there is any public policy toward trade in the world economy that represents a departure from free trade. With few exceptions, virtually all countries choose to impose restrictions on trade. In this section, we will consider some of the more widely used arguments for the protection of domestic industry. Very few of these arguments have much, if any, economic merit. The purpose here is to illustrate the fallacies embodied in the arguments for imposing tariffs that one frequently hears. In the final part of this section, we will consider a policy that is normally preferable to tariffs if there is some reason society wishes to produce more output in a particular industry than would be dictated in the free market.

Infant Government

For a developing country, tariffs can be an attractive form of taxation for several reasons. First, imports legally must pass through customs. In effect, this is a choke point where the government can easily collect revenue. The goods cannot pass into the country until the tariff is paid. The administrative costs of such a tax are also small relative to income or sales taxes. Second, gross domestic product (GDP) per capita frequently is low. Many of the country's citizens would have difficulty paying even a modest income tax. However, not all of the country's citizens are poor. The challenge is to design a tax that is based on the ability to pay. A country's tariff structure can be designed to accomplish this. Tariffs may be levied on intermediate goods or on capital equipment that is only going to be purchased by producers of final goods. These firms can recoup at least part of the tariff in the form of higher prices. However, most firms will not be able to pass along the entire amount of the tariff to consumers. In this case, the tariff acts something like a corporate income tax. Also, tariffs can be used as a highly progressive income tax. A high tariff on "luxury" consumer goods such as automobiles or air conditioners can amount to a very progressive income tax. The point is that by putting different tariffs on different imports, the government can collect revenue in a way that is something like a progressive tax on corporate or individual income. Finally, such a system has the potential to alter the distribution of income within the country.

National Defense

A common argument for tariffs is the national defense argument. A country has a legitimate need to take steps to ensure that its military forces can operate effectively if necessary. Soldiers do not fight in a vacuum. Frequently, enormous supplies of goods and services are needed at short notice in the case of potential or actual military conflict. The argument in this case is that certain industries need to be protected from foreign competition to ensure an adequate output of the industry in the case of a conflict. There are two problems with this argument. The first problem is defining which industries are essential for national defense. Because this may not be entirely clear in all cases, industries with only a tenuous connection to national defense may obtain protection. The national defense argument ultimately entails a large amount of protection in the form of tariffs or other nontariff barriers to trade.

The second problem is that a tariff is a costly means of accomplishing this end. Almost invariably, the optimal policy in this case and others is a domestic production subsidy. To illustrate the effects of a subsidy, refer back to Figure 5.1. If a country was to impose a tariff on this product, there would be a loss of consumer surplus equivalent to the area $(a+b+c+d)$. As before, areas a and c are transferred to the producers and the government, respectively. The dead-weight loss from the tariff is equal to area $(b+d)$. In the case of the tariff, domestic output increases from Q_1 to Q_3. However, the same increase in domestic production can be accomplished at a lower cost to the country by providing a production subsidy. Let us assume that the government simply furnishes the industry with a production subsidy that is equal to the price they would obtain with a tariff in place. In this case, the effect of the subsidy is to shift the domestic supply downward by the amount of the subsidy. This would shift the domestic supply curve by enough to produce the larger output associated with a tariff, Q_1 to Q_3. However, in this case the consumer is still paying the world price, P_w, for the good. Consumers can purchase the same amount of the good at the same price. The dead-weight loss is now only area b and not area $(b+d)$. Our example of protection in this case was firms located in the defense industry, but the principle can be generalized. The least expensive way to encourage domestic output of a good is through a production subsidy, not a tariff.

Infant Industries

The infant industry argument has been a staple of the economic development literature for a long time. Most developing countries go through a stage where resources are moving out of a declining agricultural sector into a growing manufacturing sector. In the initial stages of the development of a manufacturing sector, many of the industries within the sector look weak compared to world competition. The premise is that "new" industries in developing countries initially may need protection to allow them to grow in the face of more established foreign competition. The temporary protection also may allow the industry to become large enough to establish sufficient economies of scale to effectively compete in world markets. Once the industry has become internationally competitive, the protectionism is withdrawn to allow the industry to become even more efficient.

Superficially, this argument is plausible, but in practice it has been fraught with problems. The first problem is that an eligible infant industry is one that will eventually become internationally competitive. The problem for the government is picking the industries that will in fact become internationally competitive. It is an old joke among economists that any government bureaucrat who could really do this should quit being a bureaucrat and become an investor. This is just a way of pointing out that what seems easy really is not. Second, the infant industry may never grow up. Protectionism is very attractive for the producers and possibly for the workers. Industries that have been protected are frequently unwilling to give up this protection. If the government is not careful, the "temporary" protection may go on for so long that the industry never really becomes efficient. If this policy is pursued on a large scale in a country, the risk is that large parts of the manufacturing sector may become permanently uncompetitive in world markets. Once this has happened, the eventual adjustments necessary to restructure the country's manufacturing sector may be difficult. The optimal policy may be a more market-oriented approach to industrial development that emphasizes the development of a manufacturing sector based on factor abundance and comparative advantage.

Senile Industry Protection

For many developed countries, forms of protection have been designed for industries that are not new. These old, or "senile," industries may have once had a comparative advantage in world markets. However, as was indicated earlier, factor abundance can change over time. An industry in a developed country that once had a comparative advantage based on relatively inexpensive labor may be hard pressed by imports from developing countries where labor is now cheaper. The apparel industry in most developed countries is a common example. The problem in this case is how to transfer the resources from the comparative-disadvantage industry to other activities where the resources can produce more output. Some resources used in these industries cannot be easily transferred to other uses.

The argument for protecting these industries is to provide a method of moving resources out of them in such a way as to ensure that the overall output of the economy does not fall. If firms in the industry fail and the resources cannot be easily put to use elsewhere, the overall output of the economy could fall in the short run. The argument here is that temporary protection of older industries may actually increase output if the protection is gradually withdrawn as the resources reach the end of their useful life. The argument is plausible and has one advantage that the infant industry argument does not. Picking future comparative advantage industries is difficult. However, anyone can determine the comparative disadvantage industries: imports are rising, profits are falling, firms are failing, and employment in the industry is falling. Again, the difficulty lies in the execution. The protection must be temporary and should be withdrawn as the assets in the industry depreciate to the end of their economically useful lives. This process will not be easy. Unless the protectionism is withdrawn at an appropriate rate, a country could be permanently saddled with an old, inefficient industry. The protectionism in the agricultural sector of many developed countries is a case in point.

A more efficient strategy is to aid firms and workers in making the adjustment to another part of the economy. The owners of capital can be encouraged and/or subsidized to find new ways to use the capital that will earn a higher rate of return in the long run than leaving the capital in a comparative-disadvantage industry. Governments also can pursue policies to assist workers in finding new employment. This may involve subsidies for education, training, and the payment of relocation expenses. The costs of saving jobs in declining industries are very high. Compared to these costs, subsidies to firms and workers rather than protectionism may be a relative bargain for society.

Firm Heterogeneity and Trade Liberalization

In the previous chapter, we considered the effects on the industrial structure of a country that occurred as a result of moving from autarky to free trade. It was shown that trade would increase the size of the comparative-advantage industry and reduce the size of the comparative-disadvantage industry. These conclusions are not incorrect. Trade does lead to changes in industrial structure. However, those conclusions were made in the context of interindustry trade. Interindustry trade is driven by differences in factor prices that lead to countries exporting and importing very different products. Most research on firm heterogeneity is based on intraindustry trade where countries are trading similar goods. In this context trade is still leading to a reallocation of resources. This reallocation is just happening within a particular industry as opposed to between industries. A movement from autarky with intraindustry trade leads to a reallocation of resources from the least productive firms to the most productive firms. In both cases, resources in an economy are being reallocated from less productive uses to more productive uses. As we pointed out before, this reallocation of resources potentially increases the overall output of the economy and leads to faster economic growth.

The same sort of effects can occur if trade between countries already exists but there is a reduction in barriers to trade. It has been observed for a long time that the reduction of trade barriers tended to lead to a reallocation of resources within industries. Balassa (1967) made the following observation that was far ahead of his time:

> As regards the impact of tariff reductions on resource allocation, the predominance of intraindustry trade, as against interindustry, specialization in manufactured goods traded among the industrial countries is the relevant consideration. With national product differentiation in consumer goods, machinery, and intermediate goods at higher levels of fabrication, trade liberalization does not entail massive shift of resources from import-competing to export industries as presumed by the traditional textbook explanation, but leads instead to changes in the product composition of individual industries. However, tariff reductions will result in interindustry shifts of resources in the case of standardized products where international exchange is determined largely by intercountry differences in relative costs.

In terms of firm heterogeneity, lower trade barriers lead to a rise in the profits of firms that export relative to the firms that do not. In turn, this leads to firms that do not export exiting the market. Overall industry productivity rises because of this reallocation. Large reallocations of resources with industries have been observed following trade liberalization in Mexico, Chile, and Canada by Tybout and Westbrook (1995), Pavcnik (2002), and Trefler (2004). In the case of Canada, Trefler estimated that trade liberalization led to a 6.4 percent increase in manufacturing productivity.

Due to trade liberalization, the composition of the industry changes in a way consistent with the picture of an industry outlined in this section. The most efficient firms gain the most from trade, whereas lesser firms in the industry may shrink or fail. In this case the changes are in the composition of an industry. Within an industry, some firms are becoming larger and others smaller. Notice that this is different from the adjustments made with interindustry trade. In that case, entire industries were becoming larger or smaller, that is, the industrial structure of the country changed. This might lead one to conclude that the changes being wrought by intraindustry trade are not as important as the changes due to interindustry trade. However, recent research indicates that the welfare-enhancing effects of intraindustry trade perhaps are not as obvious as in the case of interindustry trade, but they are far from trivial.

Tariffs, Trade, and Jobs

The final and most common argument for tariffs is the creation of jobs in the economy. Like most arguments for tariffs, it seems plausible at first. Returning to Figure 5.1, a tariff increases the output of the domestic industry.

Presumably as output expands, the amount of employment in the industry likewise will expand. Rather simplistically, the tariff has produced more "jobs." As we will see, the tariff has not really produced any jobs, and if there are enough tariffs on imports, the total number of jobs may well be less than without tariffs.

The key to seeing this is considering employment in the industry as opposed to the overall level of employment in the economy. The tariff has created jobs in this particular industry, but there are fewer jobs in other industries. This is because consumers spend more on goods from the protected industry but less on other goods. The tariff has not increased the total number of jobs—it has just rearranged them. Protected industries have more jobs, and other industries have fewer jobs. The overall level of employment has not changed. The total number of jobs in the economy is determined by macroeconomic forces such as the rate of economic growth in the long run and the state of fiscal and monetary policy in the long run. Tariffs don't change the total number of jobs; they just put jobs in places that the market would not.

Unfortunately, in the long run tariffs may reduce the overall level of employment. As we saw in Chapter 2, there is a gain from moving resources such as labor from comparative-disadvantage industries to comparative-advantage industries. The reverse is true. Tariffs move jobs into comparative-disadvantage industries. This entails a loss in the overall output of the economy (GDP). Because the total level of employment is tied to the total output of the economy, tariffs may easily produce fewer jobs overall. Finally, an economy with a lot of tariffs will usually grow more slowly than a more open economy. The number of new jobs in the future is dependent on the rate of economic growth. The faster the growth rate, the more jobs will become available. This also works to reduce the number of jobs. The bottom line is that the number of jobs in both the short run and the long run is reduced by the presence of tariffs.

Petition of the French Candlemakers

French economist Fredric Bastiat's "The Petition of the French Candlemakers" (1873) is often used to illustrate what protection of a domestic industry from foreign competition implies. In this amusing anecdote, he illustrates the flaws arguing for protectionism.

"We are subjected to the intolerable competition of a foreign rival whose superior facilities for producing light enable him to flood the French market at so low a price as to take away all our customers the moment he appears, suddenly reducing an important branch of French industry to stagnation. This rival is the sun.

We request a law to shut up all windows, dormers, skylights, openings, holes, chinks, and fissures through which sunlight penetrates. Our industry provides such valuable manufactures that our country cannot, without ingratitude, leave us now to struggle unprotected through so unequal a contest . . . . In short, granting our petition will greatly develop every branch of agriculture. Navigation will equally profit. Thousands of vessels will soon be employed in whaling, and thence will arise a navy capable of upholding the honor of France . . . .

Do you object that the consumer must pay the price of protecting us? You have yourselves already answered the objection. When told that the consumer is interested in free importation of iron, coal, corn, wheat, cloth, etc., you have answered that the producer is interested in their exclusion. You have always acted to encourage labor, to increase the demand for labor.

Will you say that sunlight is a free gift, and that to repulse free gifts is to repulse riches under pretense of encouraging the means of obtaining them? Take care you deal a death blow to your own policy. Remember: hitherto you have always repulsed foreign produce because it was an approach to a free gift; and the closer this approach, the more you have repulsed the good . . . .

When we buy a Portuguese orange at half the price of a French orange, we in effect get it half as a gift. If you protect national labor against the competition of a half-gift, what principle justifies allowing the importation of something just because it is entirely a gift? . . . The difference in price between an imported article and the corresponding French article is a free gift to us. The bigger the difference, the bigger the gift . . . . The question is whether you wish for France the benefit of free consumption or the supposed advantages of laborious production. Choose, but be consistent."

Nontariff Distortions to Trade

In itself the abolition of protection is like the driving off of a robber. But it will not help a man to drive off one robber, if another, still stronger and more rapacious, be left to plunder him.

—Henry George

The lowering of tariffs has, in effect, been like draining a swamp. The lower water level has revealed all the snags and stumps of nontariff barriers that still have to be cleared away.

—Robert Baldwin

We have described how tariffs protect domestic industries from foreign competition. However, from the standpoint of governments and domestic producers, tariffs have a couple of disadvantages. First, they do not necessarily completely protect a domestic industry over time. Unless the tariff is prohibitively high, domestic producers still have to worry about competition from imports. In the first part of this section, you will learn about quotas that provide domestic firms with a more certain form of protection. Second, tariffs imposed by a government are a visible form of protectionism. For example, a 10 percent tariff on an imported good provides a domestic producer a 10 percent price advantage over foreign producers. Governments and both foreign and domestic producers know the size of this price advantage. If possible, governments would prefer to protect a domestic industry using a means that is not quite so visible. In the second part of this section, we discuss ways in which governments attempt to protect domestic industries without being so obvious about it. As you will learn, these forms of protectionism are becoming common in the world economy. Up until this point, we have made the assumption that the costs involved in moving goods from one country to another are zero. The existence of transportation costs constitutes an implicit form of protection for domestic producers, and in the last section of the chapter we consider transportation costs and how they affect international trade.

Quotas

One of the more restrictive forms of protectionism is the quota. Quotas restrict imports of a good to a certain quantitative level. In practice, this means that a country imposing a quota imports only a certain number of units of the good on an annual basis. Quotas are considered such an extreme form of protectionism that they are banned under international trade rules. Nevertheless, quotas still exist in various forms for five reasons.

First, not all countries are members of the World Trade Organization (WTO). These countries are still free to impose quotas. Quotas provide protection for domestic industries, but they also can accomplish another objective. For example, some countries may experience difficulties obtaining adequate amounts of foreign exchange to finance or buy all of their imports. In these circumstances, a country may choose to restrict imports through the use of a quota as a means of conserving foreign exchange. In the past, many developing countries were reluctant to join the General Agreement on Tariffs and Trade (GATT)/WTO because the elimination of quotas was a condition of membership.

Second, new members of the WTO are allowed to maintain their previously existing quotas for a specified period. For example, when a country joins the WTO, its trade regulations do not have to be in immediate compliance with WTO rules. Usually, an agreement is negotiated between the WTO and the country concerning a transition period. This transition period is designed to allow the country time to implement new trade regulations that are in compliance with WTO standards. To make this transition easier for countries joining the WTO, a lengthy transition period is normally granted. For example, when Mexico joined GATT in 1986, the transition period was 15 years. Such a situation is not untypical. From 1990 until the creation of the WTO in 1995, 31 countries joined the international trade organization, and since the WTO's creation an additional 37 countries have joined. As such, all of the newly joined members of the WTO are in the process of eliminating their quotas.

Third, some countries implement quotas on some goods in defiance of WTO rules. The U.S. quota on sugar is an example.

U.S. Sugar Quotas

Since 1816, the United States has provided protection for domestic sugar producers. As such, international trade in sugar is not a new issue for the United States and its trading partners. However, the issue has become more contentious. First, the U.S. government virtually guarantees domestic sugar producers a price that is generally higher than the world market price. Second, the subsidy to domestic sugar producers is provided through loan guarantees. As a result, the U.S. government lends the sugar farmers money and agrees to take the sugar as repayment of the loans. Thus, the government has a financial stake in maintaining the domestic price. Otherwise, the government would take a loss on this sugar transaction if prices are lower than the amount to pay off the loans. To maintain the high prices, the government has imposed a quota on imports of sugar since the early 1980s. This quota is changed annually to reflect market conditions. The following list is a partial enumeration of the effects of this policy.

1. In total, U.S. consumers lose $1.646 billion annually.
2. The average sugar producer gets $170,000 annually. The average American family loses $25 per year.
3. Because this is a quota and not a tariff, nearly 25 percent of the loss accrues to foreigners.

4. There are currently about 12,000 people employed in the sugar industry, and the implicit subsidy per job is $90,000.
5. Estimates of the jobs lost in the industry under free trade are from 2,000
   to 3,000 jobs. The cost of each job saved is approximately $500,000.
6. This does not count the loss of jobs in "upstream" industries. The industries that use sugar are somewhat smaller than they would be if their
   input (sugar) were cheaper. This would make it more difficult for U.S.
   firms attempting to compete in world markets with firms that have
   access to much cheaper sugar.
7. The program imposes losses on poor countries trying to export a product where they have a comparative advantage. The United States tries to
   aid nations in the Caribbean Basin through a program that provides for
   duty-free entry of some products from these countries. However, the
   restrictions on sugar for these countries remain in place.
8. The program has created the crime of the illegal importation of sugar.
   Sentences can go up to two years in prison and a $250,000 fine.
9. Other countries have complained to the WTO that the system is illegal.
   The U.S. system was found to be illegal under international trade rules,
   but the United States has virtually ignored these findings. This severely
   undermines U.S. credibility when it complains about other countries'
   violations of WTO rules.

If you have ever wondered why so many food products contain high-fructose
corn syrup instead of sugar, now you know. At this trade-restricted price for
sugar, it is profitable for food companies to extract sugar from corn rather
than to use sugar from sugar cane.

Fourth, international trade in textiles and apparel was profoundly distorted by the Multifibre Arrangement (MFA). As a result of trade negotiations in the Uruguay Round, the MFA was phased out by 2005. For each
developed country, the MFA managed trade in these two industries by
enforcing a quota *by product and by country* for imports of textiles and
apparel. The size of each quota was a major issue for both producers and
consumers in each industry and in each country. The previous quota protection has been replaced by tariffs. Because the system was in operation
in various forms for decades, the adverse effects of the MFA on world consumption and production of these products will linger for a long time.

Fifth, until recently world trade in agricultural products was not covered by WTO standards. For agricultural products, the use of quotas to protect domestic producers has been a prominent feature of world trade in

this sector. Quotas are extensively used by the developed countries to protect farmers from low-cost imports. The conversion of these quotas into tariffs is a major issue in the current round of WTO negotiations.

As a historical footnote, until 1999 a number of countries introduced a form of protection known as a voluntary export restraint (VER). A voluntary export restraint is an agreement in which the exporting country agrees to limit its exports to another country to a certain number of units. The primary difference between a quota and a VER is the name. For example, an importing country, such as the United States, that wanted to limit its imports of a particular product negotiates with the exporting country, such as Japan, for it to "voluntarily" limit its exports to the United States. In this case, the exporting country, not the importing one, administers the restraint—a quota. In this form, the quota (VER) on imported goods technically was legal under WTO regulations. Although such an agreement may not violate the letter of international trade law, it clearly violates its spirit. Although this form of protection has been phased out, one often hears the term VER when discussing nontariff barriers to trade. Like the MFA, the effects of past VERs can still be observed in some markets.

The Economic Effects of a Quota

In the first part of the chapter, we analyzed the effects of a tariff. In that case it was useful to separate the effects it had on consumers from its impact on producers. In our analysis of quotas we also want to separate these effects. Once again we employ a supply-and-demand model to show that the economic effects of a quota are very similar to the effects of a tariff. Figure 5.2 illustrates the effects of quotas on the domestic market for cloth for an importing country. The domestic demand and supply curves of cloth are shown as D and S, respectively. In the absence of international trade, equilibrium would occur at point E, with the domestic price of cloth equaling P.

Now, assume that this country has a comparative disadvantage in the production of cloth and decides to open its borders to trade. In this case, the country will import cloth at price P_w, and the free-trade equilibrium is located at point F. Under conditions of free trade, the domestic price of cloth would fall to the world price, P_w, with Q_1 amount of cloth being produced domestically and the amount Q_1 to Q_2 being imported. Remember, if a tariff were imposed in this market, the domestic price of cloth would rise. As a result, domestic production of cloth would expand and imports would decline. Identical effects on the domestic price, domestic production, and the amount imported can occur if the government imposes an import quota.

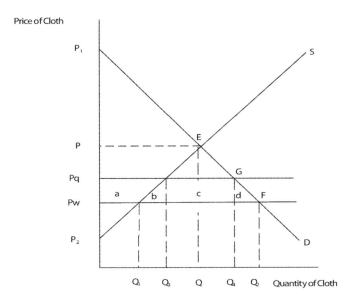

Figure 5.2   The Effects of a Quota.

Let's assume the government imposes an import quota that restricts the supply of imported cloth to X units. The imposition of the quota changes the amount of cloth supplied to the importing country. For all prices above the world price, P_w, the total supply of cloth in the importing country would equal the domestic supply, S, plus the quota amount, X. This total supply of cloth in the importing country is illustrated by the supply curve S+Q. Because the supply of imported cloth is reduced at the world price of P_w, the price of cloth will begin to rise until a new equilibrium is reached at G. In this case, domestic consumers are harmed as consumer surplus declines by areas (a+b+c+d). Like our analysis of a tariff, domestic producers benefit as they produce more of the product and sell it at a higher price. The increase in producer welfare (surplus) by imposing a quota is represented by area a. In addition, there are efficiency losses of areas b and d. Remember, the small triangle b represents the cost of resources transferred from their best use to the production of more cloth. In a free market, this represents a loss to society, as these resources would have been used to produce a product in which the importing country has a comparative advantage. Transferring resources to the quota-restricted industry necessarily entails a loss of resources to some other, more productive industry. Finally, area d is a consumption effect caused by a quota as consumers purchase less cloth.

The matter of who receives area c is the only difference between a tariff and a quota. In the case of a tariff, area c is the amount of tariff revenue the domestic government collects. In the case of a quota, area c accrues to the foreign producers and makes them more profitable. The net welfare loss to the quota-imposing country is larger under a quota. The country loses areas (b + c + d) under a quota but only areas (b + d) under a tariff. With a tariff, the domestic government gains revenue, area c, which can be spent on the provision of public goods. With a quota, area c is lost to the foreign producers. Two methods are available for a government or society to capture area c from foreign producers under a quota. First, the domestic government could auction quotas to foreign producers in a free market. The advantage to this auction quota method is that the domestic government would gain area c, which now accrues to foreigners. The limited quota supply would go to those importers most in need of the product who would pay the highest prices. Another method available to a government to capture area c is to convert the quota into an equivalent tariff. The conversion of a quota into a tariff has several advantages. First, tariffs are legal under the WTO and quotas are not. If foreign firms find the quota sufficiently restrictive, they can perhaps petition their government to complain to the WTO for relief or an alternative remedy. Second, calculating a tariff equivalent for an existing quota is relatively easy to do. To calculate a tariff equivalent, one would take the difference between the good's world market price and its quota-constrained domestic price and divide that difference by the good's world market price. Calculating these tariff equivalents has become an important process in world trade. In phasing out the MFA, the developed countries did not forgo protection in these industries. Rather, they simply converted their quotas into tariff equivalents. This process also is occurring in the developing countries as they phase out their quotas to bring their countries into compliance with WTO standards. Also, the trade negotiations in agricultural products would allow countries to replace their quotas with equivalent tariffs.

Finally, and most importantly, a tariff is much less restrictive in the domestic market when the domestic demand for the product increases. In the case of a tariff, the price would remain constant at P_t and the additional demand for cloth would cause additional imports of cloth. However, in the presence of a quota, the domestic producers supply the increase in demand. In this case, the foreign producers of cloth also gain as the price they receive for their product increases. The important point is that the losses for consumers and society are much larger in the case of a quota than in the case of a tariff when demand increases.

Although quotas reduce foreign competition in the short run, the long-run anticompetitive effects may be greatly diminished for several reasons. First, quotas may entice foreign firms that are exporting to the domestic market to engage in foreign direct investment (FDI) in the quota-constrained market. If the domestic market in the importing country is large enough and the barriers to exporting are sufficiently high, foreign firms may find it profitable to build production facilities in the importing country. This effect is analogous to firms building plants to jump over high tariffs. Second, when an importing country enforces a quota, the quota is stated as a specific number of units without regard to their price. In this case, the exporters have a clear incentive to export the highest-quality and the most expensive versions of the product. For example, the United States imposed a quota on imports of apparel from Italy in the 1930s. At that time, Italian apparel exports were not the high-quality items we see today. To maximize their revenue from a limited number of exports, Italian firms had a clear incentive to produce higher-quality items for export. Exports of automobiles from Japan are a perfect example of both effects. With the passing of the VER on exports of Japanese cars in the early 1980s, Japanese firms had an even greater incentive to build plants in the United States. This also gave the Japanese companies a clear incentive to export higher-priced vehicles from Japan. In retrospect, the pressure that U.S. companies placed on government officials to obtain a VER may have been a relatively short-sighted strategy. As a result, a quota or VER can be a two-edged sword. In most cases, a quota will benefit the domestic industry by raising profits in the short run. Whether this will also hold for the long run is another matter.

Other Nontariff Distortions

Quotas are usually considered the most important nontariff barrier to trade. Like tariffs, quotas have effects on international trade that are relatively easy to analyze. However, quotas over time will become less of a barrier to trade, as many quotas are or will be phased out and replaced with tariffs. If tariffs and quotas were the only trade restrictions that businesses engaged in international trade had to deal with, conducting international trade would be relatively simple. Businesses would merely need to consider whether a profit could be made given the constraint of a quota and/or a tariff. Unfortunately, governments pursue many other policies that either directly or indirectly affect international trade. These policies may not necessarily prohibit trade, but frequently they distort the amount of trade relative to domestic production. In some cases, the distortion is just a by-product of a government attempting to accomplish some other objective unrelated to international trade. In other cases, the clear goal is to favor domestic production at the expense of imports. These distortions are becoming increasingly important in the world economy. As explicit trade barriers are reduced worldwide, these other nontariff distortions of trade are becoming relatively more important.

Industrial Policy

Every country in the world conducts what is known as industrial policy. Industrial policy is the effect of government regulation on the industrial structure of the country. In some cases this policy is very specific, as the government may want to clearly favor one industry over another. In other countries, industrial policy is simply a residual effect. All governments pass regulations that affect business even if the purpose of the regulation is not specifically aimed at favoring one industry over another. Because we cannot consider every possible government policy that influences international trade, we will consider taxes and labor regulations as examples of industrial policies that can distort trade. Later in this section, we consider the effects of government subsidies and environmental regulation.

First, consider how differences in taxation could affect trade. For example, suppose that U.S. companies are taxed on the basis of gross income, both domestic and export. Further suppose that U.S. firms compete with European firms that also are taxed on the basis of gross income. However, assume that European firms do not have to pay taxes on income earned from exports. Given this situation, U.S. firms have to pay taxes on any income earned from exports to Europe, but European firms do not have to pay any taxes on exports to the United States. Obviously, this differential tax treatment will distort trade flows between the two. European exports to the United States will be higher, and U.S. exports to Europe will be lower because of the difference in taxation. The example is an extreme case, but the principle can be generalized. National differences in the level of business taxes have the potential to distort trade.

Second, consider how differences in labor regulations can distort trade. Assume that in the United States, workers are able to work a standard 40-hour week and can also work overtime. Overtime in the United States is paid at a higher wage rate, but the employer has the ability to determine the number of hours worked so as to maximize the profitability of the firm. Suppose that in Europe the work week is 35 hours with no legal overtime. Thus, to produce more output, the European firm must hire more workers. Further, assume that laying off workers in Europe is prohibitively expensive due to mandated government labor regulations. In this case, U.S. firms have an advantage over European firms because they can more easily adjust their operations to accommodate changes in demand. For European firms, this is much harder to do. Expanding output is more costly, as additional workers must be employed and trained. In addition, because laying off workers in the face of declining demand is difficult, European firms are reluctant to expand output and their workforce in the first place. In this case, U.S. firms will have an advantage in world markets relative to European firms because changes in exports can be more easily accommodated by U.S. firms relative to European firms.

Such differences in industrial policy have created some interesting issues in international trade. As tariffs have declined, national differences in industrial policy have a greater chance of altering the pattern of world production and trade. This is especially true given the increasing number of free-trade agreements between countries. Once countries have entered into a free-trade agreement that abolishes tariffs and quotas, the differences in business regulations among the countries become more important. For example, because Canada and the United States have abolished trade restrictions, resulting differences in each country's regulation of an industry can have noticeable effects on the trade flows between the two countries. If Canada decides to heavily regulate an industry that the United States does not, the industry will likely shrink in Canada and expand in the United States. The result is that as traditional trade barriers fall, industrial policy takes on increasing importance.

Strategic Trade Policy

For the last 20 years, a lively topic of economic debate has been the role and effects of strategic trade policy. In general, strategic trade policy refers to industrial policies that exporting countries pursue. Such policies are aimed at maximizing a country's exports. A country's strategic trade policy requires that the trade ministry identify an industry in which the country has a comparative advantage. The country then nurtures this industry by subsidizing its development and protecting it from imports. Once the industry has developed, it can export the product to the world market, devastating similar industries in the target countries. With foreign competition disposed of, the industry now has the monopoly power to raise prices and earn excess profits. The effective use of strategic trade policy is often applied to Japan and its Ministry of International Trade and Industry (MITI) during the 1980s, when Japanese imports of automobiles, steel, and semiconductors were flooding the U.S. market.

Within the United States, there was gloomy talk of the deindustrialization of the U.S. economy and the dominance of Japanese industries. From the start, various policy makers in the United States questioned the validity of strategic trade policy. First, the argument for strategic trade policy presupposes that employees in a ministry can spot profitable opportunities that the market cannot. Second, if economies of scale are necessary to make the policy successful, it is difficult to determine which industries will have significant economies of scale in their future development. Finally, no empirical studies ever determined if Japanese industrial policy was really any better than any other country. For example, France has had an active industrial policy for much longer than Japan, and no one ever discussed the success of French industrial policy. Research on Japanese industrial policy has demonstrated what economists have long suspected. Japanese industrial policy does not work much better in Japan than it does anywhere else. The empirical test to determine this was that there should be a positive correlation between how fast Japanese industries grow and the government's support of the industry. In fact, the correlation is negative. Japanese trade bureaucrats do what most governments do, which is support industries that are having a hard time competing with imports.

This result is not surprising. In 1776, Adam Smith wrote in *The Wealth of Nations* on the "folly and presumption" of government attempts to intervene in free markets.

> The statesman, who should attempt to direct private people in what manner they ought to employ their capitals, would only load himself with a most unnecessary attention, but assume an authority which could safely be trusted, not only to no single person, but to no council or senate whatever, and which would no-where be so dangerous as in the hands of a man who had folly and presumption enough to fancy himself fit to exercise it.

Of course, the same logic would apply to strategic trade policy.

Technical Barriers to Trade

An even larger and more difficult protectionist problem to address is technical barriers to trade. Technical barriers refer to a country's national standards for health, safety, and product labeling. Even when these regulations are designed solely for the protection of the domestic population, they can distort international trade. For example, most firms produce products primarily for domestic consumption, and the exportation of the product provides a secondary source of demand. However, when a firm decides to export its product, it will have to change the product label. In most cases, the new label will have to conform to the importing country's product labeling standards and be printed in the country's official language.

In addition to labeling changes, many domestic products that are exported are modified to meet government technical standards. A classic example is automobiles. For a U.S. firm to sell cars in Japan or in the United Kingdom, the steering wheel and other driving-related components have to be moved from the left side of the car to the right side. These product modifications are not free for domestic firms, and the additional cost amounts to a tariff on exported cars to countries with right-side–oriented cars. The numerous changes that domestic firms must make to comply with foreign governments' technical standards distort international trade.

These technical standards affect not only trade in goods but also trade in services. The negotiations over international trade in airline services offer a clear example. When the deregulated U.S. airline industry attempts to compete in a foreign market where the airline industry is heavily regulated with regard to gates, routes, landing times, fares, and safety regulations, the possibility of a trade dispute is rather high. The difficulty in resolving the dispute lies in the intent of the regulations. If the intent of the regulation is an expression of national preference and the adverse effects on foreign competitors are just a by-product of that preference, then it is difficult for U.S. firms or the government to complain to the WTO concerning this discrimination. However, if the regulation's intent is to protect the domestic industry from competition, countries can complain to the WTO or threaten retaliation. Efforts by the WTO to control these types of government restrictions have not been successful, and disputes of this kind are some of the most difficult areas for businesses and governments to negotiate in international trade.

Subsidies

Few, if any, governments in the world do not subsidize some form of business activity. Subsidies may take the form of actual money being given to a firm or industry. In many cases, the subsidy is more indirect or subtle in the form of reduced taxes for certain activities, lower utility rates, or a lower level of business regulation. In a world where trade barriers are, on average, falling, government subsidies are becoming more important. A significant subsidy to domestic business has the potential to increase the level of domestic production relative to imports. Also, a domestic subsidy could increase the level of exports to other countries. The main point is that significant government subsidies have the potential to change the pattern of trade among countries from what it would be without the influence of government.

When one thinks of subsidies and international trade, attention is usually focused on an explicit export subsidy. An export subsidy is a certain amount of money paid by a government and tied to the level of exports, such as $1 per ton. These types of subsidies clearly distort trade. They give exporters in world markets an advantage over other competitors that do not receive the subsidies. However, such subsidies are less troublesome than one might think. These subsidies are clearly illegal under WTO rules and can be legally offset by domestic tariffs. As a result, they are less common than one might think.

The other type of government subsidy is more troublesome. Consider a domestic subsidy that is given to a firm or industry that is not explicitly tied to international trade. Generally, these subsidies are being given to the firm or industry to accomplish some domestic policy objective. Most countries have some form of domestic subsidies as part of an overall industrial policy. The problem is that these subsidies can also distort trade. Trying to eliminate the effects on trade of domestic subsidies is an extremely difficult problem in world trade. As we will discuss in the next chapter, the problem is particularly acute with respect to world trade in agricultural products.

Government Procurement

One of the most obvious cases of government rules and regulations that distort trade is in the area of government procurement. Government procurement laws are laws that direct a government to buy domestically made products unless comparable foreign-made products are substantially cheaper. In a free market, consumers purchase products that are of the highest quality for any given price. However, government agencies differ somewhat from consumers in that the agencies spend public funds rather than their own money. Government purchases of goods and services are subject to constraints, and frequently governments have regulations that give preferences to domestic firms. The rationale for these regulations is that buying domestic is more beneficial to the country than buying an imported product. In this case, it seems that the mercantilists' views on international trade remain active. The issue of government procurement has become important because in most countries government purchases account for 10 to 15 percent of GDP.

Like most governments, the U.S. government has a "buy domestic" requirement when purchasing goods and services. Under the Buy American

Act of 1933, domestic producers are given a 6 to 12 percent margin of preference over foreign suppliers—meaning that a foreign producer must sell the good at a price that is at least 6 percent below an American producer's in order to win the contract. This "buy domestic" requirement means that foreign producers implicitly face at least a 6 percent tariff on all federal government purchases. For military or defense-related goods, the preference margin expands to 50 percent.

However, the United States differs from many other countries in that its government does not own private industries. In some countries, the government may own part of a particular firm or industry. For example, in many developing countries the government owns—either wholly or partially—the domestic telecommunication industry and/or public utility companies. This governmental ownership can be a serious barrier to trade when the government both owns a domestic industry and has "buy domestic" requirements. In these cases, the discrimination against foreign firms is much larger. The WTO has attempted to deal with this issue but has had only limited success. A government procurement code was adopted during the Tokyo Round of trade negotiations. It was expanded in scope as a result of negotiations during the Uruguay Round. However, countries that are WTO members are not obligated to be a party to the government procurement code. At this point, approximately 50 out of 151 WTO members are parties to this code. Rather obviously, governments seem to be very reluctant to part with this particular form of protectionism.

Corruption and International Trade

A recurring issue that comes up when discussing international trade is corruption. Unfortunately, the term *corruption* is too general for our discussion, so we need to narrow our focus to corruption in government. Specifically, corruption refers to the use of public office for private gain. In the private sector, the profit motive tends to motivate workers in firms to perform their jobs in an appropriate way. As a result, when we talk about corruption, it is almost universally understood to be corruption in government. Because we are discussing international trade, we want to further narrow our discussion to corruption in government as it relates to international trade.

What this leads us to is the passing of money from a company in the private sector into the hands of some government employee. There is a tendency to assume that any money changing hands in this manner is corruption—but legally the situation is not that clear cut. Suppose that it is routine practice in Country X to pay a customs official a carton of cigarettes to process goods through customs in the next 24 hours instead of sometime during the next week. All that has been done is to encourage the official to do his or her job at the "normal" speed. Frequently this is called a "grease payment" or a "facilitation payment." You have not paid the official to do anything illegal; you have simply paid to get the regular work of government done. Facilitation payments are common practice in many countries and constitute a small nontariff barrier to trade. They may be troublesome, but they are not the heart of the problem of corruption in international trade.

A bribe is an entirely different matter. In this case, a business has paid a government employee to do something illegal. It might be the reclassification of a shipment of goods to allow for a lower tariff or a payment to evade quota restrictions. Notice that both high tariffs and quotas on international trade tend to induce bribes to government officials. Government procurement is a large part of the problem of corruption in international trade. In a smaller country, government officials may routinely buy foreign goods because there is no domestic production of the product. Unfortunately, there is also no profit motive in government agencies. Officials may buy more expensive and/or lower-quality products with no immediately obvious effects. In such cases, it may be tempting to bribe government officials to purchase goods or services that they would not otherwise have purchased.

Bribes are usually illegal in the country where the payment is being made. However, the governments of developed countries have also moved to make it illegal for businesses in these countries to bribe foreign officials. The United States was the first country to enact such a law. Passed in 1977, the Foreign Corrupt Practices Act (FCPA) prohibits U.S. firms from engaging in the bribery of foreign officials, political parties, party officials, and candidates. Corruption in international trade became a more important issue in 1997 when the Organisation for Economic Co-operation and Development (OECD) countries committed themselves to passing laws similar to the FCPA. At this point 35 countries both in and outside of the OECD have committed themselves to the principles of the original convention. Although this convention and subsequent legislation in many countries will not eliminate corruption in international trade, at least the process of significantly reducing the problem has begun.

Ranking Countries by Degree of Corruption

In the previous section, we covered the relationship between government procurement and the potential for corruption. Although the logical connection is clear, it would be extremely interesting to know something about the degree of overall corruption in government among the world's countries. Fortunately, there is a well-known source for just this sort of information. The German organization, Transparency International, publishes an annual ranking of countries by the degree of overall corruption in government. The rankings are based on an index that measures the extent to which public officials and politicians are perceived as being corrupt. One of the best features of the index is that it is a composite that uses data from 12 different polls and surveys from nine independent institutions. The respondents to the polls and surveys are either businesspeople or country analysts. Only 177 of the world's 193 countries are included in the rankings due to a lack of reliable data for some countries. A corruption-free, political-economic environment is equal to 100 in the rankings, whereas a completely corrupt environment would be equal to 0. A number near 50 indicates a borderline condition. The entire survey can be easily accessed at www.transparency.org.

Economic Sanctions

One frequently hears from the popular press that the United States or some other government has imposed economic sanctions on another country or group of countries. The purpose of this section is to explain in a brief way what economic sanctions are, a bit of the history of sanctions, what they are meant to accomplish, and why they usually fail to accomplish the goals that caused them in the first place. The section is a logical extension of our discussion of nontrade barriers (NTBs). Although sanctions could involve just increasing tariffs, they normally involve some other prohibition on trade or investment. In a sense, the topic does not fit neatly into either international trade or finance. However, since sanctions frequently involve interference with international trade or FDI, it is convenient to cover them in this part of the book even though at times the interference may be in the area of international finance.

At the start, we need to define what economic sanctions are. Economic sanctions are the deliberate withdrawal caused by the government of normal trade or financial relationships in order to achieve foreign policy goals. No one in the private sector would, in most cases, voluntarily withdraw from a profitable economic relationship. It takes the coercive power of government to cause such an interruption. In the literature, the government imposing the sanctions is referred to as the sender country, whereas the country that is the object of the sanctions is the target country. In effect what is happening is that the sender country is attempting to impose significant costs on the target country. The hope is that these costs will induce the target country to change its policies in order to avoid these costs. In a sense, this is just another application of cost/benefit analysis. Is the target country willing in incur the costs of maintaining its current policies? One also needs to distinguish actual sanctions from the *threat* of sanctions. In some cases, the sender government will attempt to accomplish its ends by threatening to impose sanctions before actually doing so.

Sanctions can take a number of forms. The imposition of economic sanctions usually is less than the total severance of economic ties between two countries. It is not uncommon for the sanctions to be imposed on only part of the trade that is important to the target country. The sanctions may involve a suspension of imports. In this case, domestic consumers are "financing" the conduct of foreign policy. Sanctions may also involve the suspension of exports. Note that in this case certain costs of conducting foreign policy are being borne by domestic firms. The sanctions may be imposed on FDI. Domestic companies may be barred from investing in the target country. Finally, the sanctions may include or be limited to movements of portfolio capital. The aim may be to prevent the target country from acquiring capital or to "trap" its capital in foreign financial markets. This discussion presumes that the sanctions are bilateral in nature. However, in some cases the sanctions are legitimized by a multilateral organization such as the United Nations and may be imposed on the target country by a large number of countries. Finally, the WTO has the authority to allow economic sanctions against members that violate the rules of international trade.

Economic sanctions are hardly a new thing in the world economy. A documented case of economic sanctions occurred as long ago as 432 BCE. This was not an isolated incident. Prior to the 20th century, economic sanctions were commonly used. However, in the past, economic sanctions usually were adjuncts to outright warfare. Sanctions were just another way to damage an enemy's ability to engage in war. The use of sanctions as a tool of foreign policy separate from military conflict emerged after World War II. Instead of being complementary to military action, sanctions became a substitute for such actions. This makes sense because the motives for economic sanctions became much broader than just national defense. A partial list of reasons for economic sanctions includes the destabilization of obnoxious regimes, the protection of human rights in foreign countries, the prevention of nuclear proliferation, the settling of expropriation claims; combating terrorism, and the support of democracy. The attempt by a sender government to achieve these "softer" foreign policy goals calls for policy measures that are decidedly less extreme than military action.

Economic sanctions are usually imposed by large countries in the world economy with active foreign policy agendas. They are attractive because they occupy a middle ground in foreign policy between simple complaints about the target government's behavior and outright warfare. They demonstrate resolve in the issue, as the government is imposing costs on domestic consumers, domestic firms, or both groups. They may also have a deterrence effect of sending a message to the target country about how seriously the sender country perceives the issue to be.

This leads to an important question: Do economic sanctions work? It depends on how one defines success. If success is defined as the frequency with which sanctions demonstrably change the target country's behavior, then the answer is that they usually fail. There are many reasons for this. First, sanctions may be too weak a response to a serious foreign policy dispute. Second, in an era of rapid globalization, sanctions may not be effective. A country facing restrictions on its exports or imports may be able to find another buyer or seller, respectively. Third, the imposition of sanctions may invoke more support for the target country's government from both the domestic population and allies. Finally, sanctions impose costs on parts of the sender country's population. The losses to these groups may weaken support for the sanctions. However, sanctions may be effective in another sense. In some cases, the point of the sanctions is to accomplish domestic political goals. If the imposition of sanctions is politically popular in the sender country, then the effects of the target country may be less important. In any case, the use of economic sanctions has become a common part of the landscape of the world economy. As in the case of the WTO, they are now an official part of the machinery of policing world trade. Because they are so commonly used, economic sanctions must be perceived to be effective in some sense. This being the case, it seems safe to assume that we will all continue to hear or read about the use of economic sanctions as a tool of foreign policy.

Labor and Environmental Standards

Two of the more controversial aspects of the debate over globalization are the issues of labor and environmental standards and international trade. The argument of the opponents of globalization usually proceeds along these lines. It is asserted that the more intense competition fostered by globalization drives companies engaged in international trade to aggressively cut costs. This forces companies to try to reduce their labor costs in any way possible. With respect to environmental issues, it is asserted that companies will tend to locate production processes in countries where environmental regulations are low. In both cases, this creates "a race to the bottom" as companies will endlessly attempt to cut both labor and environmental costs. Over time, this would tend to produce ever poorer working conditions and an increasingly polluted global environment. If this argument is correct, then the solution would be some form of global standard with respect to labor and environmental regulations. In effect, the standards that prevail in the developed countries would be imposed on the developing countries as a condition of international trade. If such rules became embodied within the international trade rules, this would constitute an important nontariff barrier to trade. In this section, we will discuss both the labor standards and the environmental standards arguments.

All countries regulate their domestic labor markets with respect to wages, conditions of work, and occupational safety. These labor standards and their enforcement vary from country to country. It has been empirically shown that wages and working conditions are positively correlated with GDP per capita. As GDP per capita increases, wages and working conditions also improve. In developed countries, there is a concern over the ability to compete with countries that have lower labor standards for wages, working conditions, and occupational safety. The fear is that countries with "low" standards will enjoy an "unfair" advantage over countries with higher standards. To a large extent the argument is over comparative advantage. As we illustrated in Chapter 3, developing countries tend to have a comparative advantage in labor-intensive products. Companies will tend to produce such goods in countries where unit labor costs are low relative to the developed countries. This is not so much a "race to the bottom" as it is a firm's trying to take advantage of a country's comparative advantage. The placement of labor-intensive production in developing countries increases these countries' specialization in products in which they have a comparative advantage and, over time, will increase relative wages through factor-price equalization within the country. For these reasons, the developing countries view the drive to impose a developed country's labor standards on them as a condition of exports as nothing more than thinly veiled protectionism. They point out that when the now-developed countries were at the same level of economic development, labor standards were low. As these developing economies become wealthier, labor standards will become more like those now observed in developed countries. The proponents of the "race to the bottom" argument on labor standards no doubt are well intentioned. However, such standards would tend to rob the developing countries of one of the best avenues available to reduce the level of poverty.

Sweatshops

The United States has recently become concerned about imports of products from developing countries that are produced in "sweatshops." But just what is a sweatshop? Generally, one imagines a sweatshop to be a plant where low-wage workers work long hours under poor working conditions. Unfortunately, all of the adjectives (*low-wage*, *long*, and *poor*) are relative terms. A hard reality is that Bangladesh is not Kansas. What seems to be impossibly long hours in the United States may be the average work week in many poor countries. For example, many of our grandparents worked what we would consider to be very long days or weeks. Even college students once went to class on Saturday mornings. By a developed country's standards, working conditions in poor countries are, in some cases, appalling. However, these standards were once common in what are now developed countries. In 1870, the average American worked approximately 3,000 hours per year as opposed to nearly half that time now. Per capita GDP in the United States in 1890 was approximately $2,500, or equivalent to what a worker in Guatemala, Jamaica, or the Russian Federation now earns.

The same is true with respect to a discussion of wages. Although many workers in developing countries may be poorly educated, they are not irrational. They are willing to work in factories because their next best opportunity is *worse*. Attempts to impose wages and working conditions equivalent to those in developed countries would reduce these countries' comparative advantage in the production of products intensively employing unskilled or semiskilled labor. Such an imposition might make some in the developed countries feel better, but it would not make developing countries or their citizens better off.

The same type of argument applies to national differences in environmental standards. Environmental standards are laws that apply rules concerning environmental health to the manufacture of products. Again, the "race to the bottom" argument is that companies will move pollution-intensive plants to countries with low environmental standards. Many countries with high environmental standards fear that countries with low standards and/or enforcement may enjoy an "unfair" advantage in industries that are relatively pollution intensive. Superficially, this argument has some merit. Countries do have different environmental standards. This opens up the possibility that globalization could lead to a concentration of pollution-intensive industries in parts of the world where environmental standards are low. However, there is not a substantial amount of evidence that this actually occurs. To illustrate why this in general is not occurring, we need to look at two important aspects of pollution within the world economy.

First, consider the issue of the location of a new plant in the world. A large number of factors go into deciding where to locate a plant. Among these are the proximity to natural resources, coupled with the proximity to the final market. Firms will frequently locate plants so as to minimize transportation costs. Comparative advantage matters, and plants will tend to be located with respect to minimizing capital or labor costs. Trade barriers are part of the location decision, as well as local taxes and business regulations. Among this multitude of factors, environmental costs would no doubt be considered. However, it is not the only factor involved. If it were, firms would clearly locate the majority of pollution-intensive plants in areas of the world known for their low environmental regulations. Researchers in this area have attempted to empirically verify that firms tend to locate pollution-intensive plants in low-regulation regions. So far, the evidence indicates that this does have a small effect on plant location and trade flows. This result should not be too surprising. Lowering pollution costs is just one among many factors involved in plant location.

Second, pollution levels seem to be related to GDP per capita. In a famous paper, the economists Gene Grossman and Alan Krueger showed that for low-income economies, pollution and GDP per capita were positively related. This means that as economies grew richer, pollution levels increased. However, once a certain level of GDP per capita had been reached, the relationship became the reverse. Pollution levels decline with increases in GDP per capita for low- and middle-income countries. The overall relationship looks like an inverted U and is known as the environmental Kuznets curve. If this relationship is correct, it has interesting implications for the debate over globalization and pollution. For very poor countries, it seems that the faster economic growth that may accompany a more open economy may initially worsen the level of pollution. However, once a certain GDP per capita is reached, pollution levels begin to fall even as economic growth continues. If the empirical results are correct, the problem of pollution levels in developing countries is somewhat self-liquidating beyond a certain level of GDP per capita. This produces the interesting result that the antidote for pollution is more economic growth.

The central question concerning environmental standards is whether the environmental policies of the developed countries should be applied to the developing countries as a precondition for trade. This type of nontariff barrier would not have the same devastating effects on developing-country exports that labor standards would. However, it would reduce the comparative advantage of some developing countries in some pollution-intensive goods. This would tend to slow the economic growth of these countries. In turn, this might actually increase pollution levels if it slowed the transition of countries from the left side of the environmental Kuznets curve to the right side. Second, it appears that plant location decisions are not very sensitive to environmental standards, as other locational factors seem to dominate these decisions. However, any such regulation would tend to put more plants in the developed countries and fewer in the developing countries. Again, this would tend to slow down the rate of economic growth in the developing countries. The response of the developing countries is that this sort of regulation should be left to the domestic government to determine so that a level of environmental standards appropriate to the country's level of economic development can be set.

Given the strength of the developing countries in the WTO, global standards on labor and environmental issues are unlikely. However, the debate has had a positive effect. It has stimulated research on economic development, wages, working conditions, and environmental standards that probably would not have occurred in its absence. As a result, our understanding of how labor standards and environmental standards affect international trade is much better than it was a decade ago. A possible compromise to this policy issue may lie in the trade negotiations that the United States has conducted with Mexico and is now conducting with other developing countries. In these agreements, all parties commit themselves to rigorously enforcing their own domestic labor and environmental standards. Many developing countries have fairly rigorous labor and environmental standards, but these standards may not be strictly enforced. For a developing country to have lower labor and environmental standards than the United States is not unusual. GDP per capita in such countries may be substantially below the U.S. level. However, the standards written into law presumably reflect appropriate standards for the country's level of development. If the trade agreement requires the local level of standards to be enforced, the agreement may both improve labor and environmental standards and not significantly hinder the rate of economic growth necessary to improve the standard of living in the country.

Transportation Costs and Trade

The supply and demand model that we used to analyze the effects of trade barriers also can be used to show the effects of transportation costs on international trade, prices, and domestic production and consumption. Up to this point, we have assumed that transportation costs between countries are zero. With zero transportation costs and perfect competition, a single world price would result for a good after free trade opens up between countries.

The effects of transportation costs can be seen by comparing trade in a single good under conditions of zero transportation costs between countries to a condition in which transportation costs are positive. To think about this we can refer back to Figure 5.1. With positive transportation costs, the quantity of cloth traded is lower; imports by the United States and exports by India both have decreased. In addition, the consumption of cloth in the United States has declined, whereas the production of cloth in the United States has increased. For India, the consumption of cloth has increased, whereas the production of cloth has decreased. Thus, the effect of transportation costs is to move the price of cloth and the quantities traded partially back toward the no-trade situation. As such, transportation costs act as a barrier to trade, much as tariffs and other nontariff barriers do. Indeed, if transportation costs were equal to or greater than the no-trade price differences between the United States and India, there would be no trade between the two countries. You may be able to think of numerous goods that are not typically traded between countries for just this reason.

Often, the analysis of trade between countries distinguishes between tradable and nontradable goods. This distinction is determined by transportation costs between countries. Nontradable goods are those goods whose transportation costs are so large that it makes trade unprofitable, whereas tradable goods are those whose transportation costs are low enough to make it potentially profitable to trade the goods between countries.

One can get a sense of the effects of transportation costs on trade by estimating what economists call a gravity model. The model posits that trade will be negatively related to the distance between countries and the size of GDP of both countries. The gravity model simply puts this logic into a more formal model. For example, the model would predict that trade between the United States and India would not be as large as the trade between the United States and Canada. At this point, our primary interest is on the effect of distance on trade. The empirical estimation of the gravity model can shed some light on the degree to which distance acts as a barrier to trade. In these empirical estimates of the effect of distance on trade, the effect is as expected: negative. No one study gives a precise result. However, the general results of these models suggest a rough proportionality. If the distance between countries increases by 10 percent, then trade tends to decrease by about 10 percent. This is exactly what the model we developed in the previous section indicates. What the simple model was unable to convey was the *magnitude* of the effect. However, one should be cautious in using this result. This is the effect of distance between countries on overall trade. The effects on any particular industry could be greater or less depending on the particular transportation costs associated with that industry. To summarize, the results of the gravity model show that distance affects trade flows in the same way that government-imposed trade barriers do. Distance adversely affects trade in much the same way tariffs and quotas do.

Case Study: Time as a Trade Barrier

As they say, "time is money." This is very true in international trade. With improvements in technology, transportation by water in the world economy has become very cheap. It also is slow. It takes an average of 20 days to transport goods between the United States and Europe. The trip from Europe to Asia is an average of 30 days. One of the advantages of thinking in economic terms is that it frequently allows one to consider factors that are real but not obvious. Lengthy shipping times are a good example. If the goods are perishable, it is obvious that shipping times may increase spoilage and reduce the value of the cargo. Less obvious is that time in transit increases the costs of holding inventory and the goods are depreciating during the voyage. For certain goods where product characteristics change rapidly, there is the risk of obsolescence. In a period of rapid technological change, demand may be uncertain as tastes and preferences change quickly. In this circumstance, moving goods quickly from producer to consumer may be critical. This effect may be magnified in the presence of global supply chains. In a supply chain, the late delivery of components could lead to very expensive losses due to lost production of the final product.

An innovation of modern times is the ability to transport goods between countries using air transportation. The use of air transport can cut shipping times from weeks to literally days. This method of transportation is cheap, and yet is also expensive. Typically, it costs six to seven times more to ship the same weight by air as opposed to water transport. Even with this cost differential, air freight is growing much faster than water transportation. Over the last several decades, the use of air freight has grown nearly three times as fast as water transportation. Also, this growth shows up in trade measured by the value of imports as opposed to measures of units. Recently, 36 percent of U.S. imports by value came in via air freight. An analogous figure for exports was 58 percent for shipments outside of Canada and Mexico. This makes sense because air freight should be more common for goods with a higher value-to-weight ratio. U.S. exports are more likely to fall into that category than U.S. imports. Other OECD countries are reporting similar trade patterns by mode of transportation.

For goods with a high value-to-weight ratio, air freight appears to be an attractive option, especially in the presence of global supply chains. An interesting question is just how valuable is air freight. Another way of putting this is to think of an increase in the time of transit as just another trade barrier. More precisely, we could think of it as an ad valorem equivalent. Each day lost in transit means that the "tariff" is higher. Thus, time becomes something like a trade barrier, and 20 days in transit implies a much higher tariff than 2 days in transit. A recent paper by Hummels and Schaur (2013) offers a glimpse into what this time tariff may be. Using an extensive database on U.S. imports by transportation mode, it is possible to calculate the premium that firms are willing to pay to reduce transportation costs. Their estimates indicate that each day in transit is equivalent to an ad valorem tariff of 0.6 to 2.1 percent. This estimate makes intuitive sense. If this were not the case, then the growth rates of air transport mentioned earlier and the cost differential would be far harder to explain.

Bibliography

Balassa, Bela. 1967. *Trade Liberalization Among Industrial Countries*. New York: McGraw Hill.

Bergsten, C. Fred. 1987. *Auction Quotas and U.S. Trade Policy*. Washington, D.C.: Institute for International Economics.

Cline, William R. 1983. "The Micro- and Macroeconomics of Foreign Sales to Japan," in William R. Cline (ed.), *Trade Policy in the 1980s*. Washington, D.C.: Institute for International Economics.

Copeland, Brian R. and M. Scott Taylor. 2004. "Trade, Growth, and the Environment," *Journal of Economic Literature* 42(1): 7–71.

Gillespie, Kate and J. Brad McBride. 1996. "Smuggling in Emerging Markets: Global Implications," *Columbia Journal of World Business* 31(1): 40–54.

Graham, Edward. 1996. *Global Corporations and National Governments*, Washington, D.C.: Institute for International Economics.

Grossman, Gene M. and Alan B. Krueger. 1995. "Economic Growth and the Environment," *Quarterly Journal of Economics* 110(2): 353–77.

Hufbauer, Gary Clyde and Kimberly Ann Elliot. 1994. *Measuring the Costs of Protection in the United States*. Washington, D.C.: Institute for International Economics.

Hummels, David L. and Georg Schaur. 2013. "Time as a Trade Barrier," *American Economic Review* 103(December): 2935–59.

Krugman, Paul. 1997. "What Should Trade Negotiators Negotiate About?," *Journal of Economic Literature* 35(1): 113–20.

Levinson, Marc. 2006. *The Box: How the Shipping Container Made the World Smaller and the World Economy Bigger*. Princeton, NJ: Princeton University Press.

Maddison, Angus. 1995. *Monitoring the World Economy: 1820–1992*. Paris: OECD.

New York Times. 1997. "In Principle, A Case for More Sweatshops," June 22: 5E.

Niroomand, Farhang and W. Charles Sawyer. 1989. "The Extent of Scale Economies in U.S. Foreign Trade," *Journal of World Trade* 23(4): 137–46.

O'Rourke, Kevin H. and Jeffrey G. Williamson. 1999. *Globalization and History: The Evolution of a Nineteenth Century Atlantic Economy.* Cambridge, MA: MIT Press.

Pavcnik, Nina. 2002. "Trade Liberalization, Exit, and Productivity Improvements: Evidence from Chilean Plants," *Review of Economic Studies* 69(1): 245–76.

Sawyer, W. Charles and Richard L. Sprinkle. 1984. "Caribbean Basin Economic Recovery Act: Export Expansion Effects," *Journal of World Trade Law* 18(3): 429–36.

Transparency International. 2013. *Corruption Perceptions Index, 2013.* Berlin: Transparency International.

Trefler, Daniel. 2004. "The Long and the Short of the Canada-U.S. Free Trade Agreement," *American Economic Review* 94(4): 870–95.

Tybout, James R. and M. Daniel Westbrook. 1995. "Trade Liberalization and the Dimensions of Efficiency Changes in Mexican Manufacturing Industries," *Journal of International Economics* 39(1): 53–78.

CHAPTER SIX

History of U.S. Trade Policy

Those that don't know history are doomed to repeat it.

—*Edmund Burke*

Introduction

In the first five chapters of the book, we introduced material that was necessary to understand before beginning the primary subject of the book. A sort of barrier to entry to understanding modern trade policy is the lack of understanding of the basic economics that lies underneath it. The purpose of this chapter is conceptually similar. Modern trade policy has roots going back to antiquity. Virtually any country or political entity will have some policy concerning trade with foreigners. Even perfectly free trade is a "policy." As in almost any area of government policy, actions of governments in the past have an influence on current policy. In many cases, modern governments end up "reinventing the wheel." Often they have forgotten past policy actions and end up making policy mistakes simply because their historical knowledge is weak. Trade policy in the United States is no different. The United States has over 200 years of accumulated experience in trade policy, both good and bad. The result is that current policy and proposed changes in policy frequently have historical antecedents. Our purpose here is to touch on the highlights of the history of trade policy that have strongly echoed through U.S. history and that still influence trade policy debates in the 21st century.

The chapter is divided into five sections that move through the history of the country. The next section covers the thinking of the founders of the country on international trade. This period ended abruptly when trade policy became enmeshed with the larger issues leading to the Civil War. Post–Civil War trade policy follows the development of the United States from an important country to the dominant economy of the world. Again, there was an abrupt change related to the onset of the Great Depression. As we will see in the last section, the greatest trade policy disaster in the history of the United States was recognized as such and a remarkable turnaround was begun.

The Beginnings of U.S. Trade Policy

No country was ever ruined by trade, even seemingly, the most disadvantageous.
—*Benjamin Franklin*

Even before its official establishment as a country, the British colonies of North America engaged in a substantial amount of trade. This external trade constituted approximately 20 percent of the income of the British colonies. In what would today seem to be a familiar pattern, the colonies caught the wave of a long-run commodity boom. Starting in the 17th century, the colonies exported large amounts of food and raw materials to Europe. These included coal, fish, furs, grains, indigo, naval stores, potash, rice, rum, timber, and tobacco. This pattern of comparative advantage held for centuries. Until the 1960s, the majority of U.S. exports were food products and other commodities. The flip side of this comparative advantage was comparative disadvantage. From the beginning, the colonies and later the United States were dependent on Europe for imports of manufactured goods. As we will see, this pattern of trade created some anxiety on this side of the Atlantic that still resonates in modern trade policy.

To understand modern trade policy, it is very useful to think about how the leaders of the colonies thought about trade in the decades leading up to the revolution. As the quote at the beginning of the section indicates, there was a natural predisposition to view international trade in a favorable light. Obviously, trade was critical to the survival and prosperity of the colonies. In addition to Franklin, Thomas Paine, Thomas Jefferson, John Adams, and others were basically free traders. In part, this was an extension of a change in the intellectual environment of the Enlightenment. Franklin had personally met Adam Smith. Thomas Jefferson had gone so far as to assert that free trade was a "natural right." The American predisposition to free trade thus had two sources. The first was the practical realization that the colonies were and would be for some time dependent on trade to earn the money necessary to buy imported products that could not be produced locally. Second, thinking on the other side of the Atlantic was turning in that direction as well. In one of those interesting historical accidents, *The Wealth of Nations* was published in 1776. The ideas expressed by Smith were well known before the publication of his book. Some of

Smith's basic ideas can be traced back to the ideas of Bernard Mandeville (*The Fable of the Bees*) who was writing in the early 18th century. The point is that the men who eventually wrote the foundations of U.S. trade policy generally felt that free trade was the optimal policy. They were soon to discover that in a world riddled with trade restrictions and practical politics, free trade was not possible. What followed was 250 years of agonizing about trade policy. Frequently, the political leadership charged with actually making trade policy has a predisposition to free trade. At some level they realize that it is the optimal policy. On the other hand, that is not the world we live in. Thus, the making of trade policy from the beginning has been a process something akin to loss minimization. Free trade is not possible, but attempts are made to minimize the damage of restrictions on trade. It helps to keep this in mind when watching the formation of trade policy. If policy makers seem vaguely uncomfortable about what they are doing, there is a reason. They frequently are torn between what they know is best for the country and what is politically feasible.

The colonial leaders were aware of these sorts of trade-offs. To start, there is no exact explanation of the relative importance of the various causes of the American Revolution. At this point, it is sufficient to assert that trade policy was a nontrivial part of the problem. Like most governments of the time, the British government was wedded to a policy of mercantilism. To review what was covered in Chapter 3, mercantilism was a policy designed to maximize the trade surplus of a country. Policies were pursued that were designed to both limit imports and maximize exports. A diluted form of mercantilism is still alive and well in modern formulations of trade policy. However, in the 18th century, mercantilist trade policy formed the bedrock of government policy with respect to international trade. This was particularly true with respect to the policy of a colonial power toward any colonies. The British colonies of North America were no exception. As the 18th century progressed, the colonies found themselves caught in the crossfire of both mercantilism and trade relations with Europe that were being increasingly put under strain by the political conflicts in Europe.

Trade based on comparative advantage helped to make North America more prosperous in the colonial period. Unfortunately, the territory was open to the conflicts between Britain and France that spilled over from Europe to North America. From 1659 to 1815, these conflicts interfered with trade and at times led to military conflicts within North America. Trade was bringing the region prosperity, but trade also was making the colonies vulnerable to any interruptions in that trade. These disruptions can be seen in modern trade policy in the mild form of economic sanctions the United States and other countries sometimes impose on other countries. In the colonial era such disruptions of trade were more severe and more in line with what one would anticipate in a wartime environment. The colonial experience with mercantilism primarily took the form of a series of Navigation Acts beginning in 1651. The purpose of these acts was to maximize the amount of gold and silver being earned by Britain on trade being conducted by the American colonies. The particulars of the various acts and their subsequent amendments are too numerous to go through here. However, in all their variants the acts tended to increase the benefits of colonial trade to Britain and reduce the benefits to the colonies. The main vehicle of this was restrictions on the transportation of goods. In the main, goods being exported from the North American colonies had to be shipped to Britain before they could be shipped to another country. This restriction reduced what American exporters could earn as Britain effectively became a monopsonist, that is, the only buyer of American goods. Further, any goods imported into the colonies had to first pass through Britain or another British colony. Of course, this tended to increase the cost of imports in North America. Finally, this trade could only be conducted in British ships, which included ships from the colonies. The result was that the colonies could benefit from trade, but the total benefits were being substantially reduced by these restrictions. They were not only reduced, but it was crystal clear who some of the gains from trade were being transferred to.

Although the losses to the American colonies were not huge, they were concentrated. Both producers of export goods and merchants were bearing a substantial portion of the losses of the gains from trade. Trade between the colonies and Britain was not balanced. The value of manufactured imports usually exceeded those of the exports of commodities. As time passed, the debts of the producers and exporters to the British tended to increase. As would be familiar to someone in the 21st century the mixture of a trade deficit with a country coupled with substantial debt owed to the same country is a recipe for strained international relations. The Stamp Act of 1765 marked a turning point in the situation. The previous Navigation Acts had been loosely enforced and, in some cases, such as the Molasses Act of 1733, were widely evaded. The Navigation Acts were widely viewed as restrictions on trade that were a larger part of British trade policy, that is, mercantilism. In this sense, the North American colonies were being treated no differently than other British colonies. The Stamp Act was enacted not to regulate trade, but to raise money for the British defense of North America. In turn, this raised the thorny issue of taxation without representation. For colonial leaders already weary of the long costs imposed by mercantilism, the Stamp Act was the final straw. The act tended to radicalize American leaders and set in motion a process culminating in outright revolution. This makes trade policy important in the United States if, for no other reason, then the fact that it contributed to the eventual dissolution of the political union with Britain. A number of other factors contributed to the conflict, but British trade policy was an important part of the mix.

The formation of a new government very quickly left the American leadership with the task of quickly engaging in the process of formulating a trade policy. It is one thing to complain about British trade policy, but quite another to actually formulate a workable replacement. With trade with Britain disrupted by the revolution, the new U.S. government quickly turned to increasing trade with its one dependable ally, France. Benjamin Franklin led a delegation to Europe to seek recognition, assistance, and commercial treaties. In 1778, the United States negotiated its first trade agreement with France. In seeking this treaty, American negotiators were attempting to establish two principles that are still cornerstones of U.S. trade policy in the 21st century. The first was reciprocity. Of the two principles, it is the easiest to understand. Reciprocity means that the United States will only grant trade concessions if it can obtain concessions from the other party. In a simplistic sense, this seems completely reasonable. As we will see in the next chapter, it is not officially written into U.S. trade policy. However, it has effects on trade policy that are subtle but important. First, this means that the United States cannot unilaterally reduce barriers to trade except in very limited circumstances that only cover a small portion of trade. Without a substantial change in U.S. trade law, free trade in the United States is not a legal option. Second, to lower trade barriers, the United States has to find another country that is also willing to reduce trade barriers. In this case, the United States is something like a person attending a dance without a partner. Perhaps a partner can be found, but perhaps not. If a partner can be found, it may not be the most preferred partner. If one is ever puzzled by the choice of partners the government makes in trade negotiations, you now know why. The United States can only negotiate with countries willing to reciprocate. Because this principle was instituted 250 years ago, it is unlikely to change soon. And although it may not be optimal, there may be a reason for its durability. For better or worse, it seems fair. It also contains the traces of mercantilism. There is something of a hidden assumption that lowering trade barriers is imposing a "loss" on the country. The willingness to suffer that loss needs to be matched by another country's willingness to do likewise. This is not a perfect principle, but it could be worse. Sometimes a good outcome—lower trade barriers—occurs for the wrong reason.

The second principle the new nation was seeking in trade negotiations was nondiscrimination. In a largely mercantilist world, discrimination in trade was the norm. Aside from mercantilism, various trade agreements

routinely granted rights of access to some countries that were more favorable than to others. As a starting point, the new nation was attempting to
gain better access to foreign markets. Because countries usually had multiple trade agreements in force, there were normally varying levels of access
to their domestic markets. Understandably, any country in this environment
would be seeking access that is equal to the best access available. The gold
standard in this regard was what is known as unconditional most favored
nation status (MFN). What this means is that the United States was seeking access automatically equivalent to the best access accorded another
country. In the treaty with France and other attempts by American negotiators, they found that obtaining both reciprocity and most favored nation
status was not possible. However both principles became deeply embedded in subsequent U.S. trade negotiations. Virtually all modern trade negotiations conducted by the United States are reciprocal in nature. During the
19th and early 20th centuries, the United States and other countries were
seeking MFN status in trade negotiations. It was difficult to achieve and
led to a world of myriad trade agreements with multiple levels of protection by product and by country. In the modern world, complaints about the
complexity of trade agreements are legitimate. As we will see, one of the
great achievements of post–World War II trade policy has been the widespread acceptance of the concept of MFN. The complex world of trade
negotiations today would have seemed like a dream to the trade negotiators of earlier eras. The earlier discrimination by product and by country
has been replaced with discrimination primarily by product only. There
are frequent calls for discrimination by country due to the trade imbalances
discussed in Chapter 2. Such calls now are routinely ignored in the formation of trade policy. Although modern trade policy is imperfect, all countries understand the necessity of resisting country-specific discrimination.
You now know why.

Moving past trade policy during the American Revolution, the country
faced a more immediate trade policy problem that was *internal*. The first
attempt to form a lasting government yielded the document known as the
Articles of Confederation. This document was in operation in various forms
for the United States from 1777 to 1789. Although it was a workable document for a revolutionary government, it quickly became apparent that it
was a flawed document for operating the government of a new country. In
terms of trade policy, the problems were twofold. First, the new government needed money to finance the repayment of the war debt and to finance
the operations of the new federal government. Until the 20th century, virtually all governments needed a tariff as a source of revenue. In a simple
economy, a tariff is a convenient vehicle for achieving this. Imports enter a

country via a number of strategic locations such as ports, roads, railroads, or, more recently, airports. It then becomes relatively easy to require foreign goods to clear customs before they can pass into the country. The tariff is then paid and the revenue is passed on to the central government. Because of the ease of collection, tariffs have been used by governments to raise revenue since antiquity. Under the Articles of Confederation, each state retained its own separate trade policy with the central government having only limited rights in this regard. Without a reliable vehicle for raising revenue, the operation of any central government was difficult at best.

While important, tariff revenue was not the primary trade policy problem under the Articles of Confederation. Because each individual state could exercise its own separate trade policy, trade within the new country was being impeded by restrictions peculiar to each state. Individual states were levying tariffs on other states. Imagine a world in which states could protect their comparative-disadvantage industries. It was soon obvious to all that this situation was a major barrier to economic development and not just a trade policy problem. In the new constitution, which took effect in 1789, the problem was solved with the Interstate Commerce Clause. In the jargon of economics it established a customs union and a common external tariff. What this means is that the individual states could not interfere with interstate commerce. Trade among the states was now unimpeded by state-level restrictions. It also gave the federal government the sole right to regulate all trade with other countries. Tariffs and other trade restrictions were no longer set at the state level, but were unified at the national level. In one stroke, one of the major weaknesses of the Articles of Confederation had been solved.

With this basic issue resolved, the next step was to decide who in the government would determine trade policy. This is a crucial point for understanding how trade policy works in the United States. In a parliamentary form of government, trade policy is the responsibility of one of the ministries with the authorization of the prime minister. In a republican form of government, the situation can become more complicated. The U.S. Constitution specifies a separation of power between the executive and legislative branches of the government. In this case the legislative branch has the authority to regulate commerce and levy taxes such as tariffs. On the other hand, the executive branch is charged with the responsibility to conduct foreign policy and negotiate trade agreements. This arrangement has had a profound effect on U.S. trade policy. The president can negotiate trade agreements, but they are only valid if approved by Congress. With respect to tariffs, the setting of tariffs is the responsibility of Congress. In other words, neither the executive nor legislative branch of government can unilaterally set trade policy. Because there is no overall power to set trade policy in the United States, it is rarely clear who is actually determining trade policy. For the entire history of the United States, the making of trade policy has been a series of sometimes messy compromises between the executive and legislative branches of the government. It is also slow. Reaching an agreement that is amenable to foreign governments, the president, and Congress is never going to be easy. This information is very helpful in understanding how trade policy works in the United States. The executive branch has to negotiate cautiously with an eye to what will pass Congress. If one is watching trade policy in the 21st century, it is not unlike the process from the start. In effect, it was designed to be hard. However, it slowly grinds out agreements that both our trading partners and our elected representatives find acceptable.

The immediate need of the government at this point was to enhance revenue to fund the expanded functions mandated under the new constitution. As mentioned earlier, the only reliable source was the tariff. This new tariff was so important it was passed on July 4, 1789. The purpose of the tariff was strictly revenue. The average tariff was 8.5 percent ad valorem. The tariff was moderate because Alexander Hamilton wanted a dependable source of revenue for both government spending and funding the national debt. The point was to tax imports, not prohibit them. A moderate tariff also reduces the returns to smuggling. This is not a small consideration, as a glance at a map of the East Coast of the United States coupled with the dominance of imports from Europe would indicate that very high tariffs could easily have led to a substantial amount of evasion. Although the tariff was not uniform by product, it was nondiscriminatory. This was consistent with the U.S. desire for the principle of nondiscrimination to prevail in trade policy. It also made conducting trade negotiations nearly impossible. Offering "concessions" to foreign governments would have flown in the face of the desire for nondiscrimination. This makes some of the history to follow more understandable. For much of U.S. history, the government would frequently change the tariff for a variety of reasons. However, there is not much emphasis on trade negotiations. Now this is understandable. The nondiscriminatory nature of U.S. tariffs made such negotiations difficult. The principle of nondiscrimination continues today. The occasional calls for protectionism against one country, no matter how tempting, always is resisted. This is not new, but has long historical roots.

Unfortunately, things did not end there. From the beginning, there was a call to use the tariff for the protection of domestic industries from foreign competition. The result was the most famous trade policy document in American history. In 1791, Hamilton issued his "Report on Manufactures."

It was a classic proposal using trade policy as a form of industrial policy. Going back even before Hamilton, however, American leaders advocated what would today be called balanced growth. What this implies is that an economy should grow based on the growth of several sectors as opposed to heavy reliance on just a few sectors. In the late 18th century, the U.S. economy was dominated by agriculture. It had been successful producing agricultural and other commodities and trading them for manufactured goods. However, there clearly was a desire on the part of the leadership of the country to expand the manufacturing sector, both to enhance growth and reduce the dependence of the country on Europe. Hamilton's report was a clear step in that direction. The report also had intellectual roots that reverberate in the 21st century. Hamilton dismissed the idea of the French Physiocrats that agriculture was the only true source of the wealth of the country. More importantly, he disagreed with Adam Smith. His argument was twofold. First, he asserted that it is difficult to develop manufacturing from scratch. To use his phrasing, there is a natural inertia that makes this difficult. In modern terms, he was arguing that the initial development of manufacturing was akin to a market failure—specifically, a market failure that was large enough to require government action. In modern times this is a classic argument for infant-industry protection that was to become popular in the 20th century. Second, he made the more practical argument that in a world full of nationalistic trade policy, it would be imprudent to move to unilateral free trade. Again, this is an argument that is still commonplace.

However, the report was far from being an extremist tract for protectionism that it is sometimes portrayed as. Hamilton recommended moderate tariffs and a bounty (subsidies) for industry. As Irwin (2003) has outlined, the actual proposals were quite modest. In general, the proposed increases in tariffs were to change the tariff from 5 percent to 10 percent on just over 20 commodities. On the other side, there were proposed tariff reductions to zero on five raw materials. The proposed bounties were limited to five industries. This is hardly a blueprint for rampant protectionism. Again, there is another misconception about the report that it was "dead on arrival" in Congress. Irwin (2003) has conclusively shown this was not the case. Hamilton's proposed tariffs were rather quickly adopted by Congress. They represented a reasonable compromise between free trade and the demands for protection that were arising in the newly industrializing North. The bounties did not fare as well in Congress. Hamilton proposed bounties for coal, raw wool, sail cloth, cotton manufactures, and glass. Even with a short list of industries, there was little support in Congress. The arguments against bounties took two forms. Hamilton argued that the support of industry would improve the general welfare of the country. The counterargument was that once accepted, the principle of spending government money for such a nebulous purpose would lead to a government that was no longer limited in scope. Beyond this philosophical argument was a more pragmatic concern. This was that bounties would produce some degree of corruption. The argument was that the bounties would not in all cases go to industries that would increase the national welfare, but instead would be dispensed to industries that were powerful or well connected to the government. Also, there was the fear that the bounties would tend to be regionally concentrated. This is public choice being considered 150 years before the term was coined. The leaders of the government were quite right to be concerned about this issue. Once again, a precedent was set. Arguments about the level of the tariff would rage throughout the rest of American history, and the political system would achieve an equilibrium. However, the issue of paying American industries direct subsidies from the national government was never seriously raised again. Other countries have not been so lucky.

Import Substitution Industrialization (ISI)

In the material earlier, the idea of infant-industry protection was discussed. This is a small part of the history of trade policy in the United States. It is a common policy that has been pursued in a number of countries. The basic idea became much more important in the post–World War II era. The world in 1946 consisted of a small number of developed countries coupled with a large number of developing countries and colonies that were soon to become developing countries. Also, during this period the foundations of the modern theory of economic growth were being built. This led to some general conclusions about the best way to transition countries from developing to developed countries. The first conclusion seemed simple. The developed countries had moved away from agriculture into manufacturing in the process of achieving higher incomes. Rather simplistically, it was thought that by increasing manufacturing as a percentage of gross domestic product (GDP) as quickly as possible, the developing countries would increase the rate of growth of GDP. In addition, modern growth theory indicated that countries would grow faster relative to the rate of growth of the capital stock. This would increase the K/L ratio and make the labor force more productive. Also, it would tend to increase real wages. From this the idea of import substitution industrialization (ISI) was born. It was assumed that rapid growth would occur if manufacturing grew as fast as possible. Further, capital-intensive manufacturing might be particularly useful in this process.

The actual practice of ISI went much further than some tariff increases and a few industrial subsidies. Tariffs were raised—sometimes to astronomical levels. If tariff protection was not sufficient, then quotas were put in place to limit imports. Exchange rates were fixed, partially to make imported inputs for the new manufacturing industries cheaper. Industrial firms frequently had access to credit at below-market rates of interest. Taxes were reduced for firms engaged in manufacturing. With such a lavish set of subsidies in some countries, resources poured into manufacturing in developing countries. Domestic producers and workers in these industries usually earned far more than other, less favored, citizens. If all of these subsidies were insufficient, there was always the possibility of the establishment of a state-owned enterprise (SOE). Although the initial results of ISI seemed positive by the 1970s, the reality began to catch up with the policy. Governments were trying to establish capital-intensive industries in labor-abundant countries. The pursuit of these policies produced industries that were not internationally competitive and could only survive with massive government support.

The support of ISI frequently took the form of large government budget deficits coupled with the increasing indebtedness needed to finance chronic current account deficits. The strain of these policies became unsustainable in the 1970s as a result of the two oil shocks. The result was a horrific mixture of exchange-rate shocks, massive inflation, and austerity programs necessary to reduce the imbalances in the economy. As documented in Reyes and Sawyer (2015), Latin America represented all of these problems, but the region was hardly alone. Unfortunately, the retreat from ISI is ongoing. Although many developing countries may have avoided a macroeconomic crash, they are still pursing policies designed to replace imports with domestic consumption. ISI also created a visible dichotomy among the developing countries. The more successful countries industrialized along the lines of comparative advantage. Their manufacturing industries initially grew based on labor-intensive industries designed for export. As GDP increased and labor costs rose, they then moved on to industries that were increasingly capital intensive. The template for this successful form of development has been South Korea. The reverse side of that coin has been India. GDP per capita in India and South Korea were virtually identical in the 1950s.

Going past the debate over protectionism, it must be kept in mind that the tariff was nearly the sole vehicle for the national government to raise money. Tariffs were raised in 1794, 1799, and 1804 purely as a means to provide funds for short-term increases in government spending. As we move through the history of the 19th century, one needs to keep in mind that although the debates over tariffs were often about protectionism, tariffs were also heavily related to government finances. Tariffs tended to increase during the period 1790 to 1820 as government spending increased to finance the protection of a growing frontier and to build military capacity needed to protect American interests at home and abroad. Toll (2008) provides a fascinating account of the strain on the government finances produced by the formation of the U.S. Navy. In essence, such major expenditures could only be financed by revenue from the tariff.

The first decade of the 19th century was one of the most tumultuous periods in U.S. trade policy. The Napoleonic Wars created collateral damage for the import substitution industrialization. Britain attempted to blockade the continent to prevent supplies from reaching France. British ships routinely conducted searches and seizures of American ships and confiscated cargoes and ships. This was in addition to—and really more serious in an economic sense—the notorious impressment of sailors alleged to be British subjects. To make matters worse, the French were engaging in similar activities but on a smaller scale. The situation left the government with three unpalatable options. The first was to do nothing and simply deal with the situation as best as possible. The second option was to pursue retaliatory trade policies in an effort to change policy on the other side of the Atlantic. The third option was to go to war to protect American interests. The policy of the government moved along this spectrum as the situation changed. For a time, the initial reaction apparently was hope that the situation would improve. As the situation deteriorated, the government turned to trade policy. The result was the most draconian piece of legislation on international trade in U.S. economic history. In December 1807 the government put an embargo on *all* international trade. No U.S. vessel could leave for a foreign port, and no foreign vessel could enter a U.S. port. The embargo was repealed in 1809 and only lasted for 14 months. It failed because it was imposing extreme costs on the U.S. economy but had failed to change British policy. It was replaced by a series of acts prohibiting trade with Britain, France, or their colonies. The ultimate failure of these trade policy measures culminated in the United States declaring war on Britain in 1812. Perhaps *fail* is too strong a term. All through this period there were consistent calls for the United States to declare war as opposed to pursuing a very active form of diplomacy. Although trade policy did not change British policy, it may have given the country time to prepare for the eventual conflict and put the ultimate declaration of war on a firmer footing. By 1812, it could truly be said that the United States had exhausted all possible diplomatic means to avoid the war.

The Welfare Costs of the Jeffersonian Trade Embargo

As a social science, economics labors under the difficulty of not being able to test economic theory using experiments. In the emerging area of behavioral economics, we can now do this in a limited way using small groups of people. However, for larger issues one cannot test the effects of economic policy. It would be simply unacceptable to "try out" a policy on a country just to see if it worked or what actually would happen. However, sometimes economists get lucky. Occasionally, circumstances hand us a "natural experiment." This is an experiment that we would like to try but under normal circumstances would not be possible. The trade embargo is a perfect example. It allows us to go back and see what would happen to the United States if the vast majority of international trade were cut off. As economic theory would predict, the effects are sobering and indicate why the United States has wisely never engaged in extreme forms of protectionism.

As outlined earlier the embargo was started in late 1807. The embargo was initially effective because very few American ships entered European ports in 1808. For example, the volume of British imports from the United States dropped by 80 percent. But by late in the year, the embargo was losing force as repeal of the embargo was becoming almost certain. For economists, the important thing is that the embargo lasted long enough to see if what theory would predict actually happened. With a trade embargo, the prices of exported goods should fall dramatically as domestic supply increases. On the other side, prices of goods being imported should have risen. Overall, the embargo should have caused a contraction in U.S. GDP. Irwin (2005) has shown that the predictions matched what actually happened. Only four commodities (raw cotton, tobacco, flour, and rice) accounted for two-thirds of U.S. exports. The weighted average price of these commodities fell 27 percent in 1808. Imports were much more diversified, but their prices increased by over a third. Although the embargo never reached complete autarky, the import and export price changes were dramatic. So were the overall effects on the U.S. economy. Although such calculations are never precise, Irwin estimates that GDP in 1808 probably fell by 8 percent. Even for the 19th century when recessions were usually more severe than in modern times, this would have been a major recession. This brings up an interesting point about the embargo. Domestic manufacturers did not profit from it. Although competition from imports disappeared, the domestic economy collapsed. As a result, the embargo made manufacturers worse off in the short run. The research also reinforces the history of the embargo. It only lasted 14 months. The results of this natural experiment help to explain why this was so.

Tariffs as a Prelude to the Civil War

Up in Massachusetts we do not want that duty on molasses; we swap our fish for molasses, and if you shut out molasses you shut in fish.
— *Congressional Debate, 1828*

Moving past the dislocations of the War of 1812, U.S. trade policy entered a new phase that would last for over a century. The trade embargo and subsequent war exposed the dependence of the country on foreign manufacturing. This realization rekindled the debate that had begun as a result of the "Report on Manufactures." Tariffs began to climb as proponents of protectionism gained the necessary political power to obtain them. In the beginning, the support for protectionism was widespread. This trend continued well into the 20th century. For nearly 100 years there was little debate about the need for protectionism as a device to develop American industry. The only remaining debate concerned how high the tariff should be to accomplish this end. In the 21st century one frequently hears calls for increased protection of American industry. One should realize that this is hardly new in American history. From the War of 1812 to World War II, U.S. tariffs averaged 25 percent. In the majority of these years, the average tariff was over 40 percent. Today this would be considered a shocking level of protectionism. In the past it was merely routine. For most of U.S. history, protectionists have had the upper hand. Although the average tariff was high, significant trade policy disputes were still occurring.

One of the largest trade policy disputes in U.S. history focused on the height of the tariff after the War of 1812. As mentioned earlier, tariffs began to rise after the war. The dependence of the United States on foreign manufactures was made apparent by the war. The "Report on Manufactures" clearly showed that there was little support for direct subsidies to manufacturing as a means of enlarging that sector. That left the remaining policy response: tariffs. A consensus began to form that tariffs needed to be increased to support American manufacturing. The result was the first explicitly protectionist tariff. With the support of Henry Clay and John C. Calhoun, tariffs as high as 25 to 30 percent were established for products such as iron, cotton, and wool. The tariff was raised again in 1824 over the strong objections of Daniel Webster of Massachusetts, who urged the use of the tariff primarily for revenue. Part of the arguments by the protectionists was that U.S. exports were being discriminated against in foreign markets, which partially justified high U.S. tariffs. Quite correctly, Webster pointed out that there was a movement toward free trade in Britain, which was slowly reducing the problem. This is a good place to point out how important tariff issues and trade policy in general were in the 19th century. In the absence of military conflict and with a much more limited government then than now, for many years trade policy was the largest issue the government had to deal with. This debate over the 1824 tariff is a good example. Men who are still legendary senators were engaged in fierce debates over the tariff. In the modern world, such intense debates over trade policy occur, but they are rare.

Unfortunately, the 1824 tariff just set the stage for a much more serious dispute. In 1828, Congress passed the infamous Tariff of Abominations. The term *abominations* was warranted. It provided for the highest tariffs in U.S. history, even higher than the infamous Smoot-Hawley tariff 100 years later. The *average* tariff imposed on dutiable imports was 61.7 percent. The passage of the bill was, to a certain extent, a political miscalculation. It provided for high tariffs on finished manufactures, but also very high tariffs on intermediate imports. It was hoped that the latter provisions would deter support from Northern manufacturing interests and sink passage of the bill. John C. Calhoun and his supporters hoped that the bill would prove sufficiently distasteful to both protectionist Northern interests and the more free-trade–oriented Southern interests that it would not pass. The scheme failed, however, as the newer Western states voted heavily in favor the bill and overwhelmed the expected opposition in New England and the South. Although the scheme failed, it may have prevented the passage of even higher tariffs.

The Tariff of Abominations also starkly highlighted major differences in the economic interests of the North and the South. The majority of the Northern states and newer states in the West strongly supported high tariffs as a means of developing U.S. industry. Southern opposition was totally understandable in purely economic terms. As British exports declined, so, too, did imports of U.S. cotton. The quote beginning this section illustrates the effects on another sector of the economy. With a very small manufacturing sector, the Southern states were large importers of manufactured goods. With British goods now considerably more expensive, the alternative was even more expensive manufactured goods from the North. The potential economic damage to the South was large. In a situation eerily reminiscent of the aftermath of the Smoot-Hawley tariff, Congress realized it had made a mistake. In 1832 President Jackson signed a bill reducing some of the tariffs. However, some of the damage had already been done. In the Nullification Crisis, South Carolina threatened to not enforce the tariffs on the basis that they were unconstitutional as they favored one region of the country over another. The crisis passed, but tariffs would be a bone of contention between the North and the South until the beginning of the Civil

War. One should not overstate the importance of the tariff as a cause of the eventual conflict. However, it is also a mistake to think it did not matter. In a country split by a larger issue, sectional differences over trade policy were not a factor that tended to increase national solidarity.

In a sense, the Tariff of Abominations seemed to teach the country a valuable lesson about trade policy. There was a national consensus that protection was needed to develop domestic industry. However, there were limits to the exercise of this policy. Tariffs create winners and losers, and no one should be surprised if an extremely high tariff elicits a strong response from industries and/or regions where the losses are concentrated. The aftermath of the Tariff of Abominations is a perfect example. By 1832, Congress had begun a long process of lowering the tariff. Legislation provided for a gradual lowering of the tariff over 10 years. With a political change in 1846, Congress and the president again lowered the tariff. Tariffs resurfaced as an issue as both the Southern states and agricultural interests preferred low tariffs and a revenue tariff instead of a protective tariff. In particular there was concern that the tariff was unfairly favoring some sectors of the economy over others. The lower tariff was particularly effective because it stimulated imports and actually increased government revenue. The tariff was lowered once again in 1857. This lower tariff was partially a response to a change in thinking in Britain that was leading to lower levels of protection. Britain had finally repealed the "Corn Laws" that provided protection for domestic producers of basic grains. By lowering protection for landowners, the British government decided that the losses to poor urban consumers were more important. In a sense, the Tariff of 1857 was a crude form of reciprocity. The move to less protection was soon lost as a result of the Civil War. As the Southerners left Congress, Northern industrial interests quickly prevailed and tariffs were raised. This was not the last increase, however, as the Union needed even more money to finance the cost of the war.

Trade Policy in the Civil War

The Civil War was a devastating event for the United States, but it is an interesting exercise in trade policy. As the Southern states broke off from the Union, it was necessary to rewrite a constitution. Because trade policy had been a bone of contention between the North and the South, the creation of a constitution for the South allowed for a sort of natural experiment to see what the South would do freed from the constraints of national politics.

Article I, Section 8 of the Constitution of the Confederate States of America provides the answer. The key information it contains is "nor shall any duties or taxes on importations from foreign nations be laid to promote or foster any branch of industry."

Thus the tariff was a uniform tariff of 10 percent. Clearly Southern sentiment was for a low tariff that did not provide special protection for manufacturing. On the export side, the Confederacy pinned its hopes on the ability to finance the war via exports of cotton. This inability to finance the government through tariff revenue led the Confederate government to print excessive amounts of paper currency to finance expenditures. As usual, the result was a ruinous level of inflation in the South. Despite raising tariffs, the North also found it necessary to print paper currency. However, because the North was still gathering tariff revenue, the resulting money creation and inflation were much smaller. The Union blockade of ports drastically reduced earnings from Southern exports. On the import side, the South found it continually difficult to import essential military supplies. Although trade between the two warring parties was illegal, a substantial illicit trade occurred all through the war.

A final effect of international trade during the war was the effect on the composition of Southern imports. As detailed by Ekelund and Thronton (2001), the embargo created a perverse pattern of imports. Essential military supplies were in chronically short supply as a result of the embargo. However, "luxury" items imported from Europe were freely available. All through the war, this was a puzzle in the South. This situation was extreme enough that it was a source of lower morale too. A bit of economic logic easily solves the puzzle. Blockade runners were profit-maximizing businesses. To successfully run the blockade, it was necessary to use smaller and thus faster boats. Military supplies, such as gunpowder, are cheap but bulky. In the jargon of economics, they are goods with a low value-to-weight ratio. They are usually hauled by large, slow boats, which would have been more easily captured in the blockade. The rational response of the blockade runners was to ship luxury goods, which normally have a high value-to-weight ratio. This made the blockade much more effective. It was not necessary to capture a lot of ships. Forcing blockade runners to use smaller, faster ships was accomplishing the objective.

Trade Policy in the Post–Civil War Era

Going past the disaster of the Civil War, U.S. trade policy entered a fairly tranquil era. As we will see, Congress changed the tariff frequently during the end of the Civil War to the start of the Great Depression. However, the changes were to a certain extent just an extension of the domestic political process. In the second half of the 19th century the political landscape had become recognizable to modern Americans. There was a firm two-party system composed of Democrats and Republicans. Then, as now, on some issues each party had a distinct bias. In the late 19th century each party had a consistent view of international trade policy. Following the Civil War, the Southern Democrats maintained their affinity for lower tariffs. The country was still heavily agricultural, and this sector of the economy was dominated by those in favor of lower tariffs and freer international trade. The Republican Party, on the other hand, was staunchly protectionist. Their backing came from industrialists and workers in protected industries. This was in general true. However, each party contained elements that deviated from the general stance of the other party on trade. Another way of putting this is that each party was not exactly homogeneous in their opinions of international trade. Further, trade policy was still important. The government obtained most of its revenue from tariffs so the tariff was also bound up in the larger issues of the government's finances. Although the average tariff in this period was declining, it was not a smooth, continuous descent. Even with a limited government, a growing nation necessitated an ever larger and more costly government to perform basic functions. The result was a series of compromises between the two parties on tariffs that would satisfy the need for revenue, placate several influential interest groups, and not cause excessive damage to the welfare of consumers. Results of a study by Irwin (2007) indicate that the tariff policy may have accomplished this. Using data from 1885, he estimates that the tariff was redistributing less than 10 percent of GDP. Consumers were losing 4 percent of GDP, and import-competing industries were gaining 3.3 percent. Tariffs had the usual costs and benefits, but the results were not dramatic.

The issue became more contentious in the late 19th century. The United States had become the world's largest and most efficient economy. Given these circumstances, President Grover Cleveland in 1887 launched a blistering attack on high tariffs. A battle ensued over tariffs that would last through successive administrations for the next 20 years. This also represented the high-water mark of international trade policy as a political issue. Presidential and congressional campaigns were fought, won, and lost on the issue of the tariff. For good reason, the consensus on protectionism that marked much of the 19th century was dying. A combination of market size, industrial capacity, and low unit labor costs had given the United States both the ability to export and little fear of imports from more efficient competitors. The argument was now back to protectionism versus a revenue tariff. However, protectionism was no longer obviously necessary. This extremely contentious period ended with the election of Woodrow Wilson in 1912. With complete Democratic control of the government, tariffs were swiftly lowered. These low tariffs held, with the notable exception of an increase necessary to fund U.S. involvement in World War I. The return of Republican administrations in the 1920s led to slightly higher tariffs but in the context of the early 21st century they could not be considered extreme. The period from 1880 to 1912, where tariffs both were extremely contentious and were a major political issue, had come to an end.

Globalization: A History

When one considers the term globalization, it usually has a time dimension. In the 21st century we usually associate globalization with the increasing amount of trade occurring in the world. Also, we normally tend to think of a somewhat smooth and continuous process occurring over decades. This is true in a modern sense, but did globalization exist prior to modern times? Economic historians are certain that it did. However, there is some contention about the form that it took. One view is that globalization has been with us stretching back to antiquity. One can make a legitimate argument from historical records that globalization goes back 5,000 years. In a sense, this is definitely true. However, the extent of this trade was small relative to modern times. A second view is that globalization was like a "big bang" that started around 1500 and was powered by two events. The first was Christopher Columbus stumbling into the Western Hemisphere in a search for spices in the Far East. The second was the completion of the journey around the tip of Africa by Vasco de Gama in 1498. This ended the centuries-old overland spice trade from Asia to Europe. Both events triggered a large increase in trade that changed the world economy. However, the extent to which this increase in trade affected the world economy is a matter of debate. It ranges from the profound to the view that although it was important, it did not change the life of the average person very much. A part of this view is that the transportation technology of the time—wooden sailing ships—made only the transportation of luxury goods profitable. A more recent view is that globalization really became significant for the world economy in the late 19th century. The development of the steamship changed the nature of world trade. Steamships caused a dramatic drop in the costs of transporting cheap and bulky commodities such as coal, grains, and oil. This affected U.S. trade policy because the costs of goods were dropping even in the absence of any changes in tariffs. The movement of these goods then both triggered a boom in the world economy at the time and produced permanent changes in the way the world economy works. O'Rourke and Williamson (2004) have shown that although the evidence on the first two propositions about globalization is questionable, the effects of the transportation revolution are not. As an aside, a significant component of modern globalization is the rapid transfer of information around the world. By the 1870s, much of the world was linked by telegraph. To a large extent, the steamship and the telegraph created the modern world economy.

The Smoot-Hawley Disaster

Moving into the second decade of the 20th century, tariffs were still a non-trivial political issue but they had moved to the back burner. The same Democratic versus Republican split on low or high tariffs still remained, but it was less prominent. The onset of the Great Depression in the late 1920s caused a resurfacing of the issue in the United States. Herbert Hoover was elected president in 1928 on a campaign promise to increase the tariff on agricultural products. On election, Hoover sent Congress a bill requesting such an increase, but coupled with a decrease in tariffs on manufactured goods. From there, things went badly wrong as outlined by Irwin (2011). Two Republican leaders in the Senate and the House, respectively, were Reed Smoot and Willis C. Hawley. Separate versions were passed in both the House and the Senate that raised tariffs on agricultural and industrial products in 1929. In reconciling the two versions, tariffs were raised to the higher levels in the House version. A substantial amount of "log rolling" occurred as votes for higher tariffs on some items were traded for higher tariffs on other items. The result was a tariff bill that included rates only barely lower than the Tariff of Abominations 100 years earlier. The whole process of the bill winding its way through Congress took over a year, and there was a substantial amount of resistance. In early 1930, over 1,000 economists signed a petition opposing it. A number of prominent business and financial leaders went to the White House to personally argue that President Hoover should veto the bill, as his opposition to it was well known. Further, he had made a commitment to international cooperation, which the bill would soon destroy. In the end, he signed the bill under pressure from his party. The retaliation from U.S. trading partners was more than swift. Even before the bill was passed, the government had received threats of retaliation from nearly two dozen countries. Our largest trading partner, Canada, reacted immediately with higher tariffs on U.S. exports. Other retaliatory measures were soon to follow. Effectively the result was a global trade war where the majority of countries were increasing their tariffs in retaliation for rising tariffs in their trading partners. Rather than a unilateral increase in tariffs that occurred in isolation, the United States had fired the first shot in what was to become a global trade war.

The relationship between Smoot-Hawley and the Great Depression is complex. One sometimes hears the erroneous opinion that it was the primary cause of the Great Depression. In the main, the Great Depression was caused by a financial crisis that led to a serious contraction in the banking system and an inappropriate monetary policy response. Smoot-Hawley did not cause the Great Depression, but it clearly made a bad situation worse. Initially, the high tariffs seemed to work as industrial production and payrolls increased, but the effects were short lived. From 1929 to 1933, imports decreased 66 percent from $4.4 billion to $1.5 billion. On the other hand, retaliation took a toll. Exports decreased 61% from $5.4 billion to $2.1 billion. Not all of these declines can be traced to higher tariffs. GDP also was falling substantially as the global depression took hold. This means that not all of the fall in trade was due to higher tariffs. Madsen (2001) has estimated the effects on trade that were the result of higher tariffs and the effects of the fall in GDP due to the Depression He estimates that world trade during the Depression declined by about a third. Nearly half of this decline was related to the decline in world GDP. Eight percent of the decline was increases in tariff rates, and another 6 percent is attributable to increases in nontrade barriers (NTBs). Because of deflation, effective tariffs increased and accounted for 5 percent of the decline. Many of the tariffs incorporated into Smoot-Hawley were specific tariffs, and the ad valorem rate increased as prices fell. A more cautious analysis indicates that Smoot-Hawley did not cause the Great Depression, but it was a part of the severity. In any event, the public seemed to understand the damage. Senator Smoot, Congressman Hawley, and Herbert Hoover all lost their bids for reelection in 1932. Franklin Roosevelt campaigned on a promise to lower tariffs. Although the Roosevelt administration did not lower tariffs substantially, it did overhaul U.S. trade policy in a way that still has an influence in the 21st century.

The Fundamental Reform of Trade Policy

With the elections of 1930 and 1932, the Republican majority that had passed Smoot-Hawley changed to a strong Democratic majority. As one would expect, this led to a major change in U.S. trade policy. As Irwin (1998) points out, Congress did not really "learn" from the mistake of Smoot-Hawley. The change occurred primarily because of a change in which party was controlling the government. However, the changes that were to come were much more fundamental than the tinkering with tariffs that had been prevalent in the late 19th and early 20th centuries. The Smoot-Hawley tariffs had ignited a global trade war. This had inflicted major damage on U.S. exporters. A new form of trade policy needed to be constructed that would not only lower U.S. tariffs, but also lead to a reduction in foreign trade barriers. What was necessary was not just the unilateral changes in tariffs by Congress, but a policy that would negotiate lower trade barriers in other countries. The new policy took time to formulate. The Roosevelt administration was initially concerned with legislation designed to foster a recovery in the domestic economy. Because trade policy was contentious, the political decision was made to delay the introduction of what was then a radically new form of trade policy.

Prior to this time, the trade policy in the form of the setting of tariffs was a jealously guarded prerogative of Congress. To some extent, the problem was that the tariff was the main source of revenue for the government until the 1920s. As tariffs became less important for revenue purposes, there was more flexibility in setting the tariff to obtain other objectives, such as the opening up of foreign markets. There also was the problem that the results of a trade negotiation constituted a treaty that needed a two-thirds majority in the Senate to pass. However, without much notice to Congress in 1923 the U.S. government moved to a policy of unconditional most favored nation. This meant that the lowest tariff charged any country would be charged to all. Prior to this, MFN status was only conferred on a strictly reciprocal basis. This was rare because until the post–World War II era, the United States signed few major trade agreements. The accidental combination of the reduction of the importance of tariff revenues and use of unconditional MFN helped set the stage for a new era in U.S. trade policy.

What was needed was a policy that would not just change U.S. tariffs unilaterally, but also would reduce both U.S. and foreign tariffs at the same time. In early 1933, President Roosevelt announced his intention to seek congressional authority to engage in trade negotiations. The Reciprocal Trade Agreements Act (RTAA) was introduced in early 1934. RTAA gave the president the authority to negotiate trade agreements with other countries, and the agreements did not have the status of treaties. This was important because it reduced the votes needed for approval from two-thirds to a simple majority. The president was authorized to negotiate for a period of three years, but the negotiating authority had to be periodically renewed. The results of trade negotiations, coupled with unconditional MFN, meant that if the United States lowered tariffs for any country, tariffs would automatically be cut for all countries. The basics of RTAA set the stage for all future U.S. trade policy. In general, there is a sequence of events. The president requests authority from Congress to negotiate. For many years, this was referred to as "fast track" legislation. Since 1974, the formal term has been Trade Promotion Authority (TPA). Once the president has this authorization, the negotiations between the United States and another country or countries can commence. The finished agreement is then brought back to Congress for final approval with no amendments allowed. The lack of amendments is necessary to allow the negotiators to proceed, but it does not exclude Congress from the process. Any administration must be extremely careful in the negotiating process to produce an agreement that will obtain congressional approval. Frequently, there are complaints that the negotiations are lengthy. The time taken in negotiations is partially a function of getting an agreement that can obtain the necessary majority in Congress. Since 1934, RTAA has been the fundamental legislation governing U.S. trade policy. It marked a dramatic change from congressional leadership in trade policy to executive branch leadership with oversight by Congress. Although the responsibility for trade policy in the United States is more diffused than in many countries, it has allowed the country to move past the endless tinkering with tariffs and the inability to sign trade agreements that were the hallmarks of trade policy before 1934.

RTAA was a conceptual milestone in U.S. trade policy, but the timing of its passage was unfortunate. The world economy was just beginning to recover from the Great Depression. Understandably, the focus of the governments of the major trading nations was on domestic recovery, and trade negotiations were not at the top of the agenda. In spite of this challenge, the United States signed trade agreements with 21 countries covering 60 percent of U.S. trade. Under the circumstances, this was no small accomplishment and provided institutional knowledge of trade negotiations that was in short supply prior to RTAA. One of the interesting features of RTAA was that negotiating authority was vested in the executive branch but it was unclear which department would take the lead in negotiations. The State, Commerce, and Treasury Departments could all claim to have a stake in trade negotiations. The interesting battle that ensued was between the president's chief adviser on foreign trade, George N. Peck, and Secretary of State Cordell Hull. The fight turned out to be more important than a simple government turf battle. Peck was suspicious of the timing of tariff cuts, as he was concerned about the effects on the economy and farmers in particular. Operating from the State Department, Hull was more insulated from domestic economic pressures and was more focused on the foreign policy and broad economic benefits of trade agreements. The result was that without a formal mandate, the State Department was responsible for U.S. trade policy until 1962. The events surrounding the outbreak of World War II put trade negotiations in the background until late in the war. However, the basic outlines of U.S. trade policy had been worked out in the 1930s. This timing was fortunate, as it laid the groundwork for the substantial liberalization of global trade that was to come in the postwar era.

Case Study: Henry George on Protectionism

The U.S. economist Henry George (1839–1897) is best known for his proposed single tax on land. However, he was also an eloquent critic of protectionism in an age when it was rampant. The following are some of his better quotes concerning the folly of protectionism collected by Harriss (1989):

"It might be to the interests of [lighting] companies to restrict the number and size of windows, but hardly to the interests of a community. Broken limbs bring fees to surgeons, but would it profit a municipality to prohibit the removal of ice from sidewalks in order to encourage surgery? Economically, what difference is there between restricting the importation of iron to benefit iron-producers and restricting sanitary improvements to benefit undertakers?"

"If to prevent trade were to stimulate industry and promote prosperity, then the localities where he was most isolated would show the first advances of man. The natural protection to home industry afforded by rugged mountain-chains, by burning deserts, or by seas too wide and tempestuous for the frail bark of the early mariner would have given us the first glimmerings of civilization and shown its most rapid growth. But, in fact, it is where trade could best be carried on that we find wealth first accumulating and civilization beginning. It is on accessible harbors, by navigable rivers and much traveled highways that we find cities arising and the arts and sciences developing."

"To have all the ships that left each country sunk before they could reach any other country would, upon protectionist principles, be the quickest means of enriching the whole world, since all countries could then enjoy the maximum of exports with the minimum of imports."

"What protection teaches us, is to do to ourselves in time of peace what enemies seek to do to us in time of war."

"However protection may affect special forms of industry it must necessarily diminish the total return to industry-first by the waste inseparable from encouragement by tariff, and second by the loss due to transfer of capital and labor from occupations which they would choose for themselves to less profitable occupations which they must be bribed to engage in. If we do not see this without reflection, it is because our attention is engaged with but a part of the effects of protection. We see the large smelting-works and the massive mill without realizing that the same taxes which we are told have built them up have made more costly every nail driven and every needle full of thread used throughout the whole country."

Bibliography

Eckes, Alfred E., Jr. 1995. *Opening America's Market: U.S. Foreign Trade Policy Since 1776*. Chapel Hill, NC: University of North Carolina Press.

Ekelund, Robert B. and Mark Thornton. 2001. "The Confederate Blockade of the South," *Quarterly Journal of Austrian Economics* 4(1): 23–42.

Harriss, C. Lowell. 1989. "Guidance from an Economics Classic: The Centennial of Henry George's 'Protection or Free Trade," *American Journal of Economics and Sociology* 48(3): 351–56.

Irwin, Douglas A. 1998. "From Smoot-Hawley to Reciprocal Trade Agreements: Changing the Course of U.S. Trade Policy in the 1930s," in Michael D. Bordo, Claudia Goldin, and Eugene N. White (eds.), *The Defining Moment: The Great Depression and the American Economy in the Twentieth Century*. Chicago: University of Chicago Press.

Irwin, Douglas A. 2003. "New Estimates of the Average Tariff of the United States, 1790–1820," *Journal of Economic History* 63(2): 506–13.

Irwin, Douglas A. 2004. "The Aftermath of Hamilton's 'Report on Manufactures,'" *Journal of Economic History* 64(3): 800–21.

Irwin, Douglas A. 2005. "The Welfare Cost of Autarky: Evidence from the Jeffersonian Trade Embargo, 1807–09," *Review of International Economics* 13(4): 631–45.

Irwin, Douglas A. 2007. "Tariff Incidence in America's Gilded Age," *Journal of Economic History* 67(3): 582–607.

Irwin, Douglas A. 2011. *Peddling Protectionism: Smoot–Hawley and the Great Depression*. Princeton, NJ: Princeton University Press.

Lovett, William A., Alfred E. Eckes, Jr., and Richard L. Brinkman. 2004. *U.S. International Trade Policy: History, Theory, and the WTO*. New York: M. E. Sharpe.

Madsen, Jakob B. 2001. "Trade Barriers and the Collapse of World Trade during the Great Depression," *Southern Economic Journal* 67(4): 848–68.

O'Rourke, Kevin H. and Jeffrey G. Williamson. 2004. "Once More: When Did Globalization Begin?," *European Review of Economic History* 8(1): 109–17.

Reyes, Javier A. and W. Charles Sawyer. 2015. *Latin American Economic Development*. 2nd ed. London: Routledge.

Toll, Ian W. 2008. *Six Frigates: The Epic History of the Founding of the U.S. Navy*. New York: W.W. Norton.

CHAPTER SEVEN

U.S. Trade Policy in the Postwar Era

When goods don't cross borders, soldiers will.

—*Frederic Bastiat*

Introduction

As we will show in this chapter, history matters. Following on the heels of the last chapter, we now move into the more recent history of U.S. trade policy. The most recent news on trade policy in the United States frequently contains veiled references to terms and historical events that it is assumed the reader has some familiarity with. For example, one might easily have encountered terms or phrases such as Bretton Woods, GATT, the Uruguay Round, VER, or others. Modern trade policy is a complex mix of legislation and tendencies going back to the founding of the government. However, it is something like an adaptive expectations process. Adaptive expectations is the idea that what you expect to happen is like a weighted average of what has happened in the past. However, events in the more recent past have a higher weight than events in the more distant past. U.S. trade policy is very much like that. Trade policy from the 18th and 19th centuries still affects contemporary trade policy. However, the more recent past has a far heavier weight that began with the passage of the Reciprocal Trade Agreements Act (RTAA). In this chapter, we consider the trade policy events that occurred in the 20th century that have a heavy influence on current policy. In order to do this, we will first consider the birth of the General Agreement on Tariffs and Trade (GATT). The creation of GATT set up a framework that allowed a large number of countries to simultaneously reduce tariffs. From there, the GATT broadened its approach to cover the increasingly prevalent nontariff barriers to trade. This was accomplished through a series of large multilateral trade negotiations (MTNs). However, the ability of GATT to enforce international trade rules was severely limited by its structure. In the late 20th century, this led to the creation of the World Trade Organization, (WTO) which has enforcement capabilities that GATT lacked. In the 21st century the ability of countries to reduce trade barriers further via MTNs seems severely diminished. This is leading to a new wave of bilateral or Regional Trade Agreements that seem to represent the future of trade liberalization. In this chapter we will work through these issues in order to allow you to make more sense of what you may be reading and hearing. The material is not "hard" in a technical sense, but it is essential background material to be able to understand modern trade policy.

The Birth of GATT

> *The purpose of the whole effort is to eliminate economic warfare, to make practical international co-operation effective on as many fronts as possible, and so to lay the economic basis for the secure and peaceful world we all desire.*
> —Franklin D. Roosevelt

The catastrophe of World War II brought international trade negotiations to a global halt. Despite the turmoil of the war, some thought was still being given to recovering from the trade policy disasters of the 1930s. Both the U.S. and the UK governments felt that the trade policies following World War I tended to be focused on a "beggar thy neighbor" approach to trade. This view is a variant of the mercantilist approach to trade covered in Chapter 3. Countries pursuing this policy are attempting to shut out imports to improve domestic economic conditions while simultaneously making their trading partners poorer. As the quote at the beginning of the chapter indicates, such policies are not conducive to good relations between countries. The founders of the post–World War II international economic order were very mindful of this. This is easy to forget in the 21st century. To be clear, trade restrictions were not the cause of the two world wars. However, much like the U.S. Civil War, trade barriers in many cases were not exactly improving international relations. The result was that in the 1940s and 1950s, trade liberalization was thought to be a necessary condition for regional or world peace. It also works. Countries that trade extensively with each other rarely go to war. Each side simply has too much to lose. The problem was finding a way forward to accomplish broad-based reductions in tariffs to roll back the increases of the 1930s. The tariff escalation of the Great Depression was large and global. As a result, the bilateral trade negotiations that were the standard prior to World War II were not going to yield significant progress over any reasonable time frame. The practical manifestation of this was the Atlantic Charter negotiated between the United States and the United Kingdom in 1941. Although the agreement had no practical significance in the short run, it committed both countries to pursuing trade liberalization policies that were much more broadly based than had been historically the case. The United States was committed to liberalization. As the world's largest economy, the government realized that the rest of the world could only recover if there was some access to the vast U.S. market. For this to occur under unconditional most favored nation (MFN), it was going to be necessary to negotiate trade agreements that involved reciprocity from many countries of the world.

The practical formation of GATT was begun in 1944. The United States and the United Kingdom had conceived of a grand plan to create institutions that would help to generate postwar prosperity on a global basis as opposed to each country pursuing purely national economic interests. The creation of these institutions was the goal of the famous Bretton Woods conference in New Hampshire. The conference created two out of the three institutions. The first order of business was formulating a new international monetary system. The classic gold standard had collapsed under the pressures of the Great Depression. Virtually all governments wanted a return to a fixed exchange-rate system, but realized a return to the gold standard was not feasible. As outlined by Steil (1994) the solution was a fixed exchange-rate system with the dollar tied to gold and all other currencies fixed to the dollar. Unlike the gold standard, such a system was not automatic and had to be "managed." The International Monetary Fund (IMF) was set up to manage this dollar-exchange standard. It made short-term loans to countries with temporary current account deficits in exchange for changes in economic policy that would correct those imbalances. The second task was to build an institution that would provide financing for the postwar reconstruction of the countries of Europe and Asia. This involved the establishment of the International Bank for Reconstruction and Development, which is usually referred to as the World Bank. As opposed to the IMF, it primarily makes long-term loans for infrastructure projects. There was supposed to be another institution created at Bretton Woods. There was a strong desire to create an institution that would both subject international trade to a set of rules and police the world trading system. Until this time, the world trade system was virtually a free-fire zone where countries were free to pursue policies that were in their own national interests. With the global economy under the massive stress of the Great Depression, the logic of this led to rampant "beggar thy neighbor" policies that severely damaged world trade and left no one better off. The lesson learned was that the world economy badly needed, as Dam (2001) put it, rules of the game. The process of obtaining both the rules and the organization to enforce the rules has not been easy. The basic idea was to set up an organization to be known as the International Trade Organization (ITO). However, it soon became clear that remaking the world trading system was a more formidable task than setting up new financial institutions such as the IMF or the World Bank. This actually makes sense. The establishment of the IMF simply was a return to the familiar world of fixed exchange rates. In a sense, governments just returned to a different version of the international monetary system that had been in existence prior to the 1930s. The establishment of the World Bank likewise was not much of a change. Governments had been borrowing money for infrastructure projects for centuries. The World Bank simply made this process more accessible for a larger group of countries.

The process of establishing the ITO involved a radical change in the way governments conducted trade policy. In the past, countries were free to set whatever trading arrangements that they felt would maximize national welfare. In a sense this was necessary as the correlation between tariff revenue and total government revenue was very high. Governments naturally needed the freedom to raise and lower tariffs to cover variations in the cost of even running limited governments. By the 1940s, this link between tariff revenue and total government revenue was being broken. Trade policy now was becoming a branch of a more general industrial policy. Every country has some form of explicit or implicit industrial policy designed to affect the composition of industry in a country. Obviously, trade policy can be a powerful tool of industrial policy. Trade policy was becoming less important for revenue purposes, but it was becoming much more important in terms of economic development. This set up an obvious clash between domestic economic policy and establishing a new world trading order. Membership in virtually any international organization entails a loss of sovereignty. Organizations have rules. A country's membership in an organization implies that in that area the rules of the organization supersede domestic law. Effectively, governments lose sovereignty in a particular area as a result of membership in the international organization. In some cases, the loss of sovereignty may be small or the rules of the organization are close to the rules that the country would have adopted in any case. In the case of trade policy, the loss of sovereignty is possibly large and the rules may be substantially different from what the country would prefer. Thus the process of getting to a multilateral trading system was both long and difficult. The whole process eventually was to take over 50 years.

As outlined by Irwin, et al. (2008), the genesis of the GATT occurred in the middle of World War II. Despite the exigencies of dealing with the war, the British and American governments already were planning the creation of a new trading system. The GATT first was conceived in the United Kingdom in the early years of the war. In 1941, a British civil servant, R. J. Shackle, working at the Board of Trade, wrote a memorandum advocating a number of international economic issues that needed to be addressed after the war. This is strategic thinking at its best. At this point, it was unclear exactly who was going to win the war. Only someone with almost hopeless optimism and a clear vision would have even been thinking along these lines. Part of his memorandum advocated a new multilateral trading system free of the old system of bilateral agreements and trade preferences. At the time, it was a truly radical idea. However, it was just an idea. As the memorandum circulated in the Board of Trade, it aroused the interest of James Meade. What Meade did was to take Shackle's general idea and transform it into something more operational. In the usual way of bureaucracies, he wrote a memorandum to a memorandum entitled "Proposal for an International Customs Union." In the memorandum, Meade recommended an organization with open membership, no discrimination against other members, and to eliminate very restrictive forms of protectionism. He also recommended some type of enforcement mechanism for the organization. Meade's proposal met with general approval, and it moved up the bureaucratic ladder at the Board of Trade. Despite facing opposition from the Treasury Department, the proposal became the British basis for a vision of an open postwar trading system. Now the problem became one of selling it to the Americans. The solution to that problem occurred in the second half of 1943. From September to October of 1943, a delegation from the United Kingdom met with their U.S. counterparts in Washington, D.C. The negotiations were a complex mix of trade policy and international monetary relations issues. There were major differences of opinion on the monetary side that were not settled until the Bretton Woods conference. The trade policy debate was more about the details of an agreement. Both the United Kingdom and the United States were committed to a more open world trading system. The disagreements were over how to get there. Both the debate and the solutions are worth reviewing because trade policy in the 21st century is changing in a way that would have been familiar to negotiators from both sides.

Of the two sides, the British were more committed to liberalizing trade using a true multilateral system of trade negotiations. The economists involved on the British side comprised a truly stunning group. It included James Meade, Lionel Robbins, and John Maynard Keynes. Their views were not uniform. Meade and Robbins were much more comfortable with the idea of reducing barriers to trade than was Keynes. Keynes was wary over the idea of liberalized trade for an interesting reason. Keynes was involved with both the trade and monetary issues of building a new postwar international economic order. Unlike his colleagues, he was concerned about the postwar balance of payments situation of the United Kingdom and the overall macroeconomic situation the country would face after the war. Being very concerned about the latter, he was not sure if a much more liberalized trading system would be compatible with full employment after the war. Keynes was not alone. One of the driving forces for all countries involved in the process was the fear of the world economic situation after the war. Historically, the end of wars brought about an economic contraction. In the United States, the recession that followed World War I was a case in point. Policy makers on both sides of the Atlantic were extremely concerned about the possibility of a return of the depression after the war. As a result, Keynes had a not illegitimate concern that liberalizing trade at too fast a rate might have adverse macroeconomic consequences in the short run. Also, in a more general way, Keynes was not as committed to free trade as were some of his colleagues. However, the entire delegation was committed to multilateral trade negotiations. They also were committed to state trading, which is a very 21st-century economic issue. In addition, the British were deeply committed to maintaining trade preferences for current and former colonies. This issue will reappear later in the guise of trade preferences, not for colonies, but for developing countries in general. The British were committed to trade liberalization but with some significant exceptions. The American position was not as complicated because the U.S. economy was more market oriented and colonial entanglements were few. The British and American views were different on two main points. First, multilateral negotiations were a radically new form of trade negotiations. The Americans were ready to negotiate, but were much more comfortable with a traditional bilateral approach. Notice that in the 21st century, the United States has returned to bilateral negotiations. Historically, what followed may have been the exception and not the rule. Second, the United States was very much opposed to the idea of preferences. The Americans were in favor of unconditional MFN and felt colonial preferences might lead to other deviations from MFN. However, at the end of the conference both countries had agreed on the broad outlines of a postwar process of liberalizing trade on a multilateral basis. Given that such strategic negotiations were occurring in the middle of a global war, this was no small accomplishment.

Despite coming to a general agreement on liberalizing trade, little else was accomplished over the next year. Although many in the British government were in favor of liberalizing trade in principle, it was considered risky. This was true because of the perceived financial fragility of the British economy. The end of the war brought political changes to both the United Kingdom and the United States. The result was that in both countries, the movement to liberalized trade slowed to a crawl. As is usually the case, international trade issues are virtually never at the top of any country's agenda. In a move from war to peace coupled with changes in government in the United Kingdom, it is more than understandable that trade policy was put on hold. This was less true in the United States. Although there were political changes, they were more changes in leadership than changes in basic policy. The U.S. government, particularly the State Department, was still pushing for postwar trade liberalization. The United Kingdom and the United States finally reached an agreement on their differences in an unfortunate way. As the war ended, the Truman administration abruptly ended financial aid to the British. For the United Kingdom, this was a catastrophic event. At that point, there was no way the British economy could pay for necessary imports of food and fuel without external assistance. To prevent an economic collapse, it was essential for the country to be able to obtain loans from the United States. To this end in late 1945, the British Treasury Department dispatched a delegation to the United States to obtain temporary funding. Of course, the British delegation included John Maynard Keynes. Noticeably absent from the delegation were Meade and Robbins. This was important as everyone understood that there would be no agreement on financing for the United Kingdom in the absence of an agreement on liberalizing trade. The end result was that both sides got part of what they wanted. On the British side, they ended up with an American commitment to multilateral trade. The Americans were unable to obtain an end to British colonial preferences. However, the British were willing to reduce these preferences if the Americans were willing to substantially reduce tariffs. There were other issues to negotiate, such as cartels, subsidies, and particularly agricultural policy. However the main agreements were reached. The United States would continue to support the United Kingdom financially. In addition, the two countries had reached an agreement on how to proceed toward a new multilateral trading system. Getting all of this done by December 1945 was no small accomplishment. It was at this point that what had been negotiated for over two years was released to the public. In the usual way of bureaucracies, the State Department released a document entitled "Proposals for Expansion of World Trade and Employment." This was clever marketing. How could anyone be against the expansion of both trade and employment? The bland title hid the outlines of a radically different trade policy, both for the United States and the world.

Keynes, Meade, and Robbins

In the earlier section, these three names crop up again and again. There is a reason for this. The most famous economist of the 20th century was John Maynard Keynes. He is best known in the United States for his path-breaking work in macroeconomics and his authorship of *The General Theory of Employment, Interest, and Money*. What is less well known is that from 1914 until his death in 1946, Keynes held a number of advisory posts in the British government. He was given these posts because he was good at it. In this regard, he made his reputation early. Keynes participated in the British delegation that helped draft the Treaty of Versailles. He was deeply critical of the treaty and wrote his criticisms in *The Economic Consequences of the Peace*. The book was an immediate best seller and made Keynes the most famous economist of the interwar years. Keynes was instrumental in setting up the postwar monetary system where his expertise was strongest. However, he frequently clashed with both Meade and Robbins because his commitment to free trade was much less pronounced. Unfortunately, we will never know how Keynes would have viewed the development of the world trading system as he died in 1946.

During the first half of the 20th century, most of the best economists in the world were in the United Kingdom. One could not find two better examples than James Meade and Lionel Robbins. In the 1930s, Meade studied economics at Oxford and Cambridge and later taught economics. After a brief stint at the League of Nations, he returned to the United Kingdom and worked for the government during the war and stayed until 1947. Meade then moved to the London School of Economics and wrote several books on international economics. One of the books helped earn him a Nobel Prize in Economics in 1977. What is much less well known about Meade is that one can argue that what eventually came to be the GATT was his early writings on a multilateral trading system. Although less distinguished than Meade, Lionel Robbins was a well-known economist. After serving as an officer in the British army, he studied at the London School of Economics and taught there for much of his career. His work with the British government on trade matters was just an interruption in a long academic career. The influence of Robbins is with us today. He was the first to advocate subsidizing students in higher education. He is also the author of the famous definition of economics: economics is the science that studies human behavior as a relationship between given ends and scarce means, which have alternative uses. Neither Meade nor Robbins could match the brilliance of Keynes. However, together their view of how the post–World War II international trading system should work prevailed.

The United States moved quickly once the general outline of a postwar trading system had been announced. In late 1945, the United States invited a number of countries to participate in negotiations to reduce tariffs. At the same time, the United States proposed negotiations to be held under the auspices of the newly formed United Nations (UN). The purpose of the UN group was to formulate a charter for the ITO that originally been envisioned by Meade. Because this would take some time, the United States pushed for a protocol to reduce tariffs and set up generally agreed-upon rules that eventually would become part of the ITO charter. This initial protocol was to eventually become the GATT. Domestic politics in the United States delayed further negotiations until November 1946. At that time, meetings were held in London on the new system that included countries other than the United Kingdom and United States. A subsequent meeting was held in the United States, which produced the first written draft of the GATT. This was necessary to prepare for the first round of tariff cuts that were negotiated in Geneva in April 1947. These tariff cuts were codified in a "Protocol of Provisional Application," which became the GATT. Notice the word provisional. The intention was that the document would become part of the ITO charter that was still being negotiated. Negotiations on the creation of the ITO continued and culminated in the "Havana Charter" for the ITO in 1948. This draft charter was ambitious in scope, covering trade, international trade in services, investment, and several other issues. Ultimately, it was too ambitious. In 1950, the United States announced that it would not participate in the ITO, which effectively killed it. By accident, the provisional document, or the GATT, became the basis for the postwar international trading system.

Under these circumstances, the GATT became by default a fallback position. It was never intended to be a comprehensive global agreement. It just became so by accident. Whatever the case, the GATT worked for over 50 years. Part of the success was due to simplicity. Because the GATT technically never was a formal organization, it never had members—only contracting parties. In order to be a contracting party, the rules were relatively simple. First, a country had to grant unconditional MFN status to all other contracting parties. Countries could still discriminate, just not against other contracting parties. Second, a contracting party could not use quotas as a means of protection. This did not mean that a country could not protect an industry. It simply meant that the protection had to be in the form of tariffs. Initially, the GATT had 23 members. By 1994, it had added exactly 100 members. Its simplicity partially accounted for its success. Countries could join by agreeing to two simple trading rules. Further, when a country joined, it was given a "reasonable" period of time for its trade policy to be in compliance with the GATT. By the 1980s, this transition period normally had become 15 years. For most countries, this meant they had 15 years to convert quota protection into tariff protection. The GATT was primarily composed of Organisation for Economic Co-operation and Development (OECD) nations. Over the years, participation by the developing countries grew.

The GATT Learning Curve

As outlined earlier, a multilateral trading system for the world was a radical departure from the way trade negotiations had occurred for hundreds of years. Historically, two countries would negotiate a purely bilateral trade agreement. As Dam (2001) has pointed out, GATT created "rules of the game" for global trade. But because there were no global "rules of the game" in the modern sense, international trade became a messy environment where countries were free to discriminate among trading partners and by product. Older trade agreements could cover any part of trade that the partners considered amenable. In such a world, tariff discrimination was the norm and not the exception to the rule. Even worse, countries were free to impose quotas on any product category where this was politically convenient. Mixing public choice with such a system resulted in the situation famously described by Henry George. He wrote this in 1886, and by the 1930s things obviously had not improved.

> To introduce a tariff bill into congress or parliament is like throwing a banana into a cage of monkeys. No sooner is it proposed to protect one industry than all industries that are capable of protection begin to screech and scramble for it.

With the adoption of GATT, there was a radical change or discontinuity in trade negotiations. GATT's contracting parties had to agree to unconditional MFN treatment of all other contracting parties. In the context of GATT, this is the nondiscrimination principle. Thus, a tariff cut made on one product became a tariff cut on that product for all contracting parties. Every country had a tariff schedule containing thousands of different tariff lines or product categories. At the original multilateral trade negotiation held in Geneva in 1947, the potential number of tariff cuts was bewilderingly large. One solution was for countries to announce overall cuts in tariffs. However, this flies in the face of reciprocity, which also is one of the main principles of the GATT. It is difficult for any country to cut tariffs without obtaining such concessions from other countries. As Paul Krugman

(1999) has pointed out, mercantilism still lives in trade negotiations. It would make perfect economic sense for a country to unilaterally adopt free trade. That would maximize a country's welfare. However, that is not going to happen. The world of trade negotiations fundamentally is mercantilist. Countries will only reduce trade barriers if another country will reduce its barriers. Even at the initial MTN, this was a formidable task with only 23 countries. Where to begin? As pointed out by Winters (1990) the trick is to realize that multilateral trade negotiations really involve a large number of *bilateral* negotiations. Where negotiations really start is in the time period before negotiations even begin. Virtually every country has a ministry or department of international trade. Invariably one of its functions is to promote exports. As a result, the ministry or department is in close communication with firms in the country that export. As a result of this relationship, the government will hear complaints about trade barriers in another country that are hampering exports. Indeed, most ministries will have a list of trade barriers in a number of foreign countries that its exporters find objectionable or unreasonable. Each country has a comparative advantage in some products and a comparative disadvantage in others. As a result of exporter complaints, governments are well aware of trade barriers in foreign markets that would boost exports by the largest amount. The government also is obviously aware of the comparative disadvantage of the country. This is where its own trade barriers are high. Thus, a trade negotiation becomes something like finding a dance partner. Each country's trade negotiator will arrive at an MTN armed with a list of trade barriers in foreign countries that it would be advantageous to reduce. The negotiator will seek out their counterpart in the country where a particular trade barrier for a particular product category is at the top of the list. The other country also has a similar list. The two countries can now negotiate. One country will liberalize in one product if the other country will liberalize in another product. The depth of the cut for either country will depend on the relative intensity of the country's desire to obtain better market access in the other country. In any case, both negotiators have an incentive to make tariff cuts. All countries are trying to help their exporters. The tariff cuts that are necessary to obtain these other tariff cuts will be in comparative-disadvantage industries. The negotiating strategy is then to try to maximize cuts for your comparative-advantage industries while minimizing cuts for your comparative-disadvantage industries. In the end, a bilateral negotiation has yielded tariff cuts in both countries that will expand both trade between the two countries and overall world trade. However, this is an example of a tariff cut on two different products in two countries. Keep in mind that the optimal tariff for a firm with a comparative advantage is zero. As a result, each negotiator may well be requesting tariff cuts for an individual product in every country in the negotiation that has a comparative disadvantage in that product. The list of desired tariff cuts for any trade negotiator for any country is quite lengthy. For large countries, the list is sufficiently large that negotiators may specialize. It must be kept in mind that negotiators have an external constraint. Any tariff cuts that they negotiate may have to be politically acceptable. The GATT and later the WTO have never made democracy a criterion for being a member of the international trading system. However, in a democratic system, trade liberalization becomes subject to the public choice constraints that were discussed in Chapter 5. The bargain a negotiator has made has to be acceptable in two senses. First, it must not just be a token cut, but a cut large enough to convince the domestic industry that it will be able to increase its exports. Second, the cuts made in comparative-disadvantage industries must not be so large as to substantially injure the industry in the short run. The ultimate decisions about the negotiations are normally made back in the country's capital and not on the front lines of the negotiations. As one can imagine, the volume of communications between the government and the trade negotiators is large. There may also be substantial communications between the government and industries that will be affected by the results of the trade negotiations. Trade negotiators may have set limits to their negotiations before they start, or they can constantly check their offers and the offers of their counterparts in the other country or some combination of the two. In any event, a multilateral trade negotiation is likely to be lengthy because the number of tariff concessions a country would like to receive for its comparative-advantage products is likewise lengthy. A final point is that the introduction of the modern tax systems is making such negotiations possible from the start. Prior to the 1920s, the situation we are describing would not have been possible due to revenue constraints. The large-scale reduction of tariffs around the world that occurred under the GATT fundamentally was made possible by the newer forms of tax revenue.

From this material, one might wonder why trade negotiations matter very much. The discussion would indicate that even a multilateral trade negotiation might not accomplish very much. Each country would request a few tariff cuts from another country. The obvious result is that the two countries would cut tariffs on a variety of products. This is where the GATT provision of unconditional MFN comes in to play. Suppose that country A reduces tariffs on a product to obtain a cut in country B. Country A has cut the tariff not just for country B but for all other contracting parties to the GATT. The same holds true for country B. It has not just cut the tariff for country A, but for many other countries as well. The result is what superficially looks like a tariff cut on two products for two countries compounded into a tariff cut for two products and all the contracting parties to the GATT. Prior to the GATT, bilateral trade agreements usually did not have much impact on world trade. However, what are essentially bilateral trade negotiations coupled with MFN can have a powerful effect on world trade. The first GATT MTN in Geneva in 1947 is a perfect example of this. At that time, only 23 countries were contracting parties. However, the negotiations yielded *45,000* tariff cuts. On face value, the numbers don't seem to add up. A bit of arithmetic solves the problem. Each tariff cut was applied to 23 countries. The division indicates that, on average, each country cut fewer than 2,000 tariffs. This seems to be a large number until one considers what was mentioned earlier. Each country has thousands of different tariffs. For example, the United States currently has over 12,000 tariffs. According to Irwin (1995), in this MTN, the United States cut tariffs on 50 percent of the products that had a tariff in place. The average tariff cut was 35 percent. One may have noticed a problem here. The way the tariff cuts are being negotiated, there is a very real problem of countries being free riders. For example, a country could theoretically participate in an MTN and offer no concessions to any other contracting party. It could sit on its hands, so to speak. In this case the country would still potentially benefit from the unconditional most favored nation (MFN) nature of the negotiations. In the early MTNs, this problem was dealt with by attempting to offer concessions on a principal supplier basis. This meant that countries would trade concessions on products for which they were the principal supplier for each other. However, this process can only be taken so far, and by the 1960s a new approach to concessions was devised.

Once the template was set in the first Geneva MTN, other MTNs quickly followed. The second MTN was held at Annecy, France, in 1949. Less was accomplished in this round. Only 13 countries participated, and the number of tariff cuts dropped to 5,000. The third MTN followed quickly in 1950. It was held in Torquay in the United Kingdom. Thirty-eight countries participated, and the result was 8,700 tariff cuts. After three quick initial MTNs understandably the fourth was held in 1956 in Geneva. The number of countries participating dropped to 26 and the amount of tariffs cut was relatively small. However, tariffs were not the major issue. The major issue was the entry of Japan into the GATT. Bringing such a large and important country back into the postwar international economy clearly was the most important accomplishment of this MTN. Even as late as 1956, some countries were still reluctant to readmit Japan to the world trading system. The fear at the time was the comparative advantage of Japan in textiles and apparel. Less than 60 years ago, Japanese exports looked like those of a successful developing country. The Dillon Round of 1960 was named after U.S. Secretary of State Douglas Dillon. Unfortunately, the number of countries participating dropped to 26. In addition, the amount of tariff cuts achieved was relatively small. The Dillon Round exposed the limits of what the original MTNs could accomplish. Countries were finding it harder to make tariff cuts that, in the words of J. Michael Finger (1979), could be internalized. What this meant was that it was becoming harder and harder to make tariff cuts that could be matched by cuts for principal suppliers. With this possibility diminishing, the negotiations were becoming more difficult. It was now necessary to find a different but still similar template for future MTNs.

The Major Multilateral MTNs

The solution to this problem came with the first "major" MTN, the Kennedy Round. It also was the first MTN to move past simple tariff reductions into new areas of international trade. Because the United States was the world's dominant economy at the time, its participation was critical. Another reason for the round was the emergence in the late 1950s of the European Economic Community (EEC), which would eventually become the European Union (EU). The fear in the United States at the time was that the formation of the EEC would cause a loss of exports to Europe. Congress authorized U.S. participation under the Trade Expansion Act of 1962. This MTN officially began in 1964 and was concluded in 1967. The length of the round indicates that it was more comprehensive than previous MTNs. Sixty-six countries participated in the Kennedy Round, which represented 80 percent of world trade. Tariff reductions were the primary focus, with the goal of reducing tariffs by 50 percent with a minimum of exceptions. This across-the-board strategy was an attempt to get around the product-by-product negotiations that seemed to be producing fewer and fewer results. This approach was not altogether successful. Although the major countries engaged in linear tariff cuts, 36 countries opted out of that system. This divide led to general tensions in the negotiations and contributed to the three years it took to negotiate. Despite these problems, the MTN achieved a 35 percent reduction in tariffs, except for chemicals, steel, textiles, and other sensitive products. Other items on the agenda did not prove to be as productive. World trade in agriculture has been in disarray since the formation of the GATT. The Kennedy Round was the first MTN that tried to address this issue. A 15 percent reduction was negotiated on agricultural tariffs, but many of the main trade-distorting agricultural policies remained in place. A third objective was the removal of nontariff barriers (NTBs) to trade. Because this issue was not really addressed, NTBs proliferated in the 1960s and 1970s. A final issue was an attempt to aid developing countries. This came in the form of Part IV of the GATT. It established the principle that developing countries accord reciprocity to developed countries in trade negotiations. Whether or not this was beneficial to the developing countries is still debated.

Moving from the Kennedy Round to the Tokyo Round is an example of the "bicycle theory" of international trade negotiations formulated by C. Fred Bergsten. The bicycle theory posits that international trade negotiations are like a bicycle in the sense that both must keep moving forward or they will stop. In the post–World War II world, the application of the bicycle theory went something along these lines. The process started when the U.S. Congress authorized the president to negotiate a trade agreement. The next step was the actual negotiations, such as the Tokyo Round. After the conclusion of the MTN, the tariff cuts would be phased in over a number of years. During this interim period, planning would begin for the next MTN. The plans for a new MTN would be presented to Congress to allow U.S. participation, and thus the process would continue. Bergsten's fear, and he was not alone, was that if the process ever stopped it might not restart. We will return to that thought but for now the process was running smoothly.

Of the major MTNs, there is almost always less said about Tokyo. The implication is that it was somehow a failure. It began in September 1973, and that was not an auspicious time to start. The very next month, there was a conflict in the Middle East, and the price of oil skyrocketed from $3 to $12 a barrel. The effect on the world economy was dramatic, and the macroeconomic fallout from this event lasted for years. Unlike the Kennedy Round, the Tokyo Round occurred not in an environment of global prosperity, but one of serious macroeconomic problems. The round ended in the summer of 1979 just before the second major oil shock hit the world economy. In the overall economic turbulence of the 1970s, it is easy to miss the Tokyo Round. Under the circumstances, it just didn't seem very important. However, that characterization is unfair. One hundred and two countries participated in the round, which is a substantial increase from the Kennedy Round. The accomplishments were not inconsequential. The first was a lowering of tariffs on tropical fruits and vegetables by the developed countries to increase exports from developing countries. Tariffs on industrial products by developed countries were reduced by an average of 34 percent. A new tariff-cutting formula was introduced that reduced the highest tariffs by a larger amount than for lower tariffs. The result of this was that the range of tariffs from high to low was reduced. One of the major achievements of the Tokyo Round was to shift the focus of negotiations in the direction of areas that are related to trade but are not tariffs. A number of changes were made to make the GATT more efficient and easier to work with. The sense of failure of the Tokyo Round comes from a number of agreements where there was not a general consensus. What followed was the development of "plurilateral" agreements among a minority of contracting parties. Four of these agreements were negotiated with regard to government procurement, civil aircraft, bovine meat, and dairy products. The first two agreements are still in force, and the last two were terminated in 1997. The agreement on civil aircraft has been useful in reducing the acrimonious trade disputes that were once routine in the aircraft trade. The agreement on government procurement has not been as successful. Viewed as a whole, one can argue that the Tokyo Round was a success. Large tariff cuts were negotiated, and some progress was made on negotiating trade issues that had never been discussed before. It is unfortunate that the round always is seen as being less successful than it actually was.

The difficulties associated with the Tokyo Round and the generally poor condition of the world economy led to a hiatus in MTNs. The next MTN, the Uruguay Round, took years to conceive and even longer to complete. It was born at a meeting of the GATT trade ministers in late 1982. The agenda for the round was far larger than any previous round. In addition to tariffs the areas covered were trade in services, trade in intellectual property, trade in agriculture, and trade in textiles and apparel. To further complicate the negotiations, 123 countries were participating. The round was launched in 1986, and it was anticipated that the negotiations would take four years. That proved to be optimistic. The marathon negotiations were not concluded until 1994. Although the negotiations associated with the Uruguay Round were both contentious and long, the accomplishments of the round were substantial. First, tariffs were cut by approximately 40 percent. With all of the other issues involved, this achievement tends to be neglected. Second, there was some agreement on Trade-Related Intellectual Property (TRIPS). The protection of intellectual property in the world economy was recognized, and minimum obligations between countries were recognized. Third, the General Agreement on Trade in Services (GATS) was founded. International trade in services is now a fifth of world trade and is growing faster than world trade in goods. Prior to the Uruguay Round, there were no internationally recognized rules for trade in services. GATS is a start in that direction. It obligates all countries to pursue a policy of unconditional MFN with respect to trade in services. Unfortunately, this is only a start. The hard work of defining legal protectionism in services has just begun. Fourth, there was progress on reforming international trade in agricultural products. Prior to the Uruguay Round, international trade in agricultural products was a virtual free-fire zone where countries faced few constraints on protection for their farmers because the original GATT document allowed practices such as quotas that were not allowed for industrial products. Also in use were export subsidies, import bans, variable tariffs, and minimum domestic prices. As a result of the negotiations, trade in agricultural products and trade in industrial products are generally under the same set of rules. In particular, countries were obliged to convert any quota protection into tariffs. This left world trade in agricultural products less distorted by trade barriers. However, the hundreds of billions of dollars being spent annually in the developed countries to support agriculture are still strongly distorting world production and trade. In the end, the Uruguay Round ended with some successes. However, the main success was creating a place to start. World trade in intellectual property, services, and especially agricultural products had never been seriously considered. On these issues there is at least now a way forward.

From the GATT to the WTO

One of the greatest accomplishments of the Uruguay Round was the creation of the WTO. However, the WTO did not appear out of thin air. This was less of a creation than the modern habit of renaming something that already existed. The text of the GATT was adopted in 1947. It still forms the core of what are now the rules of the WTO. As a result of the Uruguay Round, substantial revisions were made, which are now referred to as GATT 1994. Further revisions are being made as the world economy evolves and as more forms of trade and trade-related issues are added to the rules. However, the rules are not an organization. The GATT was an agreement, and as pointed out earlier, it did not have members but had contracting parties. Unofficially, however, the GATT was also an organization. The GATT Secretariat in Geneva handled disputes among contracting parties, collected statistics on world trade, and produced reports on international trade issues. Effectively, the GATT started out as an agreement, but it was becoming an organization. It was not a replacement for the failure to establish the ITO. The central flaw was that the GATT had no effective enforcement mechanism. Under the GATT, a country could file a complaint that another country was violating its obligations. The GATT had no effective method for resolving disputes, and cases often dragged on interminably. Under the WTO, if countries cannot resolve a dispute, a panel is set up to make a determination of fault. If a country is found to be at fault, either it can correct the fault or the WTO will sanction legal retaliation by the country being harmed. The determination of fault occurs within a six-month time frame. If all avenues of the case are pursued, the whole process could take a year. This is the main difference between the old GATT and the new WTO. The former had rules but could not enforce them. The latter both has rules and an enforcement mechanism. Almost exactly 50 years after the decision to not form the ITO, the WTO was born. The learning curve did not have a steep slope, but neither was it flat.

The way forward to liberalizing world trade through MTNs is now cloudy. The bicycle of trade negotiations kept moving with the Doha Round. Like the Tokyo Round, it was launched at an unfortunate time in November 2001. World attention was focused on terrorism, and trade negotiations were not exactly on the top of most government agendas at that time. To make matters worse, the negotiations were scheduled to be completed in four years. This was going to be even harder than before because now 157 countries are participating. The agenda for the round is ambitious. In addition to cutting tariffs, the negotiators are seeking to improve market access for agricultural products, improve rules on intellectual property rights, and improve market access in services. In addition, 20 other, more technical issues are to be discussed. From a bad start, things got worse and never really recovered. Between 2001 and 2008 there were just seven meetings of the world's trade ministers aimed at salvaging the round. Since 2008, there have been several attempts to salvage the round, but negotiations have not resumed. Essentially, the round has died but no one has officially signed the death certificate. As Blustein (2009) points out, the Doha Round and subsequent trade negotiations are foundering on one essential point. The developing countries represented by India, Brazil, China, and South Africa are insisting that the developed countries grant concessions without reciprocity. They have a point, as "special and differential" treatment for developing countries is embodied in the GATT. However, the situation is complex. First, not all developing countries are equal. When that provision was negotiated in the 1960s there was widespread absolute poverty in virtually all developing countries. However, over the last half-century great strides have been made in reducing global poverty. Special and differential treatment may still be acceptable for what is now referred to as low-income countries. However, the developed countries are not willing to make concessions on a nonreciprocal basis for the group of middle-income countries.

This is now the fundamental impasse for MTNs. Without some agreement on this basic problem, the chances for further trade liberalization using the MTN framework seem low.

This leaves two alternative pathways for the future. The first is to continue to pursue multilateral negotiations but to limit the scope to a very narrow area. During the 1990s, negotiations sponsored by the WTO yielded trade liberalization in telecommunications, information technology, and financial services. Although the overall agenda of the Doha Round is faltering, work continues on narrower areas where there is some prospect for success. Given the number of countries that are now WTO members, it may be impossible to negotiate large agreements as in the past, but perhaps agreements can be made by sector. This is especially true when one considers that the agreements mentioned earlier do not involve all WTO members. In the case of telecommunications, 69 countries reached an agreement. The number of countries involved in the information technology agreement was 81. Further, countries that were not originally involved in the agreement can join it at any time. In both cases, the countries involved accounted for the vast majority of international trade in these sectors. Perhaps this is a way forward. It allows a group of countries that wish to liberalize in a certain sector to do so. Further, the agreements provide a template on how liberalization should occur in a particular sector. For world trade in services to become more open, this may be essential. Notice that two out of the three sectoral agreements are in services. Each service sector has its own special characteristics that may need a separate agreement. The same trade rules may work for both cars and shampoo. However, that may not be the case for insurance and airline travel. Although promising, such agreements may have a hidden cost. As pointed out by Aggarwal and Ravenhill (2001), if trade negotiations move in this direction, to a certain extent this is an admission that the era of large MTNs is over. This may be a painful thought for those committed to the concept of MTNs as a process of liberalizing trade, but it remains to be seen whether or not MTNs are a viable process in the 21st century.

Types of RTAs

The multilateral system and the Uruguay Round are important and should not be abandoned or jeopardized. But multilateralism moves at the pace of the slowest. Regional integration can open economies further and faster. It should be given free rein.

—*Rudiger Dornbusch*

What is clearly viable in the 21st century as an alternative to MTNs is Regional Trade Agreements (RTAs). Regional Trade Agreements are trade agreements between two or more countries that reduce trade barriers for only those countries that are members of the agreement. These reductions in trade barriers differ from the reduction of trade barriers on a multilateral basis. Under MTNs, tariffs and other barriers to trade are reduced for all countries that are members of the WTO. As such, multilateral reductions in trade barriers are nondiscriminatory. Because tariffs and other trade barriers are reduced for some countries but not for all, Regional Trade Agreements and the associated reduction of trade barriers are discriminatory. As a result, the negotiating countries that are a part of these agreements obtain a margin of preference over other countries that are not a part of the agreement. Currently 379 Regional Trade Agreements are in force between countries. The global trading system has seen a dramatic increase in the number of Regional Trade Agreements over the past 15 years. Although the recent growth of Regional Trade Agreements began in the 1990s, the seeds of this development were sown in the 1980s. Part of the trend toward regionalism occurred because of the difficult and sometimes slow progress in the multilateral trade negotiations during the Uruguay Round. In addition, during this period the United States began to implement the regional trade agreement approach to trade by signing a free trade agreement with Israel, followed by Canada, and the North American Free Trade Agreement (NAFTA).

Although Regional Trade Agreements between countries strike at the very heart of MFN, they were codified as an exception under Article XXIV of the original GATT agreement. The reasoning behind this exemption is relatively straightforward. The implementation of a regional trade agreement entails both benefits and costs. In simple terms, the reduction of trade barriers increases the amount of trade between the countries involved, and the countries that are not a part of the agreement lose some trade. If the gains in new trade are greater for member countries than the losses to nonmember countries, the volume of world trade expands and the world economy is better off. However, this total benefit is not free, as there are some losers.

There are various degrees of international economic integration between countries, and Regional Trade Agreements between countries tend to change over time. The different degrees of international economic integration can be placed along a continuum. On one end of the continuum is a Regional Trade Agreement between countries that provides a limited reduction in trade barriers. On the other end of the continuum is an agreement among a group of countries to act as if the group is a distinct country in every economic respect. There are a number of different possibilities between these two extremes. Consider a Regional Trade Agreement where two or more countries reduce or abolish tariffs on a limited number of products. This level of economic integration is referred to as a preferential trade agreement. Generally, this type of agreement is illegal under the rules of the WTO. WTO regulations state that in order for a Regional Trade Agreement to be legal, trade barriers must be lifted on "substantially all" of the trade between the two countries. Like many rules and regulations of the WTO, it is possible to obtain a waiver from this restriction. An example of a regional preferential trade agreement is the 1962 U.S.-Canadian Agreement on Trade in Automobiles and Parts. By the early 1960s, the U.S. automobile industry had spread north of the border into Canada. As a result, U.S. manufacturers were paying tariffs on what were essentially intrafirm transactions. To reduce the cost of production, it made sense to eliminate the trade barriers in automobiles between the two countries. As a result, GATT granted a waiver for this preferential trade agreement.

The second level of economic integration is a free-trade area (FTA). In an FTA, the countries agree to eliminate tariffs and other nontariff barriers to trade between each other. First, in order for a free-trade area to be legal under international trade law, it must cover "substantially all" trade among the members. In general, this statement means that the reduction of trade barriers must cover nonagricultural products. The European Union has free-trade agreements with countries such as Israel and Turkey that only cover such trade. Second, the agreement must be completed within a reasonable period of time. Almost all trade agreements between countries are "phased in" over time. In practice 15 years has become the reasonable limit. Further, a free-trade agreement may cover more than just trade in goods. The free-trade agreements the United States has with Israel, Canada, and Mexico include trade in services, portfolio investment, and foreign direct investment (FDI). With these qualifications, a free-trade area between countries is usually *less* than the name implies. Just because two countries have signed a free-trade agreement does not mean that trade between these two countries is or will become identical to trade between, say, New Hampshire and Vermont.

Finally, with an FTA each country maintains its own separate national tariff schedule. For example, an automobile company exporting from Japan to the three NAFTA countries would face three different tariffs. Because each country uses its own tariff schedule, trade deflection may occur within a free-trade area. Trade deflection is the diversion of exports to a country within a free-trade area that has lower tariffs on a specific good. For example, suppose the tariff on cars is 4 percent in the United States and Canada and 20 percent in Mexico. A car exporter to this free-trade area has an incentive to ship cars to, say, San Diego, pay the 4 percent U.S. tariff, and then ship the car to Mexico to sell it to a Mexican customer. In this case, the exporter is attempting to avoid the 20 percent tariff on cars to Mexico. Thus, when the national tariffs of the free-trade area members are very different, exporters have a clear incentive to try to evade the higher tariffs. This problem can also arise if the member countries have large differences in quotas or other nontariff barriers. Differences in tariffs and/or quotas can also lead to the establishment of "screwdriver plants." These plants are designed to provide minor assembly work on a product that is essentially produced in a foreign country but assembled within the free-trade area to avoid the higher tariffs.

A third level of economic integration is a customs union. A customs union is similar to a free-trade area but with two differences. First, a customs union has a common external tariff for member countries, which means that each country replaces its own national tariff schedule with a common tariff schedule. For example, a U.S. firm exporting to countries in the EU faces one tariff schedule—the tariff on computers is the same for Germany as it is for Portugal. The second difference between an FTA and a customs union is not all FTAs include trade in agricultural products, services, and financial flows. However, most customs unions include a very broad range of international trade. Thus, the level of international economic integration implied by a customs union is usually "deeper" than the level of integration implied by a free-trade area.

The final two types of economic integration are somewhat more difficult to define. The fourth level of economic integration is referred to as a common market. This is a customs union with the addition of factor mobility between member countries. Restrictions on the mobility of capital and labor are eliminated, and these factors are free to move within the member countries. Recall that the free mobility of capital allows for a more efficient allocation of capital within the common market and results in additional output. In addition, the mobility of labor allows for a more efficient allocation of human capital within the member countries and results in additional output. However, allowing the free mobility of workers between countries is not a minor issue because any substantial wage differentials among the member countries may induce a large migration between countries that would noticeably affect national wage rates.

The last form of economic integration is the creation of an economic union. This is an agreement between countries to maintain a free-trade area, a common external tariff, the free mobility of capital and labor, and some degree of unification in government fiscal and monetary policies. Thus, there are two additional requirements for an economic union. The first requirement is the creation of a common currency. This implies the abolition of each country's central bank and the creation of a common central bank. The advantages of a common currency are much like the advantages of lowering tariffs. Every time one national currency has to be changed into another, a fee is charged. These transaction costs are similar to a tax on international transactions. Even if the tax is relatively small, the volume of transactions among closely allied economies can make the absolute size of the tax relatively large. The second requirement is that each national government has to align its national policies with those of the other member countries. The policies that need to be aligned between countries cover such issues as tax rates, antitrust law, labor regulations, environmental regulations, and so forth. As such, any national policies that tend to distort trade flows would be candidates for harmonization. The world economy does not yet have an economic union that contains many countries. However, the European Union is determinedly moving in that direction.

Case Study: The European Union

Guided by treaties that scarcely anybody can understand, towards a destination on which nobody can agree, the European Union has survived, and often thrived for almost half a century.

—*Robert Cottrell*

The world's largest and most successful Regional Trade Agreement is the European Union (EU). Now 50 years old, the EU currently contains 27 countries with a combined population of 459 million and a combined gross domestic product (GDP) larger than the United States. The European Union began its development in 1951 with the formation of the European Coal and Steel Community (ECSC). This agreement provided for the elimination of tariffs and quotas for the coal and steel industries between Belgium, France, Italy, Luxembourg, the Netherlands, and West Germany. The basic idea of the ECSC was to promote free trade in two important commodities (coal and steel) as a deterrent to future military conflicts in Europe. Although we usually view trade arrangements as economic creatures, frequently a political goal is also involved. In this case, the goal was to reduce the probability of another European military conflict. The basic premise behind the ECSC was that the more closely integrated countries are economically, the less likelihood of war between them.

In 1957, the countries involved in the ECSC signed the Treaty of Rome, which provided for the elimination of tariffs and nontariff barriers to trade between member countries and the institution of a common external tariff. This treaty established the EEC as a customs union, which has been continually enlarging itself to cover more and more of Europe. In 1960, most of the countries not included in the EEC formed an alternative preferential trade arrangement called the European Free Trade Association (EFTA). This organization provided for free trade in nonagricultural products among its members. In addition, EFTA provided for free trade in these products between itself and the EEC. In 1967, the EEC and ECSC merged to form the European Communities (EC). Over time, the enlargement of the European Union has occurred mostly as countries within Europe left EFTA and joined the EU. Thus, while the EU membership grew, the EFTA membership declined. The United Kingdom, Ireland, and Denmark joined the EC in 1973; Greece joined in 1981; Spain and Portugal joined in 1986; and Austria, Finland, and Sweden joined in 1995. In addition, 10 countries became members in 2004. These countries include Cyprus, Estonia, the Czech Republic, Hungary, Latvia, Lithuania, Malta, Poland, Slovakia, and Slovenia. The newest members, Bulgaria and Romania, joined in 2007.

As the EU has "widened" to include more countries, it has also "deepened." What this means is that the EU has always been something more than a customs union. Technically, all that a custom union requires is a common external tariff and eliminating most of the trade barriers between member countries. However, from its beginning the EU has had something extra called the Common Agricultural Policy (CAP). Under the CAP, all of the countries in the EU subsidize their agricultural sector in a similar manner. When countries form a Regional Trade Agreement, free trade in agriculture is potentially a problem. This is because to one extent or another every country subsidizes its farmers. If the subsidy schemes among countries vary, free trade in agricultural products becomes problematic. To solve this problem, the EU adopted a common agricultural policy for all members. Belgian farmers are subsidized in the same way as Portuguese farmers. All member countries provide revenue to the EU, and the EU, rather than each national government, pays subsidies to farmers within the EU. Currently, approximately half the EU total budget is spent on farm subsidies. The CAP guarantees prices for all farm commodities within the EU. Further, the EU purchases whatever farmers cannot sell on the open market. In addition, farmers are protected by a variable levy (tariff) from international competition. If farm prices within the EU decline, the tariff rises and vice versa. Because the support prices are generous, there has been a problem of chronic oversupply of agricultural commodities in Europe. In addition, the surplus agricultural commodities are sometimes dumped on world markets to reduce the EU losses.

As a result, the common agricultural policy has created constant trade frictions between the United States and other, more efficient producers of agricultural commodities such as Canada, Australia, New Zealand, and many developing countries in selected products. Such countries not only lose exports to the EU, but at times suffer losses in other export markets when the EU sells or dumps its agricultural surpluses. Demands by countries that the EU reform the CAP in order to produce less damage in international trade of agricultural products delayed the completion of the Uruguay Round and is similarly proving to be a difficult issue in the Doha Round. In all likelihood, any future negotiations concerning world trade in agriculture will have as its central issue the common agricultural policy. The situation is politically charged because European farmers, particularly French farmers, are very active in their defense of the system. This problem is likely to be very contentious in the years ahead because many of the newest members of the EU have large agricultural sectors.

Aside from agriculture, the EU is taking a number of steps to create a full economic union. Beginning in 1985, an EU commission set about determining the steps necessary to create a genuinely barrier-free internal market in the EU. This commission listed hundreds of actions that member governments needed to take in order to create something like a unified market. Most of the governmental actions were completed by 1992, with much fanfare about the single market. The Maastricht Treaty of 1992 laid out plans for a new European currency (the euro) that replaced 12 of the separate national currencies in January 2002. This treaty also completed the evolution of the EU into a true common market. Barriers to the movement of labor and capital among the countries were removed. Capital and labor are now free to migrate in the EU in the same way they can migrate within a country.

The future evolution of the EU is uncertain. The EU has one of the major characteristics of an economic union: a common currency. However, a true economic union has other characteristics. To achieve a true economic union, the EU would need to have other characteristics such as a common fiscal policy, common levels of business taxation, common labor laws, and commonality in any other regulations that distort economic activity. In some areas, noticeably competition policy, this commonality is a reality. However, in other areas such as taxation and labor regulation, there are still large disparities within the EU that distort economic activity. The issue is further clouded by the uncertainty over the degree of sovereignty that member countries wish to hand over to a supranational body such as the EU. This issue is evident in the refusal of the United Kingdom, Denmark, and Sweden to abandon their national currencies. What is clear is that the EU is moving in the direction of creating an economic union. However, the speed with which it will move on the various issues is another matter. The only certainty is that this evolution should be an interesting economic and political process to observe.

Bibliography

Aggarwal, Vinod K. and John Ravenhill. 2001. "Undermining the WTO: The Case Against Open Sectorialism," *East-West Center Analysis Paper No. 50.*

Blustein, Paul. 2009. *Misadventures of the Most Favored Nations: Clashing Egos, Inflated Ambitions, and the Great Shambles of the World Trade System.* New York: Public Affairs.

Dam, Kenneth W. 2001. *The Rules of the Global Game.* Chicago: University of Chicago Press.

Finger, J. Michael. 1979. "Trade Liberalization: A Public Choice Perspective," in Ryan C. Amacher, Gottfried Haberler, and Thomas D. Willett (eds.), *Challenges to a Liberal Economic Order.* Washington, D.C.: American Enterprise Institute.

Irwin, Douglas A. 1995. "The GATT's Contribution to Economic Recovery in Post-War Europe," in Barry Eichengreen (ed.), *Europe's Postwar Growth.* New York: Cambridge University Press.

Irwin, Douglas A., Petros C. Mavroidis, and Alan O. Sykes. 2008. *The Genesis of the GATT.* New York: Cambridge University Press.

Krugman, Paul. 1999. "What Should Trade Negotiators Negotiate About?" *Journal of Economic Literature* 35(1): 113–20.

Steil, Benn. 1994. *The Battle of Bretton Woods: John Maynard Keynes, Harry Dexter White, and the Making of a New World Order.* Princeton, NJ: Princeton University Press.

Winters, L. Alan. 1990. "The Road to Uruguay," *Economic Journal* 100: 1288–1303.

CHAPTER EIGHT

The Institutions of U.S. Trade Policy

During my tenure as Special Trade Representative, I spent as much time negotiating with my domestic constituents (both industry and Labor) and members of Congress as I did negotiating with our foreign trading partners.

—*Robert Strauss*

Introduction

In the United States, one has to ask an awkward question: Who runs U.S. international trade policy? In a normal country, there is an obvious answer. For the vast majority of countries in the world there is a ministry or department of international trade. Most countries have a cabinet of ministers such as foreign relations, health, social welfare, etc. With respect to economics, the usual setup is to have a ministry concerned with domestic economic activity and a ministry concerned with international economic activity. This makes sense for two reasons. First, domestic economic activity and international trade are sufficiently different from international trade. There is a reason that there is a whole separate area in economics devoted to international economics. Second, international economics is not only different, it is quantitatively large. As we saw in Chapter 1 in many countries international trade is a high percentage of total economic activity measured by the ratio of imports plus exports divided by gross domestic product (GDP). Relatively speaking, this ratio for the United States is rather low. However, even in the United States international trade is over 25 percent of GDP. In this situation one would expect that the United States would have a Cabinet-level Department of International Trade. A quick look at the U.S. Cabinet shows that such a department doesn't exist. The United States is the only developed country without one. You can now understand why trying to determine what is happening in U.S. international trade policy is difficult. No one has ultimate responsibility for trade policy, and no one has the authority to unilaterally execute it. This means that understanding

U.S. international trade policy requires some knowledge of several institutions in the government that have a substantial influence on trade policy.

To start, this will require a bit of history to understand how the current system works. The primary institution in trade policy is the office of the Trade Representative. As we will see, this office has a lot of responsibility for trade policy but very little actual authority. One can see a problem already in terms of basic management principles. In addition to the Trade Representative, the Commerce and Treasury Departments are involved in the formulation and execution of trade policy. Another major government agency involved in trade policy is the U.S. International Trade Commission, which is a small, independent agency not attached to any larger government department. Finally, as international trade has become more complicated, a number of other government departments and agencies have an influence on trade policy. If you are having trouble understanding the evolution of U.S. trade policy, the institutional environment in which it operates makes this inherently difficult. The purpose this chapter is to provide you with the basic institutional knowledge that will make understanding trade policy less difficult.

Institutional History

The history of trade policy in the United States became complicated from the beginning. The Constitution gives Congress the authority to raise revenue and set tariffs. The executive branch is given the authority to negotiate treaties with foreign countries. As McGillivray, et al. (2001) has shown, this division of authority set forth in the Constitution does not bode well for setting up institutions to administer trade policy. Given the republican form of government in the United States, there is the immediate potential for trade policy clashes. With two parties dominating the political system, it frequently is the case that the majority in Congress and the president will be from different parties. Under these circumstances, a coherent trade policy is going to be difficult to achieve. Looking back, this is the trade policy history of the United States until well into the 20th century. Trade policy in this early era was set on a path by Alexander Hamilton. As secretary of the Treasury, he advocated a moderate tariff but one with the capacity to develop American industry behind protectionist tariffs. As an aside, there is one notable peculiarity in the development of U.S. trade policy. After Alexander Hamilton, the presence of the secretary of the Treasury in the making of trade policy was negligible. However, until the early 20th century, tariff revenue was the primary source of income for the federal government. The absence of the secretary of the Treasury in the making of trade policy for much of U.S. history is peculiar. What evolved out of Hamilton's trade policy was an American form of protectionism that sought to protect U.S. manufacturing from foreign—mostly European—competition. The protection was deemed necessary for the industrialization and diversification of the U.S. economy. The structure of the U.S. government and a basic principle of U.S. trade policy conspired against the active pursuit of trade agreements with other countries. The executive branch of government could negotiate trade agreements as treaties. However, any agreement must pass the Senate by a two-thirds majority. Although not impossible, this is a relatively high bar. In addition, the United States was committed to the principle of most favored nation (MFN). In a practical sense, this means that each country pays the same tariff on a product. The combination of these factors made it almost impossible for the United States to negotiate trade agreements in the 19th century. Another factor was that there was frequently a split between the attitude of the State Department toward trade agreements and the attitude of the Senate. On average, the State Department was interested in negotiating trade agreements with foreign countries as a way to reduce trade barriers abroad. Opposition from the Senate took two forms. First, the Senate frequently had a strong bias toward reducing tariffs. A second objection was constitutional. To negotiate a trade agreement, it is necessary to lower American tariffs. In a very narrow view of the Constitution, only Congress has the power to do that. Except for two purely market-opening trade agreements with China and Japan in the 1840s, trade policy was almost exclusively conducted by Congress. Aside from tariff increases associated with national defense, the two major political parties settled into a predictable set of positions on trade policy. Almost invariably, the Republican Party was associated with high tariffs. The tariff policy espoused by the Democrats was more nuanced. Like the Republicans, they were amenable to protecting domestic industry from foreign competition. The real debate was over the degree of protectionism necessary to accomplish that goal. In general, they felt that a lower level of protection would provide adequate support for industrial development. This was particularly true in the aftermath of the Civil War. The United States was in the process of becoming the world's largest economy. Because the United States was beginning to eclipse the United Kingdom, the argument for protecting U.S. industry against European competition was becoming ever weaker. Where the two parties had a substantial difference was in terms of consumer interests. Of the two parties, the Democrats consistently made the case that tariffs that were too high inflicted undue damage on the consumer. To a certain extent, this was a regional issue. After the Civil War, the South became a bastion of support for the Democratic Party. Now recall that public opinion in the

South had historically been in favor of lower tariffs. On the other hand, the Republican base was in the Northern industrial part of the country. In a political sense, the stance of the two parties with respect to tariffs was understandable.

On a more practical level, there were few formal institutions involved in international trade policy. Collecting data on foreign trade is done by the U.S. Treasury. In the 19th century this was a critical function of government as it was the primary source of revenue. From 1790 to 1820, the Treasury Department made annual reports to Congress on foreign trade and revenues from tariffs. The system was refined to provide more detail in 1821. In 1866, the data were further refined, and a new Bureau of Statistics was established in the Treasury Department. In 1903, the collection of trade statistics was transferred to the Department of Commerce. A final reorganization moved the data collection process to the Bureau of the Census. If housing the collection of trade statistics in the Bureau of the Census seems unusual, imports and the collection of customs duties were frequently problematic.

The problems started early. By the time of the American Revolution, British customs in America were handled by Americans working under British supervision. As a result, the Americans were in charge of enforcing British restraints on trade that they did not agree with. The Revolution transferred the administration of customs to the individual states and later to the new national government. As Price and Keller (1989) point out, the new Customs Service got off to a bad start. It was politicized from the beginning by Alexander Hamilton. Hamilton ensured that the majority of the new employees were aligned with the Federalist Party. This started an unfortunate trend. For much of the rest of the 19th century, the Customs Service was tied to whichever political party happened to be in power. In this period, the Customs Service was handling a huge amount of revenue derived from imports entering the country. As the century progressed, this revenue was expanding at a rapid rate. Coupling this ever-larger revenue stream with political appointees is a recipe for corruption. Unsurprisingly, it was common knowledge during the period that there was corruption in the Customs Service. This was particularly true of the Customs House in New York, where the majority of U.S. imports passed through. In 1838, Samuel Swartout took his stolen funds and left for the United Kingdom to escape prosecution. His successor, Jesse Hoyt, did exactly the same thing in 1841. The Customs Service was involved in the run-up to the Civil War. President Andrew Jackson used it to blunt the Nullification Act passed by South Carolina in 1832. During the Civil War there was chaos in captured Confederate ports and ports in border states. The Treasury sent out an investigator, Charles Cooper, to sort out the mess. Incredibly, the Confederacy had hired him to do the same job. On the other hand, the Customs Service was a haven for gifted people who were allowed to work on projects with no immediate benefit to society. This has a notable pedigree in economics as Adam Smith for a time held the position of commissioner of Customs in Scotland. In an American context, both Herman Melville and Nathaniel Hawthorne held posts in the U.S. Customs Service. Reading the first chapter of *The Scarlett Letter* gives a good example of life in a customs house in the 19th century.

The post–Civil War era in the United States is widely known as the Gilded Age. It was during this period that the U.S. government was moving from a system of the civil service being staffed by political patronage to one staffed by professionals appointed on some system of merit. This is a radical change for any country to go through, and in the United States the Customs Service was a focal point of that change. One needs to consider that the United States in the 19th century was by the standards of the 21st century still a developing country. Although the statistics are not precise, a sense of GDP per capita in the 19th century can add some perspective. In 1800, GDP per capita in the United States was a bit over $1,000. By 1900, it was over $6,000. During the century, the country had made the transition from what we would now call a low-income country to a middle-income country. In any country, this transition usually brings dramatic changes. It is not surprising that there was a substantial amount of corruption in politics and the government. It is also not surprising that corruption was becoming an issue during the Gilded Age. The average American was now prosperous enough that issues such as government corruption mattered. Corruption in the Customs Service is a textbook example. If poorly supervised, a port of entry offers ample opportunities for corruption. It is not unknown in a poor country for goods to pass through customs and never be recorded. Another common occurrence is underinvoicing. Customs officials routinely assess duties based on documents presented by the importer. If the importer underreports the value of the goods on the document, then the amount of tariff due likewise is reduced. Finally, customs officials can misclassify goods. If the tariff on a product is 40 percent and the tariff on a similar item is 20 percent, then it is relatively simple for a customs official to make a "mistake." The result is that under the right circumstances, a corrupt customs official can make a substantial amount of money. There was also a substantial amount of smuggling. As Diaz (2015) has documented, the United States has a long, difficult-to-control border that made smuggling both easy and profitable. After the Civil War, the Grant administration began to reform the Civil Service. These efforts continued in the Hayes administration. This set off a contentious battle between a wing of the Republican Party that supported the patronage system and another wing in favor of civil service reform. The leading opponent of reform was Roscoe Conkling who was a U.S. senator from New York. Unsurprisingly, he also was in control of positions for the customs house in New York. He clashed with newly elected President James Garfield over implementing reforms in New York. In an odd turn of fate, the assassination of President Garfield had an impact on civil service reform. Garfield was followed in office by Chester A. Arthur. Arthur was a friend of Conkling's and had served as the head of the customs house in New York. Although there is no indication that Arthur was personally corrupt, he was well aware of corruption in the Customs Service. The result was that he strongly supported the faction in the Republican Party working for civil service reform. The reformers were too early. Real civil service reform would not occur until early in the 20th century. However, in the preliminary political battles over civil service reform, reform of the Customs Service was a constant example of a larger problem.

The U.S. Trade Representative

As we have previously discussed, prior to the Reciprocal Trade Agreements Act (RTAA), Congress was responsible for the conduct of trade policy. Although this was a workable situation in the 19th century, it became problematical in the 20th. The disaster of Smoot-Hawley created a new trade policy embodied in the RTAA. In effect the RTAA transferred much of the authority for trade policy from Congress to the president. Congressional input into the process was still there though, as the president has to obtain negotiating power from Congress. Also, Congress must approve any negotiated agreement. Once the RTAA had passed, there was the question of who in the executive branch would actually be involved in trade policy. The natural candidate in this regard was the State Department. Within the State Department, the new policy was inextricably linked to Cordell Hull. Cordell Hull was a member of Congress from Tennessee who later was elected to the Senate. Shortly after his election, he was selected by the president to be the secretary of state. He has the distinction of holding that office for the longest period in American history (1933–1944). These were obviously tumultuous years, and his career is mostly linked to the most visible types of foreign policy. Hull's impact on U.S. trade policy is less recognized. This is understandable, as issues of war and peace are almost always more important than trade policy. However, after the passage of RTAA, the administration of U.S. trade policy was passed directly to the State Department. It is here where Hull left an indelible mark on modern trade policy. Hull was not an economist, but he had very strong opinions on trade. As emphasized by both Aaronson (1991) and Dam (2005), Hull was one of the first Americans to view trade policy as something much larger than protecting domestic industry or promoting U.S. exports. He was not naïve and understood that trade policy would always be bound by domestic politics. His service in the House and the Senate had taught him that. However, his views on trade were much broader. For Hull, trade was an important deterrent to military conflict and promoted peace. As a result, trade negotiations were an essential part of overall U.S. foreign policy aimed reducing the probability of war. Very quickly after the passage of the RTAA, the State Department began negotiating bilateral trade agreements. With a solid Democratic majority and a popular president, the State Department went about signing trade agreements that, on a reciprocal basis, gave foreign countries substantially increased access to the U.S. market. This trend continued until the start of World War II. In the planning for the postwar economic order, Hull and his colleagues at the State Department were instrumental in planning for what became the General Agreement on Tariffs and Trade (GATT). Their vision was of a world with dramatically lower trade barriers, with the United States offering major concessions to increase the participation of other countries. This was a radical departure from previous U.S. trade policy and one that created concern in other parts of the government. Although Hull resigned as secretary of state in 1944, his policies were followed by his successors, regardless of the party represented by the president. This sense of trade as an adjunct to a wider foreign policy linked to economic prosperity in the world continues into the 21st century. However, the bureaucratic mechanism for conducting trade policy was changed. The secretary of state is appointed by the president. As a result, the trade policy of the country was being determined almost entirely by the president through the State Department. Of course, Congress is involved but only at the start and the end of any trade negotiations. With trade policy being dominated by the State Department, Congress felt that it was difficult for them to have adequate influence on policy. This was even more true of the private sector and labor. With the original operation of trade policy, both groups had an ample opportunity to influence trade policy through connections with individual members of the Congress or Senate. After the passage of the RTAA, this channel of influence was greatly diminished as the power of Congress in trade policy waned and the majority of that power had been passed to the president. Obviously, a member of the Congress or the Senate has a different constituency than the president. The result was that the ability of an industry or a labor union to influence trade policy had been diminished. A trade policy being handled by civil servants in the

State Department was felt to be less responsive to inputs from business and labor and needed to be changed.

The obvious solution would have been the establishment of a Cabinet-level Department of International Trade. This obvious solution was never pursued. As we move through the development of the U.S. Trade Representative (USTR), we will see why this never happened. Prior to 1934, Congress was responsible for U.S. trade policy. The RTAA transferred much of the responsibility for negotiating trade agreements to the president. However, the State Department was so heavily aligned with the president that the input from other stakeholders was not optimal. The overall objectives of RTAA were politically acceptable, but neither the State Department nor a new Department of International Trade could or would satisfy the objective of giving Congress and other stakeholders more input into the process of formulating trade policy and providing input into the negotiating process. The creation of the USTR became the preferred solution. As we will see, it has evolved over the decades and is arguably one of the "messiest" parts of the federal government. Although it may be an unlovely way to conduct trade policy, it seems to work.

The Trade Expansion Act of 1962 included a provision for the president through a Special Trade Representative to conduct international trade negotiations. This seems like an innocuous request, but notice that the State Department had now lost control over a significant portion of trade policy. The act also provided for the new Special Trade Representative to chair a new interagency group that would make recommendations to the president on trade negotiations. Notice what is happening here. Congress essentially is mandating that the person charged with handling trade negotiations is required to receive input on trade policy from other parts of the government. Although the president is left in charge of trade policy per the RTAA, there has been a noticeable shift in how trade policy is conducted. As a result of the legislation, President Kennedy created the Office of the Special Trade Representative (STR). The initial job of the STR was to negotiate the Kennedy Round of multilateral trade negotiations (MTNs). Congress seemed to have created a general template that was acceptable to both them and the president. What follows is an apparently long-run process of tinkering with the basic template. In the 1970s, Congress expanded the role of the STR. The Trade Act of 1974 put the STR on a firmer legislative footing by making it an official part of the executive branch. It also made it responsible for the administration of trade agreements made under the Tariff Act of 1930, the Trade Expansion Act of 1962, and the Trade Act of 1974. The act also made the office officially both accountable to Congress and the president. The STR also was elevated to the Cabinet level.

However, although it is a Cabinet-level office, the STR is not a member of the president's Cabinet. This makes the office unique in the government. It is at a very high level, but the level is somewhat ambiguous. In 1979, the STR acquired its current designation as the Office of the U.S. Trade Representative. It centralized trade policy into one office, and the role of the office was expanded. USTR was given overall responsibility for the development and the negotiation of both bilateral and multilateral trade agreements. The USTR became the principal advisor to the president on international trade matters and how other U.S. government policies affect international trade. USTR was to share with the Department of Commerce the authority to monitor foreign government compliance with all trade agreements. The USTR was given an advisory role in the operation of the Export-Import Bank, the Overseas Private Investment Corporation, and the National Advisory Committee on International Monetary and Financial Policies. USTR also became the U.S. negotiator on all treaties relating to foreign investment. In a world where trade, investment, and exchange rates are increasingly interlinked with trade, these changes actually were somewhat ahead of their time. The changes also were indicating that both Congress and the president were becoming increasingly comfortable with having trade policy managed by an office that, although housed in the executive branch, had equal accountability to Congress. The authority of USTR was further expanded under the Omnibus Trade and Competitiveness Act of 1988. One of the main aims of the act was to strengthen the sense that Congress and the executive branch were working in partnership and the USTR was the operational arm of that partnership. USTR was given even more responsibilities in the act. The USTR is the chair of the interagency committee that advises the president in the formulation and implementation of trade policy. Related to this, it coordinates trade policy with other agencies. Although this sounds mundane, it actually is quite important. What this means is that with respect to trade policy, the USTR has the authority to make decisions after consultation with other parts of the federal government. In order to influence trade policy, other agencies must first work through USTR. Further, the USTR became the principal spokesperson on international trade policy for the president. In this sense, the USTR functions somewhat like a regular member of the Cabinet. The USTR was put in charge of the administration of all trade agreements. Given the large number of multilateral and bilateral trade agreements now in place, this is a substantial responsibility. Finally, USTR was charged with reporting to Congress and the president on both nontariff barriers to trade and international commodity agreements. Under the Uruguay Round Agreements Act of 1994, the USTR was given responsibility for all negotiations occurring under the umbrella of the World Trade Organization (WTO). Because current and future WTO negotiations cover much more than simple trade in goods and services, this authorization is far more important than it looks at first glance. The Trade and Development Act of 2000 created two new offices in the USTR. One of these offices is concerned with leading all U.S. trade negotiations related to trade in agricultural products. Given the relative importance of U.S. trade in agriculture, this is again a seemingly small increase in responsibility that on closer inspection is quite large.

Despite the importance of international trade in the American economy, the USTR is a quiet government agency. It is squarely in the middle of U.S. trade policy, but there is very little discussion of its activities. Whenever a trade policy debate is occurring in the country, the USTR is right in the middle of it. On the one hand, it is actually handling the negotiating process that was initiated by the president. On the other hand, it is charged with handling input from Congress and all other parties affected by any potential agreement. It is surprising given the USTR's importance in the formulation of trade policy that its activities generally are not well understood. Its public profile is actually highest when issuing relatively routine reports required by law. Since 1986 USTR has produced a report on estimating the impact of foreign barriers to trade on U.S. exports. This report is quietly influential. When possible, it provides quantitative estimates of the effects of foreign trade barriers. It is one of the underpinnings of continued U.S. efforts to liberalize world trade. Every year the USTR must produce the Section 301 report, which refers to a section of the Trade Act of 1974. The report provides an annual documentation of violations of the intellectual property rights of American firms in the world economy. In 2006, USTR was required to produce a list of "notorious countries" where such violations are particularly prevalent. In 2010, this became a separate report from the Section 301 report. It usually is the case that these reports garner far more attention to the USTR than the more mundane work of negotiating trade agreements and monitoring the compliance of other countries with previous agreements.

The U.S. International Trade Commission

Most Senators are able to get statistics to prove anything they want, on any side of a question. I believe that if we have a permanent board composed of men who will use discretion, talent, and experience in the investigation of these subjects, they will be able to furnish data which will receive more credit than any that we have heretofore had.

—Senator Atlee Pomerene

Given the inherent messiness of U.S. trade policy, from time to time attempts have been made to put the setting of tariffs and other trade barriers on a more orderly basis. The first attempt to do so goes back to the 19th century. As we saw earlier, in the late 19th century there was a tremendous amount of debate concerning the tariff. In early 1882, President Chester A. Arthur appointed a commission to study the U.S. tariff schedule overall. Because tariff rates were high, the basic idea was to have a group of experts to advise the government on how to reduce them. In late 1882, the commission recommended large reductions in tariffs. As usual, the politics of protection went to work. The result was the largely derided Tariff Act of 1883. The result was so bad that it is usually referred to as the "Mongrel Tariff." The actual tariff reduction achieved was less than 1.5 percent in a situation where the average tariff was 35 to 40 percent. It was part of a pattern of the term of President Arthur that attempts to do the right thing did not go as well as planned.

The idea of a nonpartisan tariff commission resurfaced in the early 20th century in the Wilson administration. In 1916, Congress created the U.S. Tariff Commission. The purpose of the Tariff Commission was to provide Congress with unbiased information concerning the U.S. tariff. For more than a century prior to the creation of the Tariff Commission, information on tariffs was gathered by concerned congressional committees. In effect, the creation of the Tariff Commission passed this information-gathering function to an outside agency. This didn't have to occur. Congress could easily have done the work on its own or passed the work to the Commerce Department. However, in both cases the results might not have been an improvement on the existing system. In-house analysis would have reflected the preferences of the party in power. Likewise, the secretary of commerce is appointed by the president so any analysis originating there was subject to political influence. As Schnietz (1994) has shown, the basic idea of the Tariff Commission was to create a nonpartisan source of information on the U.S. tariff. However, the impetus for its creation was political. The tariff had been a political football since the 18th century. In the post–Civil War era it had been a predictable struggle between Republicans and Democrats favoring high and low tariffs, respectively. At the time, economics was still in its formative years, and rigorous economic analysis of tariffs that we now take for granted did not exist. Protectionists were free to recommend high tariffs because there was no economic analysis to definitively say that the position was wrong. The Democrats felt that a nonpartisan Tariff Commission would more often recommend lower tariffs than ones that were higher. The primary frustration of the Democrats was the inability to convey the idea that not all of the tariff was being paid by the foreign producers. This fallacy was one of the main devices used by Republicans in their arguments for higher tariffs. If domestic industry could be supported with higher tariffs and the foreigners were paying all of the tariff, then high tariffs increase the welfare of society. The Democrats were gambling that a nonpartisan commission on tariffs would tend to produce analysis of tariffs that provided the public with a more balanced view of the costs and benefits of higher tariffs. The original structure of the Tariff Commission was six commissioners appointed by the president. No more than three of the six could be from one political party. Overlapping 12-year terms assured that no one president could "pack" the commission. The chairman and vice chairman are selected from among commissioners who have served at least a year for two-year terms. Successive chairmen may not be of the same political party. Further, no active businessperson could serve. Salaries were generously set at $7,500 to reduce the possibility of outside influence and were the same as federal judges and members of Congress at the time. In the 21st century this would translate into a salary of over $160,000. Under current law, commissioners now serve nine-year terms.

Initially the work of the Tariff Commission was to publish studies on the effects of tariffs. The first chairman was the well-known economist Frank Taussig. At the time, Taussig was the leading American economist specializing in international trade. The work of the Tariff Commission went exactly as planned. Over the next several years, the commission produced numerous product and industry studies illustrating that tariffs increased the cost of goods to American consumers. The impact this ultimately had on the tariff debate is unknowable. However, it clearly put the argument that raising tariffs was costly to the consumer on firmer empirical ground. The Tariff Commission also had another duty. In 1916, Congress passed the Antidumping Act. This act closed an interesting loophole in the previously adopted antitrust acts. The act prohibits foreign producers from selling in the U.S. market at low prices with the intent of damaging or destroying a domestic industry. Such predatory pricing clearly is illegal for U.S. firms. The law was administered in the U.S. judicial system, but proved to be unworkable. The Antidumping Act of 1921 made the system of determining dumping workable by taking it out of the courts and putting it into an administrative process with two steps. First, the Treasury Department would determine if dumping was occurring. Next, the Tariff Commission would determine if the domestic industry was being injured or was likely to be injured in the future. If both determinations were positive, then the tariff would be raised by an amount equal to the dumping margin.

For most of its history, the Tariff Commission conducted antidumping investigations and supported the trade policy being carried out at the State

Department. A major change occurred in 1974 when the agency was renamed the U.S. International Trade Commission (USITC). The USITC has three major objectives. The first is to administer U.S. trade remedy laws that will be described in the next chapter. The second is to provide the president, the USTR, and Congress with independent and high-quality analysis of tariffs, international trade, and competitiveness. The third objective is important. The USITC maintains the Harmonized Tariff Schedule of the U.S. (HTUS). In order to accomplish this, the USITC is organized into five areas of operations. These are import injury investigations, intellectual property–based import investigations, the research program, trade information services, and trade policy support. The fact that the USITC is little known outside of Washington is a measure of its effectiveness. The work it does is hardly glamorous, but is essential to the operation of trade policy. Virtually all of the other actors in U.S. trade policy are touched by the direction in which the political winds are blowing. In its independence, the USITC is the only agency involved in trade policy that, by design, was both bipartisan and independent. The political process yields the commissioners, but the length of their terms insulates them from short-run political pressure. The staff of the USITC are civil servants that have the usual protections from political forces. The result is an agency with both a striking degree of independence and professionalism. As a result, its day-to-day work is excellent and its research has influence. This independence gives it a larger voice in U.S. trade policy than one would guess. Recall that the initial reason for the creation of its precursor was primarily political: producing research that would buttress the arguments of a political party for lower tariffs. The result in the 21st century is an agency that virtually no other country has. This is an independent agency that conducts internal research on trade policy that is immune from short-run politics. Sometimes countries get lucky and create good institutions for dubious reasons.

Who Makes U.S. Trade Policy?

We end the chapter by attempting to answer the question we posed at the beginning: Who makes U.S. trade policy? The Constitution of the United States made trade policy a shared responsibility from the beginning. Congress, subject to authorization by the executive branch, was given the authority to set tariffs. On the other hand, the executive branch was given the lead responsibility over foreign policy and the making of treaties subject to congressional approval. This means that the trade policy of the country has to be the result of a bargaining process between the executive and legislative branches of government. In this sense, trade policy is not terribly different than any other policy. These compromises go to the heart of the republican form of government that the framers of the Constitution intended. They feared the concentration of power in the hands of a dominant party that can easily occur in a parliamentary form of government. However, such a system does not guarantee absolute equality in the making of policy. This is clearly true in the making of U.S. trade policy. From the late 18th century to the passage of the Reciprocal Trade Agreements Act in the 1930s, the balance of power with respect to trade policy was clearly in the hands of Congress. Partially, this reflected the fact that tariff revenue was the major funding source for the government. Because Congress clearly has the lead authority on revenue issues, its dominance in the making of trade policy was consistent. The decline in the importance of tariff revenue coupled with the trade policy disaster of Smoot-Hawley led to the change in leadership on trade policy. The Reciprocal Trade Agreements Act shifted the lead role on trade policy from the legislative to the executive branch. From the 1930s to the 1990s, trade policy was driven by measures to liberalize trade emanating from the executive branch. Congress always had the final say in the passage of any trade agreements, but made little attempt to thwart the fundamental thrust of liberalizing trade. The passage of the North American Free Trade Agreement (NAFTA) marked a turning point in U.S. trade policy. NAFTA was granted congressional approval by a very narrow margin. Past this point, Congress has become much more activist in trade policy. The term "activist" needs to be qualified. Trade policy changes still are the result of actions by the executive branch—these are not formulated by Congress. Rather, any trade policy initiatives coming from the executive branch are carefully scrutinized by Congress. The result is that the formulation of trade policy is now far more balanced than it was prior to the passage of NAFTA. The president can no longer assume that the result of a trade negotiation will automatically pass Congress. Further, Congress has become increasingly reluctant to grant the president the needed authority to negotiate in the first place.

As a democracy, these shifts in the balance of power are related to political shifts. Historically, the Republican Party was the party of protectionism and the Democratic Party was more oriented to freer trade. From the 1930s until the 1990s, the Republican Party shifted its stance toward a more free-trade orientation as U.S. business became increasingly export oriented. This change in orientation in the party was not universal. In the Republican Party there is still a substantial minority that is deeply suspicious of the increasing globalization of the U.S. economy. The reverse was true for the Democratic Party. As imports increased, organized labor became increasingly in favor of protectionism. On the other hand, the majority of the party supports at least limited moves toward a more open U.S. economy. From the 1930s until the 21st century there was a solid bipartisan majority in Congress that was willing to let the president negotiate trade agreements. Unfortunately, the opposition to liberalizing trade in both parties has grown. The result is that there still is a majority in Congress that is willing to liberalize trade. However, this majority is now smaller and much more cautious. The really interesting aspect of all of this is that trade policy debates do not neatly split along party lines. There are significant minorities in both parties firmly opposed to further liberalization of trade. On the other hand, there is a majority in favor of more liberal trade. At this point, further trade agreements are dependent on the president and congressional leaders creating a bipartisan majority. Politically, this is no easy task. This difficulty is not purely a function of the preferences of elected officials. As we have seen, trade benefits the economy as a whole, but not necessarily all groups within the country. The benefits of trade frequently are widely dispersed and difficult to see clearly. On the other hand, the losses from trade are clearly visible. Plant closures and the resultant unemployment are very visible. In a democracy where the government routinely assists groups experiencing economic distress, it is unreasonable to ask groups adversely affected by trade to passively accept their losses. The bad news of this process is that the future liberalization of trade may well be slow and politically tedious. On the other hand, it assures that the gains and losses from trade have been carefully considered. Although this may superficially appear to be just politics as usual, public choice is at work in the background. If further gains from trade liberalization are the result of hard political battles, this is the result of the government making sure that the interests of all stakeholders in trade policy have been given the chance to influence policy.

Case Study: Trade Promotion Authority

As mentioned in Chapter 6, one of the provisions of the Reciprocal Trade Agreements Act was granting to the president the authority to negotiate trade agreements. Formal trade negotiations start with legislation enabling the president to negotiate trade agreements without explicit congressional interference. Congress is willing to allow this because any resulting agreement must, in the end, pass Congress. The original legislation provides that agreements must pass with limited time for debate and no amendments. This system became more formal with the passage of the Trade Act of 1974, which also set up the office of the U.S. Trade Representative. This act allowed negotiations until 1980 but was extended by Congress for eight more years. It was renewed again until 1993 to allow for the Uruguay Round negotiations. The expiration of negotiating authority was renewed in 2002 but expired again in 2007. Since 2007, Congress has taken a piecemeal approach. It has allowed fast-track rules for individual or small groups of RTAs to be voted on without amendment. On the other hand, Congress has been unwilling to give the president the broad authority to negotiate larger trade agreements such as the Trans-Pacific Partnership or a reciprocal trade agreement (RTA) with the European Union (EU). This hinders the ability of the United States to negotiate trade agreements because the U.S. Trade Representative is negotiating without the guarantee that the results of the negotiation will definitely be put to a congressional vote.

The story here is a familiar public choice story. Prior to the early 1990s, the attitude of Congress was that there was no harm in allowing the president to negotiate. The granting of this authority was politically routine. Congress was secure in the knowledge that the president would have to take its opinions into consideration during the negotiations to have any chance of the results being passed. After the bitter battle over the passage of NAFTA, the attitude of Congress toward the Trade Promotion Authority changed. Since the early 1990s, several presidents have found that obtaining this authority is not easy. Mercantilism is still alive and well in *both* political parties. For slightly different reasons, both the political right and left are opposed, sometimes adamantly, to globalization. In turn, this leads them to oppose any further movements toward free trade. As a result the leaders of both parties find it difficult to grant this authority without encountering stiff opposition. A number of special interest groups opposed to globalization have not been able to stop trade agreements, but they can slow them down. A useful way to accomplish this is by denying the president Trade Promotion Authority. This has made the process of negotiating RTAs more difficult. Given the virtual failure of the MTN process, slowing down the process of obtaining future RTAs has become the weapon of choice for protectionists.

Bibliography

Aaronson, Susan. 1991. "How Cordell Hull and the Postwar Planners Designed a New Trade Policy," *Business and Economic History* 20: 171–79.

Dam, Kenneth W. 2005. "Cordell Hull, the Reciprocal Trade Agreements Act, and the WTO: An Essay on the Concept of Rights in International Trade," *New York University Journal of Law and Business* 1: 709–30.

Diaz, George T. 2015. *Border Contraband: A History of Smuggling across the Rio Grande*. Austin, TX: University of Texas Press.

Eckes, Alfred E., Jr. 1995. *Opening America's Market: U.S. Foreign Trade Policy Since 1776*. Chapel Hill, NC: University of North Carolina Press.

McGillivray, Fiona, Iain McLean, Robert Pahre, and Cheryl Schonhardt-Bailey. 2001. *International Trade in the Long Nineteenth Century*. London: Edward Elgar.

Price, Carl E. and Mollie Keller. 1989. *The U.S. Customs Service: A Bicentennial History*. Washington, D.C.: U.S. Government Printing Office.

Schnietz, Karen E. 1994. "The 1916 Tariff Commission: Democrats' Use of Expert Information to Constrain Republican Tariff Protection," *Business and Economic History* 23(1): 176–89.

CHAPTER NINE

Administered Protection

*If the other fellow sells cheaper than you, it is called dumping. 'Course, if you sell
cheaper than him, that's mass production.*

—Will Rogers

Introduction

All through the book we have made an implicit assumption about trade
policy. The assumption was that all trade policy was being made by some
type of explicit government decision, such as what tariffs to change or
whether or not to participate in a multilateral or bilateral trade agreement.
In most countries, governments have chosen to delegate some of the decisions of trade policy to either a ministry of international trade or some other
government agency involved with trade policy. This process can be referred
to as either the bureaucratic track or administered protection. In our discussions of trade liberalization, we left out that international trade rules recognize several conditions under which countries can increase the level of
protectionism for an industry. Although the details vary by country, they
are all sanctioned by the World Trade Organization (WTO). The most often
used is the familiar issue of dumping. While less well known, there are also
provisions for offsetting foreign government subsidies and the temporary
protection of industries that are losing comparative advantage. The purpose
of this chapter is to familiarize you with the three different forms of administered protection. They are separate and distinct. Unfortunately, much of
the commentary on these issues isn't clear about these distinctions, and
the result is the writing sometimes creates more confusion about precisely
what is happening. Finally, trade policy does not occur in a vacuum. The
final section of the chapter reviews what we know about how the process is influenced by the parts of the economy most heavily influenced
by trade policy.

The Bureaucratic Track

Throughout most of the history of the United States, Congress was able to change the tariff on any product at any time. The ebb and flow of the need for revenue, changes in comparative advantage, and changes in the political power of industries and workers could be quickly reflected in the tariff. The Reciprocal Trade Agreements Act of 1934 (RTAA) marked a dramatic change in Congress's ability to respond to changing economic conditions by changing the tariff. What was obvious about the RTAA was that it transferred a substantial amount of the responsibility for trade policy to the president. What was less obvious is that changes in tariffs primarily came to be associated with some form of trade agreement. Rather than micromanaging tariffs on a year-to-year basis, tariffs became set by trade agreements for the long run. This became even more true with the advent of the General Agreement on Tariffs and Trade (GATT) and later the WTO. Under the GATT, all of country's tariffs were bound. What this meant was that when a country joined the GATT, it no longer had the option of increasing its tariffs under normal circumstances. This was one of the reasons that the number of contracting parties in the GATT initially was slow to increase. Once a country joined the GATT, it lost a significant amount of autonomy in setting tariffs. From that point on, a country's tariffs could only move in one direction, and that was down. As countries participated in the various multilateral trade negotiations (MTNs), they were negotiating ever lower tariff levels. Again, these new lower tariffs were bound. Once in place, they could not be raised. Over time the effect was like an ever-tightening vise. Tariffs continued to fall, and once they had fallen they could not be raised. Initially this was not too much of a problem. Recall that the average tariff in the United States after Smoot-Hawley was approximately 60 percent. Even after the initial tariff-cutting MTNs, tariffs in the United States and other developed countries were still relatively high. However, after the Kennedy and Tokyo Rounds, tariff cuts were implemented, the average level of protection under 10 percent. With the wave of reciprocal trade agreements (RTAs) being signed by the United States, the average tariff in the United States is now less than 2 percent. For many U.S. industries there now is virtually no significant protection. Further, it is hard to either raise a bound tariff or legislate punitive tariffs on a particular country. As we saw earlier, comparative advantage can change over time. The contracting parties to the GATT and the members of the WTO have been in the process of lowering tariffs for nearly 60 years. Tariff cuts that were agreed to decades ago may have been based on a pattern of comparative advantage that no longer exists. Changing comparative advantage coupled with very low tariffs can create a situation where changing trade patterns can put enormous strain on industries that are losing comparative advantage. In turn, governments find that their options in protecting such industries are limited. This situation leaves governments in the position of badly wanting to offer protection to industries with sufficient political influence but limited means of doing so. As tariffs have been reduced and trade becomes more liberalized, this puts an increasing focus on the few avenues that were provided in the original GATT (and now WTO) that allow countries to increase tariffs.

Administered Protection

One of the best examples of politics at work in international trade policy is the phrase coined by Finger, Hall, and Nelson (1982): administered protection. One of the effects of a country imposing a tariff is that domestic firms and industries gain additional producer surplus through additional sales and higher prices. Current WTO rules have made it difficult for a country to unilaterally increase tariffs on selected products. Effectively, the tariff on any particular product by a country is "bound." What this means is that any member country of the WTO cannot simply raise the tariff because of pressure from an industry or a special interest group. As a result, countries have developed several forms of what is known as administered protection.

Although there are several different forms of administered protection, they all involve increasing the tariff on a particular imported good. These forms of administered protection are sanctioned by the WTO. What this means is that it is possible for an industry in the United States or another country to obtain an increase in a tariff in a manner that is consistent with a complex set of WTO rules. The goal of these rules is to protect domestic industries from "unfair" foreign competition. As we will see, "unfair" in this case may mean something different than how most of us understand the word. It has been suggested that things have gotten to the point where the possession of comparative advantage is now an unfair trade practice. Administered protection by the United States is not trivial in size. The U.S. International Trade Commission (1995) has estimated that antidumping statutes alone cost the U.S. economy $1.16 billion per year. Protected firms and workers gain $685 million and the rest of society loses $1.85 billion.

Antidumping

The first type of administered protection that a country can impose is called the antidumping law. Technically, this is Section 703 of the Tariff Act of 1930. An antidumping law does not allow a firm to sell its product in an export market for less than it is sold for in its home market. Dumping by a firm or industry can be defined in two ways. Cost-based dumping occurs when a firm sells a product at a price below its cost of production in a foreign market. Price-based dumping is when a firm sells a product in a foreign market at a price lower than the price charged in its home market. The U.S. antidumping laws are based on either form of dumping.

Dumping by a foreign firm can occur for three reasons. First, a foreign firm may find it in their best interest to sell their product at a lower price in a foreign market for a relatively short period. This is called sporadic dumping. For example, if the foreign firm finds itself with excess inventory, the quickest way to reduce the inventory may be to "dump" the unwanted inventory in foreign markets. This is the international equivalent of a "sale." This form of dumping can occur due to the international asymmetry of the business cycle, and is sometimes referred to as cyclical dumping. For example, suppose that the Japanese economy is in the middle of a recession and the U.S. economy is in the middle of an economic expansion. In this case, it is easy to see why Japanese producers would attempt to sell excess inventory in the U.S. market. With slack domestic demand in Japan, a firm may not be able to make a profit but may be concerned with minimizing losses in the short run. So long as the firm sells the product at anything above marginal cost, losses for the firm would be minimized. Such behavior by firms is routine and would pass unnoticed in a large domestic market such as the United States. Such sporadic dumping is often seen as a part of doing business, but in an international context it can draw legal action from the industry in the importing country.

The second type of dumping, persistent dumping, is the sale of a product in a foreign market at a price below that sold in the domestic market over an extended period. If different markets have different elasticities of demand, then it is often in the firm's best interest—maximization of profits—to charge different prices in each market. This is the sort of routine price discrimination that one sees in a large domestic market. Many products in the United States sell at somewhat different prices in different regions. If the differences in these elasticities of demand between the two markets persists, then the "dumping" may likewise persist. Unlike sporadic dumping, persistent dumping may cause lasting damage to the domestic industry.

A final type of dumping is predatory dumping. The intent of a firm engaged in predatory dumping is to price its product in such a way so as to drive domestic firms out of business. Once the domestic competitors exit the market, the foreign firm then is in a position to raise prices and maximize profits in the long run. Such predatory pricing is illegal in the United States, even if no foreign firms are involved. However, no foreign firm has ever been found guilty of predatory dumping.

History of Antidumping Law in the United States

The original U.S. antidumping law passed in 1916 prohibited only predatory dumping. This law simply extended the Sherman Antitrust Act to the activities of foreign firms. The intent of the law was to create a level playing field for domestic and foreign firms. The law is still on the books. It requires showing an intent to injure. It has rarely been used and has never been successfully invoked. This is a point one should keep in mind. The legislative changes that have followed the original antidumping law have created a bias in favor of domestic firms. With the Antidumping Act of 1921, Congress loosened the requirements on antidumping to permit federal government action to further restrict imports. Under this act, foreign companies now could be charged with dumping even if there was no proof of predatory pricing. It is this act that forms the basis for current U.S. antidumping law. The Antidumping Act was incorporated into the 1930 Tariff Act and subsequently amended in 1979, 1984, and 1988. The result of these amendments has been to make it easier to restrict foreign imports sold at lower prices than similar U.S. goods. The Trade Agreements Act of 1979 was a watershed piece in the history of antidumping law. It transferred the determination of the dumping margin from the Treasury Department to the Department of Commerce. This transfer occurred because the former was not considered as understanding of the interests of domestic industry as the latter.

From its inception in 1948, the GATT sanctioned the concept of antidumping laws. Originally, antidumping laws were included in Article VI of the GATT. The Kennedy Round of the GATT led to the adoption of the GATT Antidumping Code. This code provides guidelines under which countries may act against foreign firms that engage in predatory pricing that result in material injury to an industry based in the importing country. The antidumping code simply creates the guidelines, and countries can adopt their own antidumping laws. This code was amended during the Uruguay Round of the GATT. According to the amended code, each signatory country can legislate and administer its antidumping law as long as it conforms to WTO standards.

The original intent of U.S. antidumping law was to prevent predatory pricing of foreign firms. Over time the law was amended to prevent foreign firms from engaging in price-based dumping and cost-based dumping.

The immediate and obvious problem for foreign firms selling goods in the United States is that they can be legally prevented from pursuing pricing strategies that are perfectly legal for U.S. firms. In essence, the antidumping regulations have been "captured" by U.S. firms for their own advantage. Although the announced aim of the antidumping law is to protect U.S. industry from predatory dumping, the real aim is protectionism in the form of allowing U.S. firms the option to underprice foreign competition without foreign producers being able to retaliate. This misdirection seems to be the reason for the continued existence of antidumping laws in their current form; however, obfuscation is what keeps them going. The administration of antidumping laws in the United States has now become a complex process that only a few business people, economists, and lawyers understand.

Between 1980 and 2008, U.S. firms filed 1,158 antidumping cases. On average, 40 cases are filed per year. As is frequently the case, the devil is in the details. Once a case is filed, a regulatory process is set in motion that can take from 20 days to over a year to complete. Simply put, the U.S. government conducts two investigations. First, the International Trade Administration (ITA), which is a division of the Department of Commerce, conducts an investigation to determine if the imports in question are being "dumped" and, if so, by how much. Second, the U.S. International Trade Commission (USITC) conducts an investigation to determine if the alleged dumping is harming the domestic industry or firm. In the initial stages the ITA has 20 days to determine if the imports are being dumped. If the ITA makes a negative determination, the case is terminated. If the ITA finds that dumping is occurring, then the USITC works on a separate track to determine if the domestic industry is being injured. They have 45 days to make this determination. If the USITC finds that there is no injury to the domestic industry, then the case is terminated. If the ITA finds that dumping may be occurring and the ITC finds injury, then the case continues. If after 160 days the ITA finds that dumping is not occurring, then the case is terminated. If after 235 days the ITA still is finding dumping but the ITC has now determined that there is no injury to the domestic industry, then the case is terminated. After 280 days, if both the ITA finds dumping is occurring and the ITC determines that the U.S. industry is being injured, then a final determination of dumping is made. If this occurs, then on day 287, the Department of Commerce issues an order for a tariff to be imposed equal to the difference between the imported price and the fair value that has been determined. If the duty is imposed, it can stay in place for as long as five years. Many antidumping cases are "terminated" at one point or another in the process. This is not surprising. What occurs in many cases is that the foreign firms have simply agreed to raise prices in order to avoid explicit tariffs. This "harassment" effect has been demonstrated by Herander and Schwartz (1984). The same effects have been more recently estimated in Staiger and Wolak (1994).

Countervailing Duties

The second form of administered protection is a countervailing duty. This is a tariff designed to offset the effects of foreign government subsidies for exports. Between 1980 and 2005, 474 countervailing duty cases were filed in the United States. In an average year, 16 cases are filed. Like many economic issues, there are two views on this subject. If the increase in U.S. imports does not harm a domestic industry, one possible response by the government to such subsidies would be to send a "thank you" note to the foreign government. In this case, if a foreign government wishes to subsidize the consumption of U.S. citizens, then so much the better. The United States would have a higher standard of living at the expense of some other country's taxpayers. On the other hand, although it may be perfectly legitimate to ask our firms to compete with foreign firms, it may be asking a bit much for them to compete with foreign governments. In order to prevent this, U.S. trade law allows domestic firms to petition the U.S. government for a "countervailing duty" to offset foreign government subsidies on exports. The process of obtaining a countervailing duty is similar to that of an antidumping petition.

This countervailing duty is conceptually clear; however, determining the size of government subsidies is quite difficult in practice. Two problems arise in countervailing duty cases. First, there is the difficult issue of which government subsidies can be countervailed. Optimally, one would like to countervail direct subsidies on exports. A clear example would be a government subsidy of a certain monetary amount for each unit exported. However, government subsidies to firms and industries are rarely that clear. For example, assume that a foreign government subsidizes the research and development (R&D) expenses of an industry that subsequently exports the product. In this case, can that subsidy be countervailed? In some cases, the answer is yes and in other cases no. What about industry-specific tax breaks? The list of indirect subsidies to firms and industries can go on endlessly. Indeed, it is difficult to find any firm in any country that has not received some form of a government subsidy.

This leads to the second problem with countervailing duty cases: disentangling a country's trade policy from its industrial policy. For a variety of reasons, governments subsidize one industry or another. This encouragement or industrial policy may take the form of direct subsidies, partial or total government ownership, and tax relief. However, there is a potential conflict between a government's ability to pursue an active industrial policy and a level playing field in international markets. This conflict is not yet severe, but it is unlikely to go away. Other countries have similar laws. As a result, U.S. firms that export are not immune from these effects. Any firm receiving substantial government assistance is at risk of having its exports "countervailed" in foreign markets.

Safeguards

Occasionally, a country's comparative advantage can shift more quickly than the domestic industry can adjust. This situation leads to the final type of administered protection: safeguards. Until recently, the term "escape clause" was more commonly used than safeguards. A safeguard allows a domestic industry to petition the government for temporary protection to allow the industry a chance to adjust their operations to compete with the more intense import competition. The purpose of the safeguard is to protect domestic firms, which might be profitable in the long run, from being driven out of business due to an increase in imports that has occurred in a short period.

In this case, the USITC investigates the industry and makes a determination on whether or not the industry is being harmed by imports. The final decision on whether or not to protect the industry is made by the president. Surprisingly, the filing of these petitions is fairly rare. Since 1975, approximately 75 cases have been filed. Virtually all countries have this type of administered protection, which is perfectly legal under the WTO. The escape clause may be particularly important in a period of floating exchange rates. A loss of comparative advantage coupled with an overvalued exchange rate may produce a situation where the firms might be able to deal with efficient foreign competitors or an overvalued exchange rate, but not both. When protection is granted, the tariff is usually raised on the particular good and then gradually lowered over a period of time such as five years.

An example of relief under safeguards occurred in 2002, when President George Bush imposed tariffs ranging from 8 percent to 30 percent on a variety of imported steel products. Under this relief, the new tariffs were to be phased out over a three-year period. The design of the import relief is to give the U.S. steel producers time so that they can bring the costs under control and upgrade equipment. Critics of the import relief argue that protecting the U.S. steel industry raises the cost to steel-using industries and causes a decrease in employment in the steel-using sectors of the economy.

Trade Policy and Public Choice

A government that robs Peter to pay Paul can always depend upon the support of Paul.

—*George Bernard Shaw*

The use of both tariff and nontariff barriers to trade tends to make a country as a whole worse off. However, these effects are not uniform. The gains to consumers tend to be widely dispersed and in many cases hardly noticeable. However, the losses to domestic producers and workers can be very concentrated. As a result, some firms and workers might seek protection from the government. In this chapter, we will explain why most countries provide protection to some domestic industries. We begin by analyzing the political economy of protection. Protection from imports may not be in the country's best interest, but it is in the interest of selected special interest groups. We also explain a country's structure of protection by describing why the tariff is high for some goods and low for others. We start by outlining the theory of public choice. This is a broad area involving the application of economic logic to the political process and the process of making economic policy. Once one understands public choice in general, then the application of public choice to international trade policy isn't too hard. From there we can consider a very practical application of the theory known as the structure of protection. As is usually the case in economics, we use the theory with some confidence because it has been subject to extensive empirical tests.

Given that a country as a whole gains from trade, one would expect free trade to dominate most countries' international trade policy. Trade barriers cost the economy more in lost consumer surplus than is gained by producers and the government. However, as we saw in the last two chapters, firms and workers in import-competing industries gain from trade barriers. As we will see in what follows, the interaction between the gains from trade for the country and the gains from trade barriers for producers explains the existence of trade barriers. The result is that free trade is not most countries' international trade policy.

In economics, policy refers to an action or actions that a government implements. For example, governments regulate industries and firms in a number of areas. These regulations are designed to strengthen, facilitate, supplement, or modify economic activity. In the presence of market failures, government regulation can improve the welfare of society if the benefits of correcting them exceed the costs. Such regulations are commonly observed for pollution or in the food and pharmaceutical industries. Not all government regulation of industries and firms works to the benefit of society as a whole; some regulations favor one segment of society but leave the overall economy worse off. Not surprisingly, industries and firms that benefit from regulation favor it. For example, it is illegal for firms to conspire to fix or raise prices. However, firms can legally raise prices if the government regulates and enforces minimum prices for an industry's product. In this case, firms in this industry may find it in their own interest to accept regulation if it can enhance their profitability. In an insightful paper, Pelzman (1976) pointed out that businesses and other groups in the economy could have a demand for regulation.

The existence of a demand for regulation means that there is a potential market for government regulation. In this case the government is acting something like a monopsonist (i.e., the sole supplier). One area where a market for government regulation exists is international trade. Imports of goods and services have conflicting effects. Consumers want the benefits that come from free trade, but firms and workers in the industries that compete with imports want to restrict trade. Olsen (1965) argued that there is a conflict between economic welfare and the development of special interest groups. In the United States, special interest groups lobby for changes in laws and regulations that will benefit them, although not society as a whole. Lobbying to restrict international trade has a long history in the United States and in most other countries. For example, the U.S. steel industry petitioned for increased trade barriers in 2002 and the President authorized additional trade restrictions on imported steel to protect the domestic industry. The question to be answered is why the activities of special interest groups may succeed even if the regulation they favor lowers the welfare of the society as a whole.

Over the last 40 years, economists have developed the theory of public choice to describe political behavior. However, economists are not alone. A branch of political science known as positive political science also has emerged. The premise underlying the theory of public choice is that politicians, like all individuals, attempt to maximize their utility. Utility maximization for a politician, in most cases, means maximizing the number of votes he or she will receive in the next election. This implies that politicians tend to favor programs with immediate and clear-cut benefits combined with vague, difficult-to-measure, or deferred costs. Likewise, politicians generally do not support programs with future benefits that are vague and difficult to measure coupled with immediate and easily identifiable costs.

For example, consider a country contemplating freer trade. At first, it might seem that a politician's optimal strategy for securing votes would be to favor the reduction of trade barriers. As we have shown using trade theory, the abundant factor of production gains from free trade and the scarce factor of production loses from free trade. Furthermore, there are more consumers that would benefit from lower trade barriers than there are firms producing goods that ineffectively compete with imports. For both political and economic reasons, it would seem that free trade would be the optimal vote-maximizing strategy for a politician.

Unfortunately, it is not that simple. In a democracy, individuals have an incentive to form groups designed to influence the government to pass laws that serve their collective interest. This behavior is called collective action. In the case of international trade policy, although a country benefits from free trade, the gains to individual consumers are relatively small per good consumed. Usually an individual consumer cannot quantitatively feel the gains from trade. The result is that in general individuals do not form groups to lobby the government for freer trade. In addition, tariff rates and the price increases associated with nontariff barriers to trade are not explicitly known by consumers. As a result, the effects of restricted trade may go unnoticed by the consuming public. The other group that gains from free trade is industries that have a comparative advantage. However, what these export-oriented firms are interested in is the international trade policy of other countries. As a group, these firms want free trade—or at least fewer restrictions on their exports to foreign countries. They have an interest in domestic trade policy only to the extent that they use imported inputs. The result is that these industries do not have a strong incentive to lobby for lower domestic trade barriers.

The group with a clear economic interest to lobby the domestic government concerning trade policy is the group that ineffectively competes with imports. They have a strong incentive to form special interest groups and engage in collective action to obtain protection from imports. Although protectionism is not in the country's interest, it is in the interest of this special interest group. For example, the debate over the increased protection of the U.S. steel industry focused on the gains to the steel industry and its workers versus the increased cost of steel to the U.S. economy as a whole.

Following Krueger (1974), activities that are designed to benefit a special interest group are called rent-seeking activities. Rent seeking is the act of obtaining special treatment by the government at the expense of society as a whole. For example, requesting that the government raise or not lower a tariff on a particular good is a form of rent-seeking behavior. Such behavior also may help maximize the votes a politician receives in the next election. Voting for protection may gain a politician a few additional votes from the industry, firm, and workers that receive the protection.

In this case, the politician attempts to gain the extra votes that are contingent on voting for protection and simultaneously minimize the harmful effects of protection on society as a whole. In the United States and virtually all other countries, the tariff imposed on goods varies considerably from one good to another. In fact, the U.S. tariff schedule is an extremely complicated document because tariffs are levied on very specific goods or very specific product categories. Complexity in a country's tariff schedule provides two advantages. First, a producer of a good that competes with imports can focus their lobbying efforts for protection on a particular good. For example, it is easier to gain protection for a product like imported bacon than for all imported food products. After all, consumers are not likely to notice a small increase in the price of bacon because prices on all products constantly change to reflect market conditions. However, if a tariff is imposed on all imported food products, the price increases might not go unnoticed by consumers (voters). Second, a detailed tariff schedule makes it possible for a politician to pick up votes by protecting one specific good without inducing protests from the average consumer (voter). For these reasons, most countries have developed very complicated tariff schedules and the tariffs on very similar goods may be dramatically different. In the following section, we present a more precise explanation of what causes the differences in tariffs for different products.

The Complexity of Fruit Juice

Table 9.1 is a copy of several pages of the tariff schedule for the United States. It includes the most favored nation (MFN) tariff for fruit and fruit juices that are applied to WTO member countries. Note that frozen orange juice importers pay a tariff of 7.85 cents per liter to the U.S. government. Orange juice has a tariff of only 4.5 cents per liter, and the tariff is even lower for grapefruit juice. Yet foreign-produced apple juice is imported into the U.S. duty free. Apparently, the grapefruit growers and apple growers associations are not as efficient in lobbying for their interests as is the orange growers association. Examine the different juices listed and notice the mixture of tariffs in place on each product. If you were to examine any page of the U.S. tariff schedule, you would find the same dramatic differences in tariffs by product.

Keep in mind that the tariff schedule is less complicated than it used to be. The previous *Tariff Schedule of the United States* was in use until 1988. However, the tariff schedule was considerably more complicated than the new Harmonized Tariff Schedule (HTS). The advantage of the new HTS is that it makes tariff schedules more similar across countries. This is an obvious advantage in trade negotiations and for companies exporting to more than one country. The HTS was authorized in Section 1207 of the Omnibus Trade and Competitiveness Act of 1988. It is currently in its ninth edition. If the included paragraph and the table seem horrifically dull, consider that for international trade policy specialists, this sort of material is the raw stuff of their jobs.

Table 9.1 Preparations of Vegetables, Fruit, Nuts or Other Parts of Plants

Heading/ Subheading	Statistical Suffix	Article Description	Rates of Duty
2009		Fruit juices (including grape must) and vegetable juices, not fortified with vitamins or minerals, unfermented and not containing added spirit, whether or not containing added sugar or other sweetening matter:	
		Orange juice:	
2009.11.00		Frozen	7.85¢/liter
	20	In containers each holding less than 0.946 liter	
	40	In containers each holding 0.946 liter or more but not more than 3.785 liters	
	60	In containers of more than 3.785 liters	
2009.12		Not frozen, of a Brix value not exceeding 20:	
2009.12.25	00	Not concentrated and not made from a juice having a degree of concentration of 1.5 or more (as determined before correction to the nearest 0.5 degree)	4.5¢/liter
2009.12.45	00	Other	7.85¢/liter
		Grapefruit juice:	
2009.21		Of a Brix value not exceeding 20:	
2009.21.20	00	Not concentrated and not made from a juice having a degree of concentration of 1.5 or more (as determined before correction to the nearest 0.5 degree)	4.5¢/ liter

(*continued*)

Table 9.1   Preparations of Vegetables, Fruit, Nuts or Other Parts of Plants
(*continued*)

Heading/ Subheading	Statistical Suffix	Article Description	Rates of Duty
2009.21.40		Other	7.9¢/liter
	20	Frozen	
	40	Other	
2009.29.00		Other	7.9¢/liter
	20	Frozen	
	40	Other	
		Juice of any other single citrus fruit:	
2009.31		Of a Brix value not exceeding 20:	
		Lime:	
2009.31.10		Unfit for beverage purposes	1.8¢/kg
	20	Not concentrated	
	40	Concentrated	
2009.31.20		Other	1.7¢/liter
	20	Not concentrated	
	40	Concentrated	
		Other:	
2009.31.40		Not concentrated	3.4¢/liter
	20	Lemon juice	
	40	Other	
2009.31.60		Concentrated	7.9¢/liter
		Lemon juice:	
	20	Frozen	
	40	Other	
	60	Other	
2009.39		Other:	
		Lime:	
2009.39.10	00	Unfit for beverage purposes	1.8¢/kg
2009.39.20	00	Other	1.7¢/liter
2009.39.60		Other	7.9¢/liter
		Lemon juice:	
	20	Frozen	
	40	Other	
	60	Other	

(*continued*)

Table 9.1   Preparations of Vegetables, Fruit, Nuts or Other Parts of Plants
(*continued*)

Heading/ Subheading	Statistical Suffix	Article Description	Rates of Duty
		Pineapple juice:	
2009.41		Of a Brix value not exceeding 20:	
2009.41.20	00	Not concentrated, or having a degree of concentration of not more than 3.5 (as determined before correction to the nearest 0.5 degree)	4.2¢/liter
2009.41.40		Other	1¢/liter
	20	Frozen	
	40	Other	
2009.49		Other:	
2009.49.20	00	Not concentrated, or having a degree of concentration of not more than 3.5 (as determined before correction to the nearest 0.5 degree)	4.2¢/liter
2009.49.40		Other	1¢/liter
	20	Frozen	
	40	Other	
2009.50.00		**Tomato juice:**	0.14¢/liter
	10	In airtight containers	
	90	Other	
		Grape juice (including grape must):	
2009.61.00		Of a Brix value not exceeding 30	4.4¢/liter
	20	Not concentrated	
		Concentrated:	
	40	Frozen	
	60	Other	
2009.69.00		Other	4.4¢/liter
	40	Frozen	
	60	Other	
		Apple juice:	
2009.71.00	00	Of a Brix value not exceeding 20	Free
2009.79.00		Other	Free
	10	Frozen	
	20	Other	

(*continued*)

Table 9.1 Preparations of Vegetables, Fruit, Nuts or Other Parts of Plants (*continued*)

Heading/ Subheading	Statistical Suffix	Article Description	Rates of Duty
2009.80		**Juice of any other single fruit or vegetable:**	
		Fruit juice:	
2009.80.20	00	Pear juice	Free
2009.80.40	00	Prune juice	0.64¢/liter
2009.80.60		Other 1/	0.5¢/liter
	10	Cherry juice	
	20	Berry juice	
	90	Other	
2009.80.80		Vegetable juice	0.2¢/liter
	31	In airtight containers	
	39	Other	
2009.90		Mixtures of juices:	
2009.90.20	00	Vegetable	0.2¢/liter
2009.90.40	00	Other	7.4¢/liter

Source: U.S. International Trade Commission (2014).

In most countries, the tariff schedule is as complicated as the example indicated in the box. Tariffs can vary considerably even for reasonably similar goods. This analysis of variation in tariffs by product for a country is called the structure of protection. Researchers have been studying why the tariff on one specific good is low and on another specific good is high. In reviewing the literature, Baldwin (1989) found that the research indicates that the interaction between politicians and special groups described earlier is useful in describing the structure of protection. More specifically, the research provides a list of factors that influence the probability that an industry will receive or maintain protection.

First, large industries that are important to a country are more likely to receive protection than are small, unimportant industries. This implies that it may be easier for automobile producers to obtain protection than it would be for motor-scooter producers. Second, the fewer number of firms (more concentrated) in the industry, the more likely it is protected from imports. This is because it is easier for the firms to organize and lobby the domestic government for protection when there are fewer firms. As a practical matter we measure this using the percentage of industry sales accounted for by the four largest firms (CR4). Third, it is easier for firms to obtain protection if they produce an intermediate product, such as steel, in which the voters are unlikely to notice price increases. Fourth, the potential voting strength of the industry's employees affects the degree of protection. Industries that have a larger number of employees are more likely to be protected than those that have fewer employees. In addition, if the industry is regionally concentrated and/or unionized, the workers are able to lobby more effectively for protection. Finally, industries that have a comparative disadvantage are more likely to be protected. Firms and workers in these industries have more to lose from freer trade than those industries that have a comparative advantage. This is particularly true for U.S. industries that intensively use unskilled labor.

This research indicates that an industry characterized by one or more of these factors does not guarantee it will be protected. However, if an industry has one or more of these characteristics, there is a higher *probability* that it will have a higher tariff. The same logic would apply to the existence of nontariff barriers to trade. For example, the U.S. steel industry has consistently obtained high levels of protection. The steel industry is large in terms of output and employment; the workers are unionized; the industry is highly concentrated and is somewhat regionally concentrated; and it is an intermediate product. As documented by Kreinin (1984) and in subsequent bouts of protectionism, the steel industry has been able to obtain a higher tariff than the national average for manufacturers. In addition, recent research on this issue has focused on developing more formal theoretical models to describe the process of obtaining protection. However, this newer research by Grossman and Helpman (1994) does not alter the conclusions given earlier.

Uniform Tariffs in Chile

Although there are no efficiency reasons for uniform import tariffs, there are practical political economy considerations for advocating a flat import structure.

—*Sebastian Edwards*

Economists such as Edwards (1997) have long advocated a uniform tariff that would solve a number of problems associated with a complicated tariff schedule. One, the tariff becomes easy to administer because customs officials would not have to worry about classifying a product into whatever category it might best fit. For example, is a sport utility vehicle a car or a truck? (The U.S. tariff on a car is 2.5 percent, whereas the tariff on a truck is 25 percent.) Two, a uniform tariff makes lobbying for protectionism *much* harder. If an import-competing industry wants an increase in the tariff, the tariff would have to increase on all imports. This is likely to create some resistance for several reasons:

- A general increase in the tariff is unlikely to pass by consumers completely unnoticed.
- Other industries capable of lobbying the government would likely do so.
- Firms purchasing imported intermediate products would see the increase in the tariff as a direct increase in their costs and would complain to the government. Under most supply and demand conditions, the firms could not pass all of this cost increase on to consumers and, therefore, profits would fall.
- The same would be true of firms that are purchasing imports for final sale to the consumer. Firms that export may find tariff increases especially harmful as it may dilute their ability to compete in international markets. The net result is that more firms may lose from the higher tariff than the number of firms that might gain from it.
- Add consumer preferences to the mix, and the optimal public-choice strategy for a politician may well be *lower* tariffs.

What we have just described is much like what happened in Chile during the last 20 years. In the early 1970s, Chile had tariffs that were high and very complex. These tariffs were replaced by a 10 percent uniform tariff in 1979. In response to an economic crisis in the 1980s, the uniform tariff was raised to 35 percent. Since the mid-1980s, the uniform tariff has fallen to 7 percent. A uniform tariff may be the best alternative to free trade. Corbo (1997) and others have concluded that in Chile, where it has been tried for 20 years, it appears to work fairly well.

Case Study: Harley-Davidson

In the early 1980s, the classic American motorcycle firm, Harley-Davidson, was on the brink of bankruptcy. The firm was in serious trouble due to a combination of adverse factors. First, by its own admission, Harley-Davidson had been poorly managed in the 1970s. Second, the firm was facing a flood of cheaper, higher-quality imports from Japan. Japanese firms were obviously intent on penetrating the U.S. market, but a Japanese recession was giving them even more incentive to export than usual. Related to this was a seriously overvalued exchange rate. A combination of unusually low Japanese interest rates coupled with high rates in the United States produced an exceptionally low value for the Japanese yen. At an exchange rate of 250 yen to the dollar, it was difficult for many producers in the United States and elsewhere to compete with the Japanese. Third, the United States was just emerging from a recession in the early 1980s, so domestic sales were below average even without imports. Durable goods always suffer disproportionately in a recession, particularly if they are recreational goods such as motorcycles. Finally, the dollar was becoming increasingly overvalued, making it even easier for Japanese firms to sell in the U.S. market at very competitive prices.

Faced with this situation, Harley-Davidson filed a safeguard petition arguing that the firm could survive and compete with the Japanese given some time to adjust. In 1983, the USITC recommended to President Ronald Reagan that the firm be granted relief. Tariffs were increased to 45 percent from 4 percent the first year and were to decline progressively to 10 percent in 1987. A year ahead of schedule, Harley-Davidson notified the government that it was now competitive and did not need the final year of protection. The rest, of course, is history.

Bibliography

Baldwin, Robert E. 1989. "The Political Economy of Trade Policy," *Journal of Economic Perspectives* 3(4): 119–36.

Corbo, Vittorio. 1997. "Trade Reform and Uniform Import Tariffs: The Chilean Experience," *American Economic Review* 87(2): 73–77.

Edwards, Sebastian. 1997. "Trade Liberalization Reforms and the World Bank," *American Economic Review* 87(3): 43–48.

Finger, J. Michael, H. Keith Hall, and Douglas R. Nelson. 1982. "The Political Economy of Administered Protection," *American Economic Review* 72(3): 452–66.

Grossman, Gene M. and Elhanan Helpman. 1994. "Protection for Sale," *American Economic Review* 84(4): 813–50.

Herander, Mark G. and J. Brad Schwartz. 1984. "An Empirical Test of the Impact of the Threat of U.S. Trade Policy: The Case of Antidumping Duties," *Southern Economic Journal* 51(1): 59–79.

Kreinin, Mordechai E. 1984. "Wage Competitiveness in the U.S. Auto and Steel Industries," *Contemporary Economic Policy* 2(4): 39–50.

Krueger, Anne O. 1974. "The Political Economy of the Rent-Seeking Society," *American Economic Review* 64: 291–303.

Olsen, Mancur. 1965. *The Logic of Collective Action*. Cambridge, MA: Harvard University Press.

Pelzman, Sam. 1976. "Toward a More General Theory of Regulation," *Journal of Law and Economics* 19(2): 211–40.

Staiger, Robert W. and Frank A. Wolak. 1994. "Measuring Industry Specific Protection: Antidumping in the United States," *Brookings Papers on Economic Activity, Microeconomics* 1: 51–103.

U.S. International Trade Commission. 1995. "The Economic Effects of Antidumping and Countervailing Duty Orders and Suspension Agreements," Investigation No. 332–344, Publication 2900.

U.S. International Trade Commission. 2014. *Harmonized Tariff Schedule of the United States*. Washington, D.C.: U.S. Government Printing Office.

CHAPTER TEN

Trade Policy in the 21st Century

Introduction

It is no exaggeration to say that the 20th century was the most momentous century in the history of trade policy. It started with the governments of the developed countries engaging in trade policy as they had for centuries. Tariffs were changed annually in response to the need for revenue and the need to change tariffs due to domestic political considerations. The disaster of a global trade war in the 1930s coupled with the decreasing importance of tariffs as a source of government revenue changed trade policy around the world. In the post–World War II era the various rounds of multilateral trade negotiations (MTNs) drastically reduced the tariffs of the developed countries. The developing countries were latecomers to this process but are now in the slow process of liberalizing trade. Given the major changes in trade policy in the 20th century, it is safe to say that the changes in the 21st century will be less drastic.

Although no one can say with certainty how trade policy will change in the coming decades, there are a number of general areas to watch. The first is the movement from multilateral trade negotiations to regional trade agreements. Second, the creation of the World Trade Organization (WTO) in the last decade of the 20th century was a watershed event in trade policy that is generally not appreciated. Third, a combination of the WTO and the uncertainty over future MTNs creates the possibility of a new form of trade negotiations that has already proven successful and could be a way forward for global liberalization of trade. Fourth, the developing countries are only just starting to liberalize trade and more fully participate in the formulation of global trade policy. Currently, they are at a crossroads, and how they move forward on trade policy will influence the world economy in the 21st century. Finally, this is a U.S.-centric book. Like the developing countries, the United States is also at a crossroads in trade policy. The choice that the United States makes going forward will not only affect U.S. trade policy, but also global trade policy.

Multilateralism Versus Regional Trade Agreements

One of the more contentious issues in international economics is the debate over trade liberalization. Aside from the formation and expansion of the European Union (EU), until the 1980s trade liberalization occurred mostly within the framework of the various MTNs. However, since then there has been a rapid proliferation of regional trade agreements (RTAs). Like most economic phenomenon, this development has both benefits and costs. The main difference is that the benefits and costs of RTAs cannot be perfectly calculated. This lack of certainty has developed into a situation where some economists have serious reservations about the rapid spread of RTAs. As one would expect, this group of economists emphasizes the costs of RTAs relative to the benefits. The other side of the debate does just the opposite. Their conclusion is that the potential benefits of RTAs outweigh the admitted costs. At this point, there is no precise answer to this debate.

Until the 1980s, trade liberalization was occurring primarily through multilateral trade negotiations under the auspices of General Agreement on Tariffs and Trade (GATT). Theoretically, this nondiscriminatory reduction in trade barriers is the optimum method to reduce trade barriers. If trade barriers are reduced on an MFN basis, there is only trade creation and no trade diversion. Trade creation is the increase in trade that occurs when trade barriers are lowered. Trade diversion is the loss that occurs to non-members of an RTA as they now face higher trade barriers than member countries. Trade diversion occurs only if trade liberalization is discriminatory, meaning that one country is treated differently than another country. In a perfect world, trade liberalization would occur only on a multilateral basis, with no discrimination between countries. This is one of the strongest arguments for MTNs. RTAs inherently threaten this process because they are *inherently* discriminatory. Member countries are treated differently than nonmember countries. RTAs enhance world welfare if total trade creation is larger than trade diversion. However, this enhancement may come at a high cost. First, as RTAs spread, world trade becomes more complicated. For example, what is the tariff on a particular product? With RTAs, the answer depends on which country you are talking about. Consider a current example. What is the U.S. tariff on steel? If the steel comes from Israel or Canada, the tariff is zero. If the steel comes from Jordan, one must go to the U.S. tariff schedule to see what the current status of the steel tariff is because the free-trade agreements (FTAs) with these countries are not fully phased in. If the steel is coming from a developing country, it might qualify for duty-free entry under a number of U.S. trade agreements designed to assist such countries. This is just one example of a product imported into the United States. Because there are many countries now involved in many different RTAs, world trade has become more complicated. The world trading system is at risk of going back to the situation that existed prior to GATT. Each country potentially had a different tariff for each product for specific countries. In economic terms, this causes an increasing amount of trade diversion that potentially reduces world welfare.

A second cost of RTAs is more subtle. Countries only have a limited amount of time and expertise to expend on the issue of trade liberalization. As RTAs spread, governments will spend more resources on RTA negotiations. This implies that they will expend fewer resources negotiating under the WTO framework. As a result, the process of obtaining multilateral trade liberalization becomes more difficult with the spread of RTAs. The opponents of RTAs emphasize these costs. They fear that the spread of RTAs is jeopardizing the nondiscriminatory nature of world trade that had been developed under the GATT/WTO framework. Further, they fear that RTAs tend to distract government attention away from the process of liberalizing world trade in a nondiscriminatory fashion. There is not a lot of argument among economists about these points. World trade is becoming more complicated, and the amount of trade diversion is rising. No doubt part of the problem with the Uruguay and Doha MTNs has been that governments no longer view them as the only way to liberalize world trade.

However, other economists are not so concerned about the development of RTAs. They freely admit that the opponents of the spread of RTAs are correct in the points made earlier. However, they consider other factors that make the spread of RTAs look considerably less ominous. First, it must be pointed out that RTAs are legal under the WTO. In order to be legal, an RTA must cover substantially all trade, be completed within a reasonable period, and result in an average level of protection against nonmembers that was not higher than before the agreement. This has always been the case, as RTAs normally produce more trade creation than trade diversion. Slowing the spread of RTAs probably would involve an amendment of WTO rules to make it harder for countries to form them. Such a development is unlikely. Subject to the current rules, the spread of RTAs is something like a free market where governments can engage in RTAs or not depending on their preferences.

Also the spread of RTAs may be saying something about governments' preferences for them. In the first place, suppose that two countries, such as Germany and Austria, naturally have a close economic relationship. The two countries are geographically close and share a common language. Further suppose that Germany and Austria wish to form an FTA or an even deeper RTA. In this situation, should WTO rules make this difficult for the two countries to accomplish? The point is that it would be awkward to establish WTO rules that would make an RTA easy to form for Austria and Germany but hard for the United States and Singapore. Second, there is the issue of the depth of economic integration. In chapter 7, we discussed the various types of RTAs. The difference in types is related to the depth of integration. One of the current problems with multilateral liberalization is that the depth of integration being pursued is not very deep. If one compares the agenda of the Doha Round to the current depth of integration in the EU or even the North American Free Trade Agreement (NAFTA), the issue becomes obvious. In some cases, countries want to pursue a level of economic integration that is not possible in a multilateral framework. If a country wants to pursue deeper levels of economic integration with other countries, it has little choice but to negotiate RTAs. One final advantage of RTAs relates to the adjustment of the domestic economy to higher levels of import competition. Although multilateral trade liberalization may be desirable, the adjustment costs for some domestic industries may be quite high. If trade barriers are reduced on a global basis, imports in a particular product category potentially could increase by a large amount. The costs for domestic industries in terms of lost profits and/or job losses likewise could be high. The costs for domestic industries by an RTA may well be lower, as trade barriers are being reduced for a smaller number of countries. Because the agreements are phased in over a period of time of up to 15 years, the short-run adjustment costs are even smaller. These adjustment costs and the opposition to liberalization probably are positively correlated. In this case, it may be easier for a country to liberalize trade using RTAs than through multilateral liberalization.

A useful way of summarizing this debate is to think in terms of substitutes and complements. Those who fear the spread of RTAs really fear that they are a substitute for multilateral liberalization. Economists who are less concerned about the spread of RTAs tend to view them as complementary to MTNs. MTNs move at a slow pace on a limited number of issues. Despite the complications, there is little or no support for abandoning that process. The WTO is still a work in progress. In the Doha Round, many of the negotiations involve spreading the authority of the WTO to some types of trade, such as agriculture and services, that were not adequately addressed under GATT. Such negotiations are essential to further the process of the liberalization of world trade. Even if an MTN does not produce much in the way of trade liberalization, coming up with acceptable rules for certain types of trade and other issues is worth the cost of the negotiations. The world economy needs an organization to set the rules of world trade and to referee disputes among countries. Although the WTO may no longer be the force for multilateral liberalization that it once was, its role in the world economy may still be increasing rather than diminishing.

Whither the WTO?

From the beginning of modern trade policy in the 1930s, the clear intention was to create an international organization that would formulate the rules of global trade and then enforce those rules. Unfortunately, such an organization impinges on the sovereignty of individual states to independently set all aspects of their trade policy. It took literally decades for most of the countries of the world to be able to reconcile this conflict. In a sense, the GATT was a halfway house between an agreement among the world's major trading nations and the creation of such an institution. The proposed International Trade Organization (ITO) proved to be a bridge too far in the 1940s. For all its imperfections, the GATT accomplished a tremendous amount from the late 1940s to the 1990s. As outlined earlier, how much more trade liberalization that can be accomplished through multilateral trade negotiations is questionable. The basic failure of the Doha Round has led to the impression among many that the WTO is no longer an important force in world trade.

That impression was incorrect in a number of ways. First, virtually everyone knew from the start that not allowing the ITO to become a reality was a mistake. Because the GATT was not a formal organization, its ability to actually enforce the global rules of the game was problematic. Enforcement under the GATT was left to investigative panels with little authority to enforce their judgments. In retrospect, it is surprising that countries generally followed the GATT with so little formal enforcement capacity. However, ethics and the propensity of countries to do the right thing are limited. The counterfactual question is this: Over the last 20 years, what would have happened to the world trading system if the WTO had not been created? Perhaps one could argue that world trade would have performed better in the absence of the WTO. However, if one has the sense that things would have been worse sans the WTO, then why is that true? Since the Doha Round essentially has failed, what else has the WTO accomplished? First, and most importantly, the world now has an organization to police world trade. The world trading system now has rules and a workable enforcement mechanism for those rules. Countries now routinely file complaints with the WTO over alleged violations of the agreed-upon rules of international trade. The WTO serves as an impartial arbitrator of these complaints and the judgments are made, by legal standards, promptly. What is probably more important is more difficult to see and impossible to quantify. The mere existence of the WTO and its mechanism for handling disputes reduces the amount of misbehavior in the trading system. No country enjoys being accused of violating international trade rules. Further, the resolution of a dispute now contains concrete penalties. Losing a WTO case can mean retaliation by the injured party in the form of selective trade barriers that can harm an offending country's exporters. With 20 years of experience, the system has proven its worth. At this point, very few countries would consider going back to an international trading system where the enforcement of the rules was dependent on the voluntary willingness of countries to obey them. Trade negotiations under the auspices of the WTO are another matter. Although the Doha Round is not officially dead, there is little hope of bringing it to a successful conclusion. As indicated in the first section, much of the further liberalization of world trade may well occur as a result of an increasing number of RTAs. What is often not considered is that the WTO is involved in the process of creating RTAs. The negotiation of RTAs is notified to the WTO, which maintains a global RTA database on all current and future RTAs. Also, all RTAs have to comply with standards that were set up under Article XXIV of the GATT and now enforced by the WTO. The notion that RTAs are a form of trade agreement that happen outside of the supervision of the WTO is just wrong.

Although RTAs may well prove to be a substitute for MTNs, another form of trade negotiations is occurring through the WTO. These are called plurilateral agreements. Such agreements are reached among a subset of the members of the WTO. Any commitments made among the countries can be confined to the countries signing the agreements or made open to all members of the WTO. The first such agreements were made in the Tokyo Round and were legitimized in the Uruguay Round. The two plurilaterals that came out of the Tokyo Round concerned trade in civil aircraft and government procurement. The civil aircraft agreement provides for free trade in aircraft and parts among 30 countries. It also covers conditions of trade peculiar to that industry and sets norms for government purchases and inducements to purchase aircraft. The other Tokyo Round plurilateral that is still in force is considerably more important as it covers the large area of world trade concerning government purchases. The government procurement agreement currently has 45 WTO members, with another 10 countries intending to join the agreement. A third plurilateral was concerning international trade in information technology. In 1996, 29 countries signed the original agreement. By 2014, there were 70 members. As well as adding more countries, the agreement has been expanded to cover more goods and services. In 2014, 14 WTO members began negotiating on liberalizing trade in environmental goods. Further, this agreement is envisioned as being made available to all countries on a most favored nation (MFN) basis. With trade liberalization under the MTN framework stalled, the concept of further liberalization utilizing plurilaterals has much to recommend it. A major problem with the MTN framework is the need to obtain a consensus on liberalization among 162 members. As the Doha Round has sadly demonstrated, finding common ground on many issues among an increasingly large and diverse population of countries may not be possible. Plurilaterals allow a group of WTO members to liberalize trade in way that is mutually agreeable on a limited number of product categories. Further, any initial agreement is not etched in stone. Other countries can join the agreement at a later date, and the agreement can be modified at a later date to include more products. They provide a maximum amount of flexibility under the umbrella of the WTO to liberalize trade. These agreements are potentially troubling in that they could lead to a very fragmented approach to trade liberalization. The number of countries participating varies widely, and the product coverage can be narrow. Also, they are setting a precedent for trade in particular product categories. Once the WTO has sanctioned a plurilateral, it is difficult to see that the agreement would be fundamentally changed in the future. In a sense, plurilaterals carry the same risk that RTAs carry: a further fragmentation of world trade as opposed to general agreements that are binding on all WTO members. It is far too early to predict that the future of WTO negotiations is plurilateral as opposed to multilateral. However, the longer the world goes on without a successful MTN, the likelier that outcome is. As a result, 21st-century trade negotiations could be dominated by an increasing number of RTAs and plurilaterals. The public choice argument for this may be compelling. Both RTAs and plurilaterals avoid the problem of countries free riding on MFN-based agreements. They may well be much easier to get by domestic political opposition than the sort of broad-based liberalizations inherent in an MTN. An RTA is an agreement that inherently levels the playing field for producers in both countries. A plurilateral is an agreement that each signatory country finds acceptable for a limited amount of trade. Further, the benefits do not have to be extended to countries that are not part of the agreement. The obvious spread of RTAs and the potential spread of plurilaterals indicate that this may be the case.

World Trade in Agricultural Products

The rich world tells the poor world to get rid of subsidies, but continues to spend
$1 billion a day subsidizing its own farming enterprises.

—Oxfam

Over the last two chapters you may have had the feeling that something
was missing. What has been left out of our discussion has been world trade
in agricultural products. This is odd because world trade in agricultural
products is now $1.7 trillion per year and accounts for 20 percent of trade
in goods. In developed countries such as the United States, agriculture is a
relatively small percentage of gross domestic product (GDP). However, the
sector's effects on trade are much larger. U.S. exports of agricultural products are approximately $160 billion. Our imports normally are smaller, but
the United States consistently runs a trade surplus in agricultural products.
Given this information, one might think that the U.S. Department of Agriculture would be listed as an institution involved in international trade policy. Agriculture matters a lot in U.S. trade policy. Unfortunately, the story
is not a happy one and it really has no ending. Rather, world trade in agriculture is a source of endless tension in trade policy among many developed countries and in the relationship between developed and developing
countries.

The problems in world trade in agricultural products date back literally
centuries. When agricultural products were a high percentage of GDP, it
was understandable that governments would protect agricultural interests
for the usual public-choice reasons. In the United States the story really
begins in the 20th century during the Great Depression. As part of the New
Deal designed to pull the country out of the Great Depression, the Roosevelt administration passed the Agricultural Adjustment Act of 1933, which
was designed to reduce the impact of low agricultural prices on farm
income. The act provided subsidies for farmers in cash for reduction in the
amount of land being farmed. In turn, this would reduce the supply of agricultural commodities and raise prices. The higher prices acted as a subsidy to farmers. Farmers also received cash subsidies for taking land out of
production. In the other developed countries, similar policies were being
put into place as the Depression greatly reduced the price of all commodities. Recall that the U.S. government also passed the Reciprocal Trade Agreements Act (RTAA) in 1934. This set off a potential clash between the desire
to maintain agricultural prices and the desire to liberalize the world trading system. Governments can subsidize farmers by guaranteeing high prices

and/or direct cash subsidies. Guaranteed prices for agricultural products and lower trade barriers on these products are an uneasy mix. The issue surfaced quickly as the United States sought to sign bilateral trade agreements before World War II. It became clear that maintaining high prices for U.S. farm products and liberalized trade were in conflict. In more concrete terms, this conflict substantially changed the nature of the GATT.

When the GATT was being written, special provisions for agriculture were included at the start. Article XI allowed the ability to restrict imports if they were in conflict with domestic programs aimed at reducing the supply of a product. The effect of Article XI was to allow countries to use tariffs and quotas on agricultural products to restrict the supply available in the domestic market. In essence, if there was a conflict between domestic agricultural policy and trade policy, then the former could take precedence over the latter. There was further damage in the GATT. Article XVI permits the use of both production subsidies *and* export subsidies. The only requirement of Article XVI is that countries must discuss their policies with other countries that might be affected. In the GATT agriculture was given special treatment from the start. Agricultural policy was to be set independently by each country with no effective supervision of trade. The result was that world trade in agricultural products became a free-fire zone where countries could pursue domestic policies that inflicted large losses on the farmers of other countries, and this result was perfectly legal under the GATT. As shown by Berkema, Henneberry, and Drabenstott (1989), this result occurred because of the United States. When the GATT was being written, the United States insisted on the inclusion of both Article XI and XVI. American policy makers were determined that the liberalization of world trade would not interfere with the operation of the Agricultural Adjustment Act. This attitude persisted in the early GATT rounds. The creation of the European Union (EU) in 1957 brought agriculture back into the picture. The Dillon Round of trade negotiations officially sanctioned the Common Agricultural Policy (CAP) of the EU (then European Economic Community). The United States was concerned about the CAP, but did not envision how large the program would become. During the Kennedy Round, agriculture was barely discussed. During the Tokyo Round, a critical decision was made by the GATT contracting parties. In a procedural vote, the EU separated agriculture from other areas of negotiation. This effectively swept agriculture off the table for that MTN. Agriculture returned as the main issue of the Uruguay Round. The developed countries were maintaining high prices in domestic markets to support farm income. These high prices were producing surpluses, which were disposed of using export subsidies. In effect, the developed countries were creating surpluses of agricultural products and then dumping them in world markets, which depressed prices. The losers in this process were developing countries exporting agricultural products. The result of the negotiations brought agriculture back into the world trading system in the form of the Agreement on Agriculture. This agreement has three pillars. First, nontariff barriers (NTBs) were converted into tariffs and the overall level of tariffs in agriculture was reduced. Second, the developed countries agreed to reduce, but not eliminate, export subsidies. Finally, the agreement dealt with domestic support of agricultural policies. This pillar involves a complicated set of domestic support "boxes." There are three boxes of policies that distort trade in descending order from amber to blue to green. Policies in the amber box were subject to reduction. Countries agreed to limit spending on blue-box policies, but policies in the green box were not limited. Unsurprisingly, countries chose to move subsidies to the blue and green boxes. The overall level of agricultural subsidies in the world economy continues to rise. It is currently about $500 billion per year. The easy criticism is that the Uruguay Round failed in agriculture, but this is excessive criticism. It put agricultural protectionism back under the umbrella of the WTO by eliminating quotas, and it began addressing the critical question of trade-distorting agricultural subsidies. Unfortunately, agriculture is a major reason for the failure of the Doha Round. The grand bargain being proposed there is developed-country cuts in agricultural subsidies for developing-country cuts in tariffs on manufactured products. This has created an impasse that so far has not been broken. Outside of the MTN negotiating process, the United States has quietly been making an end run on trade in agriculture. All of the 20 RTAs that the United States has signed provide for free trade in virtually all agricultural products. This is unique among the developed countries. In a world where trade in agricultural products is horribly distorted, the United States is carving out an ever-increasing space where farmers can compete in something more akin to a free market.

U.S. Trade Policy in the 21st Century

U.S. trade policy in the 21st century has changed profoundly from the 20th century. From an older system where Congress managed trade policy in accordance with the need for revenue coupled with political pressures, the system has evolved into something entirely different. First, the link between trade policy and government revenue has been broken. Second, in a sense, the argument made by the Democratic Party in the post–Civil War era is now the norm. The U.S. government now balances the interests of consumers versus the interests of producers. Further, the government uses trade policy to augment other forms of foreign policy to achieve objectives that are broader than pure economic gains and losses. The change in trade policy in the 20th century was marked by a large shift in the responsibility for trade policy from Congress to the president. From the enactment of RTAA in 1934 until the 1990s, the leadership of the president in trade policy was clear. Two political shifts occurred in the late 20th century with respect to trade policy that are changing how it is conducted in the 21st century. First, the bitter political battle over the passage of NAFTA marked a change in leadership in trade policy. Prior to NAFTA, Congress invariably gave the president the authority to negotiate trade agreements. They were willing to do this, secure in the knowledge that they possessed the final decision-making authority. After the passage of NAFTA, the granting of trade promotion authority to the president is no longer routine. The balance in Congress between more protectionist-oriented members and those with a more free-trade approach has changed. The former has learned that the easiest way to stop further liberalization is to block the process before it ever gets started. This change has occurred as a result of deep changes in the attitude concerning trade in both political parties. Traditionally, the Democratic Party has been more oriented toward the liberalization of trade due to a focus on consumer welfare and a realization that protectionism can lead to higher profits for business. The traditional Republican stance on trade was to cater to its historical constituency and support higher levels of protection. As the U.S. economy has changed over the years, the attitudes on trade in both parties have become more complex. In the Democratic Party the support for more liberal trade has eroded. The fiercest opponents of more liberal trade are now the labor unions. As the importance of labor unions in Democratic Party politics has increased, the party has moved to an increasingly protectionist stance. In something of a role reversal, the Republican Party has become much more amenable to lowering trade barriers. As the U.S. economy has become more export oriented, the attitude of business has become much less reflexively protectionist. However, the changes that are occurring in the structure of the economy are not universally welcomed in the Republican Party either. A significant portion of the party blames more open trade for changes in the economy and society that they feel threaten American welfare. Thus, the politics of protectionism have become more complex than just free-trade Democrats versus protectionist Republicans. The free-traders are now composed of a significant part of each party. Likewise, protectionism is now bipartisan. Further, the numbers of members of Congress in both camps are roughly even. This situation has not stopped the United States from moving to more open trade, but it is definitely slowing it down.

The most obvious place one can observe this is the failure of the Doha Round. As detailed by Blustein (2009), the United States walked away from the negotiations as a result of the inability to obtain any significant concessions from the developing countries. The U.S. Trade Representative did this because he had no choice. The period when the United States could grant large concessions in return for small concessions had ended. Any trade agreement without significant gains for U.S. exporters is no longer politically tenable. Because the United States is still the world's most important economy, the lack of further serious U.S. participation in future MTNs is unlikely. Understandably, this has shifted the focus of U.S. trade policy to agreements that have more clearly tangible benefits. This has skewed trade policy in one clear direction. First, since 1985 the United States has signed 20 RTAs with countries around the world. It is currently negotiating two large trade agreements with a number of countries in Asia and with the EU. Although RTAs are difficult to pass in Congress, they do ultimately pass. Congress has yet to reject an RTA that the president has negotiated. Unlike MTNs, RTAs are considered fairer than MTNs because they inherently provide free access to a foreign market in return for free access to the U.S. market. More quietly, the United States has been an active participant in plurilateral agreements within the WTO. Although the politics of RTAs can be contentious, even the protectionists in both parties waste little effort opposing such agreements. Events seem to follow the path of least resistance, so one would expect that U.S. participation in both RTAs and plurilaterals should increase over time. This also follows a kind of zero-sum game situation in trade policy that is rarely discussed. Governments only have a limited amount of resources that they can allocate to the conduct of trade policy. The rise of RTAs already has created concern that this trend is reducing the resources available to negotiate new MTNs. The logic is correct, but the concern may be misplaced. Trade liberalization is still proceeding, but at a slower pace and in a different format. One might prefer a faster pace and a grander scope of liberalization. However, trade policy in any democratic country is ultimately determined by the voters. The criticism of political leaders and trade policy officials is misplaced.

Case Study: The Trans-Pacific Partnership

The trends mentioned earlier in U.S. trade policy can be clearly seen in the contentious negotiations over the proposed Trans-Pacific Partnership (TPP) trade agreement. As is true of almost all trade agreements, the TPP is complicated. It began as a trade agreement among Brunei, Chile, New Zealand, and Singapore in 2005. The negotiations have expanded to include Australia, Canada, Japan, Malaysia, Mexico, Peru, the United States, and Vietnam. It is likely that Indonesia will join the negotiations, and other countries that have expressed an interest include Colombia, the Philippines, South Korea, Taiwan, and Thailand. It is noteworthy that China has chosen not to participate. The negotiations have been lengthy even with a relatively small number of countries. This has occurred because the agreement is exceptionally comprehensive. In addition to the usual reductions in tariffs on goods, the agreement frees up trade in services and agricultural products. It also contains provisions on foreign direct investment and the protection of intellectual property rights. It is a good example of why countries have moved away from MTNs. Such a comprehensive agreement may be possible among a limited number of countries. However, reaching an agreement of this type on a global basis would be inconceivable.

At this point the passage of the TPP in the United States is uncertain. As was described earlier, the passage of a single RTA in Congress can be contentious. In the end, they have all been granted congressional approval, but it has not been easy. Plurilateral agreements that contain some of the provisions of the TPP have been much easier to pass. The difference with the TPP is that it is large and highly visible. The number of sectors of the U.S. economy that will be adversely affected by the agreement is likewise large. The potential gains to the United States also are large, but they are less visible than the losses. The result is that the protectionists in both parties can find common ground in opposing the agreement. In a sense, TPP is not an MTN, but it is large enough to mobilize the opposition. As a result of its relatively large size, its passage is far less certain than the passage of an individual RTA. Finally, the United States also is negotiating a similar agreement with the EU. At this point, this agreement is drawing far less opposition because the negotiations have yet to be concluded. It may well be that the government has stretched its limited trade policy resources to the limit. The U.S. Trade Representative is not a very large government agency. If both agreements do not go forward, then the government may have learned a hard lesson in the reality of liberalizing trade in the 21st century. Liberalization may still be possible, but only in small amounts over an extended period. Although the protectionists may be wrong in their arguments, their views have to be accommodated in order for the process of making the United States a more open economy to be realized.

Bibliography

Berkema, Alan, David Henneberry, and Mark Drabenstott. 1989. "Agriculture and the GATT: A Time for Change," *Federal Reserve Bank of Kansas City Economic Review* March: 21–42.

Blustein, Paul. 2009. *Misadventures of the Most Favored Nations: Clashing Egos, Inflated Ambitions, and the Great Shambles of the World Trade System.* New York: Public Affairs.

Index

ABOUT THE AUTHOR

W. Charles Sawyer is Hal Wright Professor of Latin American Economics at Texas Christian University (TCU). Before coming to TCU in 2007, he taught at the University of Arkansas, Louisiana State University, the Helsinki School of Economics and Management, and the University of Southern Mississippi. In addition, he has served as a consultant for the United Nations Conference on Trade and Development and the United Nations Industrial Development Organization. Sawyer has published more than 40 articles in leading research journals and is the coauthor of three books: *The Demand for Imports and Exports in the World Economy*, *International Economics*, and *Latin American Economic Development*. He is a member of the American Economic Association, the International Trade and Finance Association, and the Academy of International Business.